HUMMEL ART

BY John F. Hotchkiss

Important Note:

Since the First Edition, First Printing was released the retail prices of new M.I. Hummel figurines increased approximately 12%.

Retail prices in Table I and II should be increased 12% in estimating the present cost of new figurines. The prices for older marks shown in Table II will also probably increase 12%. The rare items in Table III may or may not reflect this increase as their prices depend on many other variables.

Some of the reissues mentioned on page 135 have appeared at the time of this Third Printing. Some are only available in Germany. Reports have been received that some of these do not carry the latest mark, TMK-5. Prices in many cases are much higher than the suggested retail price. In view of this confusing situation, buyers should be especially cautious in purchasing items listed in this book for possible reissue.

— John F. Hotchkiss

HUMMEL ART

John F. Hotchkiss

First Edition, 1978
Third Printing

ISBN 0-87069-184-8 Hardbound
ISBN 0-87069-249-6 Softbound

Copyright © 1978 John F. Hotchkiss

Art Director, Jann Williams
Typesetting by Type-O-Graphics Two, Inc., Des Moines, Iowa
Printed by McGrew Graphics, Kansas City, Missouri
Color by Art Lithocraft, Kansas City, Missouri

Published by

Wallace-Homestead Book Company
1912 Grand Avenue
Des Moines, Iowa 50305

This book is dedicated to
THE ROCHESTER PUBLIC LIBRARY
as well as to
ALL OTHER LIBRARIES
from the smallest up to
THE LIBRARY OF CONGRESS
that have made the writing of this book
NOT ONLY A POSSIBILITY BUT
ALSO A PLEASURE

How to Use This Book

This book is intended to be used for many purposes. A few of the more important ones are to gain information about Hummel figurines, to find price information on figurines and other items, as a reference for other Hummel art, additional published material about Hummel articles, and as a directory to many dealers and collectors of Hummel articles.

To locate a figurine by name, start with the tables in Section II, where the name will be listed in alphabetical order. To locate a figurine by number, first use the Master List in Section IV. Section IV will also tell you where to find an illustration.

Guide prices for any figurine can be found by using the directions in the previous paragraph. The Table of Contents can direct you to price information on other forms of Hummel art. It is very important to read the section "Price Guides Can Help," before using any of the price information in this book. Without reading this special little section, serious errors can be made and many dollars can be lost.

For those who are interested in learning about all of the other available Hummel art, this book is divided into various categories such as prints and pictures, figurines, dolls, and others. Before starting on any of these, you may want to take a few minutes to read a little about the story behind all of these adaptations of the art created by the artist known as both Berta and Sister Maria Innocentia Hummel.

The bibliography contains numerous references to other published material for the serious or advanced collectors who may want more information than could be packed into this book.

Listed under Sources are directories for buying, selling, repairing, protecting, displaying your Hummel art. The aim was to have something for everyone and everything in its place. It is up to you whether you decide to snack or partake of the whole meal.

Contents

Introduction

HUMMEL ART is intended to provide useful information to persons interested in figurines and other articles based on the original designs of Berta or Sister Maria Innocentia Hummel. Its first objective is to provide a handy and inexpensive source of general information, including current prices and pictures for items now being produced, as well as discontinued items and rare collectors' examples.

The second important objective of this book is to provide the more than one hundred thousand owners of *HUMMEL, The Complete Collector's Guide and Illustrated Reference*, by Eric Ehrmann with essential additional information, price updates, and necessary revisions to that book. All of the additions contained herein are necessary for a complete and accurate understanding of Hummel art. This newest book, *HUMMEL ART*, will also make collecting of it more enjoyable.

The book was written and organized with the beginning collector and dealers particularly in mind. The beginner can obtain enough insight and information from it to answer most of his questions during the early stages of his hobby.

The many collectors and dealers with extensive collections will appreciate the massive coverage and unique information on the identification, authentication, and current values not only on figurines but also on all of the other types of Hummel articles now becoming very popular. Also included are sections on sources, reproductions, repairs, displaying and protecting your collection, not found in any other publication. An extensive bibliography records many other sources of further detailed information.

As an independent source for identifying, answering questions, and pricing, this book can render valuable assistance on the adaptations of Sister Hummel's art that have such a universal appeal.

10

1.

History of Hummel Art

What Is Hummel Art?

For the purposes of this book, Hummel art is any fine, decorative, or useful art form adapted from an original creative work by Berta Hummel (later Sister Maria Innocentia Hummel). The counterparts of these originals have appeared in numerous forms for over forty years. The three-dimensional figurines are the most famous conceptions of her pastels and paintings.

Her original works are not in themselves a part of this book. Some of them are in the house where she was born in 1909, and in which her mother and brother still live. Primarily, these are the ones she drew before entering the convent in 1933. More of her original drawings and paintings are in the Franciscan Convent at Seissen in West Germany. Dr. Herbert Dubler of Verlag Ars Sacra, Josef Müller of Munich wrote that they owned most of the originals for which they hold the two-dimensional rights. Some originals also exist which Sister Hummel gave as gifts during her relatively short life. Recently an original Sister Hummel made in 1939 at the request of some young girls surfaced in St. Louis.

Sister Maria Innocentia Hummel (Berta Hummel)
Hum No. H-1
"M. I. HUMMEL" BUST, 12¾". Stamped with *Three-Line* TMK-4 and incised year "1967." Number H-1. Designed by "Skrobek," year discontinued unknown. Superceded by small 5¾" bust in 1977 with TMK-5.

The three-dimensional conversion of her originals into figurines was so well executed under her supervision while she was alive that they are now classed as works of art themselves by the U.S. Department of Commerce.

Most of the remaining Hummel art in this book are two-dimensional expressions of her originals produced by photomechanical processes to preserve line and color. In this category are prints, pictures, calendars, and cards. Transfers have also been made to apply to articles such as music boxes, plates, bells, eggs, candles, and innumerable other collectibles.

Bas-relief is another form into which Sister Hummel's pictures have been adapted, principally for a series of annual plates. Production of these plates has usually been limited to the year of issue. Prints, pictures, greeting cards are a few of the two-dimensional replicas that are covered later in this book.

Hummel-like art is the term used in this book for items often referred to as reproductions. This broader term is used because variations are so wide that there is a question of whether or not they were inspired by Sister Hummel's work. Some appear to have been more likely issued with the objective of capitalizing on the worldwide appeal of her work and the approved adaptations. These "unauthorized" reproductions are usually dissimilar enough to avoid infringing on existing copyrights. Some Hummel-like examples are in two-dimensional cards and prints, but most of them are figurines of varying quality and appearance. Currently only figurines licensed by the Franciscan Convent in Seissen to be produced by the W. Goebel Company of West Germany are genuine "M. I. Hummel" figurines. Each one must be so marked in an incised facsimile of Sister Hummel's script signature. Any piece without this signature is either Hummel-like, Hummel-inspired, a reproduction, or other imitation.

The Artist —
Sister Maria Innocentia Hummel

Muted colors glowing softly . . . round, cherubic faces of children at work, at play, at worship . . . a Hummel print, a Hummel figurine. Who was their creator? Who imbued these figures with their universal appeal? Sister Maria Innocentia Hummel.

Sister Maria Innocentia Hummel was born Berta Hummel on May 21, 1909, at Massing am der Rott in Lower Bavaria. She was the third daughter of Adolph Hummel, a prosperous shopkeeper, and his wife, Viktoria.

Adolph Hummel had artistic ability, but his childhood dream of becoming an artist vanished of economic necessity. It was ap-

Sister Maria Innocentia pictured with several of her students sometime in the 1930s.

parent, however, at an early age, that Berta had inherited his artistic inclinations. At age three, she often sat drawing with a pencil on paper. Her creativity also manifested itself in theatrical activities such as the design and creation of doll costumes and the staging of German folk tales for her family and neighbors. Indeed, Berta buzzed from one creative activity to another, earning the nickname "Das Hummele," — "The Busybee."

At age six, Berta entered the elementary school of the Armen Schulschwestern at Massing. As at home, she showed herself to be a free spirit — her attention flitted from subject to subject. Her lack of discipline, however, was amply compensated for by her developing artistic talent and her sunny disposition.

Berta was admitted at age twelve to the Institute of English Sisters at Simbach, a prestigious boarding school. Here she pursued her art education under the direction of Sister Stephanie. It was Sister Stephanie who suggested to the Hummels that Berta continue her education after graduation by taking the curriculum for art teachers at the Academy of Applied Arts in Munich. Although it meant financial sacrifice for the whole Hummel family, they agreed, for Adolph Hummel saw it as the fulfillment of his own childhood ambitions.

In 1927, Berta entered the Academy of Applied Arts, attending the Berufsfachschule, a department devoted to training art teachers for elementary and secondary schools. It was here that her style developed, influenced by the works and ideas of Giotto, Michelangelo, and other masters. Her work was also influenced by the Werkbund, a German art movement that attempted to incorporate the great traditions of the Baroque and Florentine periods into contemporary design.

During this period of her life, Berta developed a close friendship with two nuns, Sister Laura and Sister Kostka, who were also staying at the religious dormitory of the Schwestern der Heiligen Familie while studying at the Academy of Applied Arts. As the friendship grew, so did Berta's interest in entering the religious life. Although she was offered a job at the Academy as a graduate teaching assistant, Berta chose to join the Franciscan religious order after graduation in 1931. On August 22, 1933, she took her final vows and became Sister Maria Innocentia Hummel.

Sister Maria Innocentia taught art to young children at institutions administered by the convent. She created a series of drawings to amuse and reward the children; these were displayed at an education symposium in 1933 and were well received. Soon after, her work became well known throughout Germany. By 1934, her drawings were appearing on postcards and she collaborated on a children's book, *The Hummel Book*, with Margareta Seeman, who wrote the verse. A biography, *Sketch Me*, written by an American Franciscan nun is now out of print.

13

It was in 1934 that her work first came to the attention of Franz Goebel, the head of W. Goebel Porzellanfabrik in Oeslau. He persuaded Sister Maria Innocentia and the convent to let him transform her sketches and drawings into ceramic figurines for the export market. It was agreed that the Siessen Convent would always have final approval of all figurine designs, since the convent also administered her artwork, granting licenses and charging royalties for the right to publish her drawings and designs in forms of which they approved.

In March, 1935, the first seven figurines were displayed at the Leipzig Trade Fair; each piece bore the mark "M. I. Hummel." The mark emphasized the fact that the figurines were created from drawings that Sister Maria Innocentia made after entering religious life.

Although her health began to decline slowly in 1937, she continued her activities in spite of hardships imposed by the Nazi government. After all, the royalties from her artwork and figurines enabled the convent to survive the increasing tax burden levied on convents.

During the war years, the arduous conditions and shortages of food, fuel, and medicine contributed to the development of a lung infection, later diagnosed as chronic tuberculosis. Sister Maria Innocentia survived to see the Third Reich crumble and peace come to Europe. However, the privations had taken their toll on her health. She died in the Siessen Convent on November 6, 1946, but left the rich heritage of over 500 sketches and paintings, now known as Hummel art.

Why Is It Called Collectible?

Is Hummel art great art? If wide acceptance is a measure of great art then surely the work of this active young "hummele," later a religious nun, must be a candidate for this classification. If great art is popular art, it must follow that her work would be classed as great art. Millions of people not only recognize "Hummel Art" when they see it, but they have been and are still willing to pay anywhere from a few cents for a postcard to thousands of dollars for the recently available large figurines. Sister Hummel's art, like that of the great masters may survive the test of time, or it may not. In any case, today, less than fifty years after most of it was created, it is cherished and enjoyed the world around not only as great art but as very collectible art.

Like so many important artists in history, Sister Hummel was deeply religious. As did these others, she directed part of her creative effort to translating her impressions and feelings into paintings of various religious subjects and events, such as her

Madonna in Red. Religious Hummel art is being actively collected, despite the present decline in general spiritual involvement, because of her ability to arouse a deep emotional response to her pious paintings.

For the same reason her other art is collectible by an even broader cross section of the population. It attracts, it is cheerful, it is motion-filled, and it tells a story. It recalls for many collectors the past when they had similar experiences. For example in Stormy Weather a young girl and boy huddle under an umbrella as protection from the elements. In this work Sister Hummel captured that moment of both awe and fear of thunderstorms so well that collectors relive similar feelings they once had or may have imagined. In the same way there were other times when as children they felt grown up and took pleasure and pride in acting the part portrayed in Doll Mother, the Pharmacist, or twenty others that stir memories and feelings.

There are many shallower reasons why Hummel art is collectible. For some it may be used only as a touch of decoration or a conversation piece. It is collectible for the very important reason that it is affordable and a good value in the eyes of the buyer. These are collectors who have not understood the message being sent.

Another attraction is the large number of models that are available which appear in a great variety of forms such as figurines, fonts, pictures, paintings, or plaques. Not all of the hundreds of Sister Hummel's work are available in each form. The grand total of combinations of subject, size, and form is in the tens of thousands — a vast reservoir from which collectors of many tastes, attitudes, and means can drink and find deep satisfaction. There are many more than just one series of look alikes that tug simultaneously at both the heartstrings and the pursestrings.

LITTLE PHARMACIST
Hummel, 322

DOLL MOTHER
Hummel, 67

STORMY WEATHER
Hummel, 71

15

Hummel art is also collectible because it fits today's life-style as well as it did that of thirty years ago. It is not a fad or style collectible as some of the Victorian art or Art Nouveau once was. Hummel art is addictive in their interest because of the variety of subjects. Two are more than twice as interesting as one, and so on. An old-time collector once commented, "One is an example, two is a pair, and three is a collection." Each addition to the group brings another and different expression of Hummel originality and is usually surrounded by some event associated with its acquisition. Perhaps the piece was a gift on a special occasion or a memento from a vacation trip.

In recent years Hummel art has been collected for another entirely different reason. It is being used as an investment that will keep up with, or maybe beat, the rate of inflation. This motive is not confined to the collecting of Hummel art, alone, but has permeated all fields of collecting for the last twelve years. While all Hummel art is not limited edition, it is being purchased as a secondary reason for its potential gain in value. The merits of this action are more fully discussed in a later section.

Courtesy, Verlag Emil Fink

Signatures on Original Hummel Art

Berta Hummel (later Sister Maria Innocentia Hummel) signed her original drawings in a number of different forms in the lower left or right corners. These signatures can be seen clearly in most two-dimensional reproductions. Generally, the most common form of her signature looks like this *M.J.Hummel*. Other examples of her work have been found that are signed just "H", "B", or "B" and "H" superimposed in a simple monogram. She also used "B.Hummel" and "M.I.Hummel." The only drawing found with a date is Stormy Weather. It is signed "Hummel '36" and is interesting because this is two years after she took her final vows. In attempting to date some of her work in order to study changes in style, no consistent relationship could be found with respect to year and the way she signed her work.

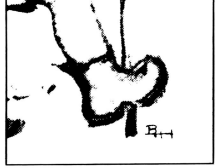

Courtesy, Verlag Emil Fink

One keen observer noticed a relationship between her signature and some of her subjects. Some of her religious paintings are signed "M.I. Hummel," an example of which is Angelic Sleep, shown below.

Courtesy, Verlag Emil Fink

No examples of this style of signature have been seen on her children or non-religious subjects. The Goose Girl (below) was the only titled drawing and box-style signature encountered.

Companies who reproduce two-dimensional versions of Sister Hummel's art usually add a monogram or symbol of copyright registration. This symbol often appears near the signature but is not part of the original drawing. Ars Sacra Verlag, Josef Müller, one of the licensees, uses the letters A & R worked into a monogram. The Emil Fink Verlag reproductions do not appear to have anything similar in the picture area or face of the reproduction.

Courtesy, Verlag Emil Fink

Courtesy, Verlag Emil Fink

Many prints, cards, or picture reproductions are cropped by the publishers in order to obtain a different composition or treatment. This cropping frequently eliminates any evidence of the Hummel signature.

Collectors familiar with Sister Hummel's style probably are not confused by the absence of a signature on some reproductions. However, the novice might find it disturbing not to be able to distinguish between a cropped piece reproduced from an original Sister Hummel painting and Hummel-like paper products such as those published by Alfred Mainzer of Long Island City, which are not copied from original Hummel art. Until the beginning collector is able to distinguish original reproductions, he might wish to collect only those items in one form or another with a Hummel signature on them.

19

2.

Adaptations of Hummel Art

What Are "M.I. Hummel" Figurines?

M. I. Hummel figurines are small ornamental figures made of porcelain, the highest grade of ceramic. These three-dimensional figurines are adaptations from original drawings and paintings of Sister Maria Innocentia Hummel. These adaptations are all approved before production by the Franciscan Convent at Siessen, Germany, where Sister Maria Innocentia Hummel lived until her death in 1946. All master models created from Sister Hummel's originals are and always have been subject to convent approval since they were first issued in 1935. A special licensing and royalty agreement between the convent and the Goebel company specifies this approval.

Authentic M.I. Hummel figurines are only made by the W. Goebel Company and can be distinguished from any other figurines in a very simple way. A genuine M.I. Hummel figurine must have a facsimile M.J.Hummel signature incised somewhere on the figure or edge of the base. Unless this incised (pressed in) facsimile signature is on the figurine, it is probably not a genuine M.I. Hummel figurine. The way this signature appears is shown on a

Opposite page, GOOSE GIRL, Hummel, 47.

21

CLASSIFICATION OF GOEBEL TRADEMARKS

TMK-1
CROWN MARK

1935
To
1949

- **1a** CROWN +
- **1b** CROWN + *Goebel*
- **1c** CROWN + U.S. ZONE

TMK-2
FULL BEE MARK

1950
To
1959

- **2a** INCISED-FULL BEE
- **2b** STAMPED-FULL BEE
- **2c** SMALL or LOW BEE

TMK-3
STYLIZED BEE MARK

1960
To
1967   STYLIZED BEE

TMK-4
THREE LINE MARK

1968
To
197?   THREE LINE

picture of a Sister Hummel bust on page 10. Although the W. Goebel Company did vary many of their other marks, collectors can be grateful that in the application of the facsimile signature they were both consistent and persistent. Some of the very small designs only two or three inches high are difficult to mark so that the resulting signature is indistinct on some, but it should be there and is worth the hunt.

M. I. Hummel figurines are not only signed but are probably one of the best marked ceramic objects that have been made since porcelain was rediscovered. This excellent marking makes collecting them a joy because of the story that unfolds when one learns to read the marks on the bottom of every piece. Because of the nearly infinite combinations and variations of markings, in almost every instance two important questions, "Who made it?" and "When was it made?" can be answered with some assurance.

Examples of this "historical shorthand" can be seen on pages 23 to 28. These twenty pictures provide enough of a story to fill a separate book. Although a separate book has not been done yet, the book *Hummel*, by Eric Ehrmann has the most information on these marks of any publication to date. It is these trademarks that answer the "Where" and "When" questions of interest to collectors. Since 1870 the W. Goebel Company has used more than twelve different trademarks although some of them are a minor variation of one theme.

The marks of interest to M. I. Hummel figurine buyers are those from 1935 to date. In this book all trademark information has been condensed to conform to the manner in which most collectors are already using it today. Five of the twelve marks that are shown in *Hummel* have come into common usage and are shown in the chart on the left numbered from one through five. The common name used in descriptions is shown above them and the period during which this mark or slight variations of it was used is below the facsimile of the mark itself.

TMK-5
CURRENT MARK

1972
To
Present   VEE OVER GEE

1. WHITSUNTIDE, 163.
Incised *Crown*, TMK-1 and
number 163. Stamped black
"GERMANY."

2. WHITSUNTIDE, 163.
Incised *Crown*, TMK-1, Number
163 (incised) 7″. Printed black
"GERMANY." Also *Full Bee*,
TMK-2, in black.

3. HEAVENLY ANGEL, 21.
Incised *Crown*, TMK-1, incised
number 21/0/1/2-6″. Unusual ½
size code. Stamped black
"GERMANY." Hollow figure,
open base.

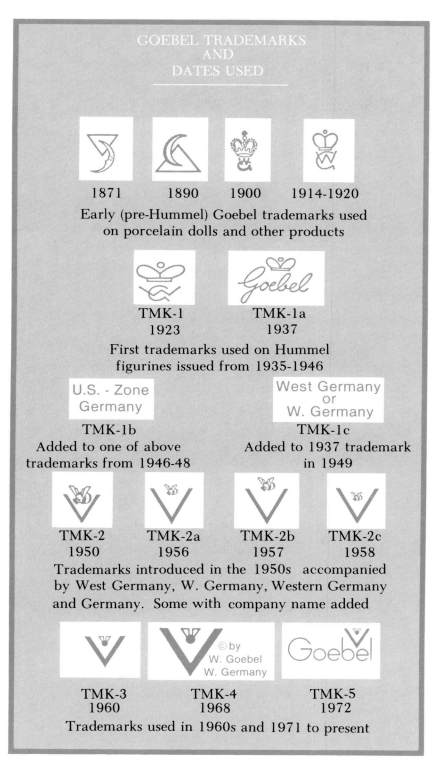

GOEBEL TRADEMARKS
AND
DATES USED

| 1871 | 1890 | 1900 | 1914-1920 |

Early (pre-Hummel) Goebel trademarks used
on porcelain dolls and other products

| TMK-1 | TMK-1a |
| 1923 | 1937 |

First trademarks used on Hummel
figurines issued from 1935-1946

TMK-1b — U.S. - Zone Germany
Added to one of above
trademarks from 1946-48

TMK-1c — West Germany or W. Germany
Added to 1937 trademark
in 1949

| TMK-2 | TMK-2a | TMK-2b | TMK-2c |
| 1950 | 1956 | 1957 | 1958 |

Trademarks introduced in the 1950s accompanied
by West Germany, W. Germany, Western Germany
and Germany. Some with company name added

| TMK-3 | TMK-4 | TMK-5 |
| 1960 | 1968 | 1972 |

©by W. Goebel W. Germany

Trademarks used in 1960s and 1971 to present

The above trademarks, dates, and comments are close approximations. Many overlapping and combinations of marks coupled with conflicting copyright dates indicate the futility of reading too much meaning and accuracy into the "shorthand" history on the bottom of some figurines. Many of these variations are visibly demonstrated in the actual pictures of figurine bottoms accompanying this chart.

4. ANGEL WITH FLOWERS, 36.
Double Crown, incised and
printed, TMK-1. Number 36
(earlier than 36/0). No "country of
origin." Incised "M.I. Hummel."

5. UNKNOWN.
Double (incised and printed)
Crown, TMK-1. Double rim base,
cream colored patina. Closed
base, small air ventholes.

Provision has been made to subdivide these periods into smaller increments to further identify the time of manufacture, if required. For example three subdivisions are suggested for the Crown Mark period from 1935 to 1949 as shown on previous page. This is accomplished by adding a sub letter to the numerical indication of this period. The subdivisions shown, namely 1a, 1b, 1c, are strictly arbitrary and can be changed or expanded as collectors desire. The five mark system has been in use by one expert collector for some time and is being used by others in slightly modified form with considerable success.

These trademarks have been applied as conscientiously as the facsimile signature "M. I. Hummel." In the early days the trademarks were also applied by incising. Later trademarks are stamped in blue ink after the first firing and before the final firing so that they are under the glaze and practically tamper-proof. A study of the pictures of the actual figurine backstamps shows that for many years only an insignia rather than the name of the manufacturer was used. The use of an insignia rather than a name is a common practice among porcelain manufacturers. In 1950 this insignia became the "Full Bee," (see mark #2). Since the words "Das Hummele" mean "busy bee" an association between this logo of the W. Goebel Company and Hummel figurines evolved to the point of confusion for many buyers. All of the trademarks shown are the logo of the W. Goebel Company itself and are used by them on all their products from figurines to dinnerware. The "V" and "Bee" mean Goebel, not Hummel. To repeat once more, the only mark that indicates a genuine 𝓜.𝓘.𝓗𝓾𝓶𝓶𝓮𝓵® approved figurine is this facsimile signature itself. Any other device has no merit and can even be misleading.

6L. RETREAT TO SAFETY, 201.
Full Bee, TMK-2. Number/size
201/2/0-4". Printed Bee in incised
circle "(c) W. Goebel" in blue,
incised date 1948. Printed black
"GERMANY." Solid bottom.

6R. PLAYMATES, 58.
Incised *Crown*, TMK-1. Number
58/0-4". No year date. "U.S.
ZONE GERMANY."

7. GLOBE TROTTER, 79.
No trademark. Stamped in black
"U.S. ZONE" and "GERMANY."
Creamy colored patina. Venthole.

8. APPLE TREE BOY, 142.
Stamped blue, *Full Bee*, TMK-2,
Number/size 142/1-6". Stamped
black "GERMANY." Hollow base,
good patina coloring. No year.

9. HEAR YE! HEAR YE!, 15.
Stamped blue. *Full Bee*, TMK-2,
with (R) at side (for registered?).
Number/size 15/0-(5¼"). Stamped
black "GERMANY." Aged patina
color, solid base.

How They Are Marked

Having pointed out how to tell who made the figurine and about when it was made, the next most important "shorthand" on the base is the combination model and size number. This is for identification and control purposes on almost all M. I. Hummel figurines. Each different model design adapted from Sister Hummel's original is assigned a number between 1 and 400, and this number is incised on the base. If a design is made in only one size this is the only designation. Puppy Love, which is model #1 has only been made in the 4½" size since 1935, and so is a good example because it merely has that number incised.

Little Fiddler, #2, is made in four sizes at present and therefore, has to have additional code marks to indicate each size in the series. The 6" size is marked 2/0 on the underside of the figurine to indicate that there are more sizes in existence and that this was the initial size issued and sometimes referred to as standard size. The 7½" size is marked 2/I. The Roman numeral "I" indicating that it is the next larger size over the original one. The 11½" is number coded 2/II. The Roman numerals are used to indicate sizes larger than the original in ascending order.

Figurines can also be made smaller than the original size. Village Boy is a good example, as it has been made in two sizes smaller than the original 6" size which is now designated as 51/0. When it was decided to issue a smaller 5¼" size, this was marked 51/2/0 to indicate it was the next smaller size or the "double zero size." In descending order from the original size, Arabic numerals are used to indicate the number of zeros. The smallest size Village Boy is 4" high and marked 51/3/0. Size marks only show relative sizes of one design. Not all /3/0 are 4" high. The 4" size in School Boy is designated 82/2/0.

Apple Tree Girl, #141 at the present time, is made in four sizes ranging from 4" to 29" and indicates how the design number and size marks are combined.

NO.	141/3/0	141/2/0	141/0	141/I	141/II	141/III	141/IV
SIZE	4"	-	-	6"	-	-	-

141/V . . . 141/X
10½"   29"

The above series shows also that there are sizes that are not currently produced and cataloged. Some of these were probably never issued and others that are now blank may have once been issued and then discontinued. The 1950 catalog shows the 4", 6", and 10½" as the ones available at that time, also. Further research may establish how many of the missing sizes may have been produced and discontinued.

While the combination of the model number and the size marks is sufficient to distinguish most figurines, there are some additional marks used. Bookends are sold as a pair and are made in

10.   UMBRELLA GIRL, 152.
Stamped *Full Bee* and incised
Full Bee, TMK-2. Number 152
(No. A or B) 5″ with "(c) W.
Goebel" in blue script but no year.
Stamped black "GERMANY."

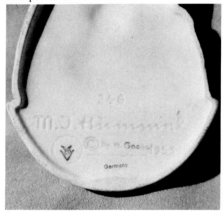

11.   FONT, HOLY FAMILY, 246.
Printed blue. *Full Bee* in incised
circle, TMK-2, "(c) by W. Goebel"
in blue over incised guideline
followed by incised 1955. Stamped
black "GERMANY."

12.   VOLUNTEERS, 50.
Stamped *Low Bee* in blue in incised
circle, TMK-2. Number/size
50/0-(6″), stamped in black
"WESTERN GERMANY." No
date, year, or copyright notice.

26

only one size. For example, Apple Tree Boy, #142, and Apple Tree Girl, #141, are used as a pair of bookends. Their numbers as bookends are 252A and 252B, respectively. The two Nativity Sets, #214 and #260, have about sixteen pieces in each of the two different sized sets. Each piece is designated by a capital letter following the set number and slash mark. St. Joseph in the smaller set is 7½″ high and designated as 214/B. In the larger set, he is 11¾″ high and is designated by 260/B. Many of these smaller #214 figures are available individually in either color or in white. St. Joseph, in color, would be marked 214/B/11, and if in white, the marking would be 214/B/W. Candy boxes are signified by a prefix. The one with the Joyful figurine, #53, on top is marked III/53. Figurines mounted on lamp bases are designated by a capital "M" preceding the figurine number. In this case, the number is the number of the lamp - not the figurine. Apple Tree Girl, #141, when used as a part of a lamp, is M229. Music boxes are just the reverse. The "M" after #388M indicates Little Band Music Box.

The combination of model design number and size code mark are known in numerous other exceptions which have appeared over the years. In some cases the model design number is followed by a decimal mark which collectors prize as a variable. Another eagerly sought one is an Arabic size code mark instead of a Roman numeral. The 7½″ size of Wayside Devotion has been found marked 28/2, instead of the usual 28/II. The actual size of the figurine does not always agree with what the size code mark or what the current catalog shows. Collectors believe that these variations were greater with the earlier trademarks than they have been in recent years. Again, such deviations from the actual marking are premium pieces. The Master Numerical List, Table IV, shows the size code marks for many sizes that no doubt have never been issued. These have been shown because of the uncertainty at this time of what has not been issued and to provide a place to record information when an example of one of them is found or is issued in the future.

Almost without exception, both a trademark and a combination design-size number have appeared on "M. I. Hummel" figurines since they were first introduced. This is not the case with the next combination mark on the underside of the figurines. The use of the company name and the copyright date accompanying it has varied greatly over the years. Currently the copyright date, copyright insignia, and the company name appear on all the figurines large enough to accommodate them. There is also a small capital "R" in a circle near the upper right-hand side of the company name trademark. This signifies that this has been registered by the Goebel Company for its exclusive use. Studying the twenty illustrations of how the figurines have been marked since 1935 will show how the application of the company name and the copyright date has varied over the years. See illustrations on pages 23 through 28.

"M. I. Hummel" Base Shorthand

Model#/Size#
(Little Goatherder

Copyright Notice

TMK- 2
FULL BEE

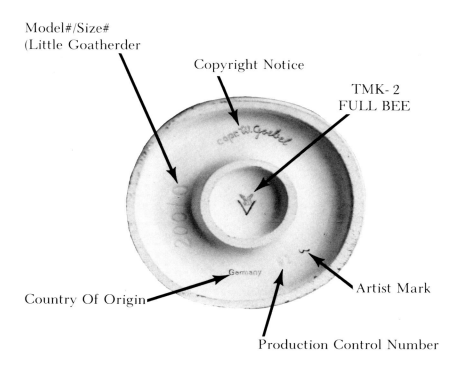

Country Of Origin

Artist Mark

Production Control Number

Model #
(Valentine Gift)

TMK-5
V over G

Special Information

Copyright Symbol

Country of Origin

Copyright Year
(Not always year
of issue)

Artist Mark

® Sometimes used
at right of TMK to indicate
"Registered"

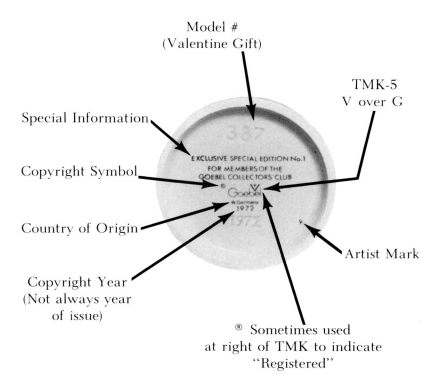

EXCLUSIVE SPECIAL EDITION No.1
FOR MEMBERS OF THE
GOEBEL COLLECTORS' CLUB

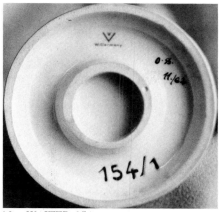

13.   WAITER, 154.
Stylized Bee stamped in blue,
TMK-3, (c. 1960). Number/size
154/1-(7″) (now discontinued) filled
with black. Marked with brush
"O.S. 11/62." Solid base.

14.   UMBRELLA GIRL, 152.
Stylized Bee stamped in blue,
TMK-3, Number/size 152/0-(5½″)
with "WEST GERMANY" at
lower right of "V". Incised copyright "(c)" followed by "W.
Goebel" stamped in black over
incised guideline. Underneath
guideline, year 1951 incised.

15.   SPRING CHEER, 72.
(5″) *Stylized Bee*, TMK-3 but
with no "(c)" with name or year.

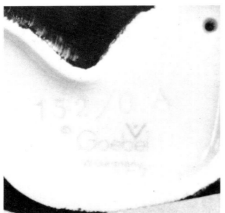

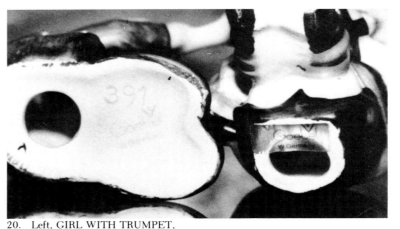

16.   Right, KISS ME, 311. *Stylized Bee*, TMK-3. Black stamp "by W. Goebel." No copyright or year. (Note: copyrighted 1955, issued 1965.) This model's doll has socks. Left, KISS ME, 311. *Three Line*, TMK-4, (c. 1968), stamped in blue followed by incised illegible "1955." This model's doll has no socks. Restyled in 1972. See Section II and III for more information.

17.   M.I. HUMMEL BUST, HU2. Large. Stamped with *Three Line*, TMK-4, and incised year "1967." Designed by "KROBEK"; year discontinued unknown. Superceded by small 5¾" bust in 1977 with TMK-5.

18.   UMBRELLA GIRL, 152B. Stamped blue, *Three Line*, TMK-4. Number/size 152/II B-(8"). Copyright year 1951 (?) incised.

19.   UMBRELLA BOY, 152A. "V over G," TMK-5. Number/size 152/0A-4¾" with incised copyright date of "1957."

20.   Left, GIRL WITH TRUMPET, 39 l. (Part of Little Band) with *V over G*" TMK-5, Number 391, copyright date "1968." GIRL WITH SHEET MUSIC, 389. Right, (part of Little Band) with "*V over G*," TMK-5. Because of small base area and unusual aluminum label.

In many instances undue emphasis has been placed on the date that is on the bottom of many, but not all, figurines. Some collectors have assumed that this is the year the piece was actually made, or if not, the year it was first issued and cataloged. This is perhaps due to the occasions when the date appeared without being associated with the copyright notice. As far as can be ascertained at this time, any dates that have appeared are the dates when the piece was copyrighted. It is not the date of manufacture. As an illustration of how different the two dates may be, The Artist, #304, was issued for the first time in 1971, but was copyrighted on October 20, 1955, sixteen years previously; therefore 1955 appears on the underside of figurines issued in 1971.

Many figurines have other small marks on the underside. Some of them are incised, small Arabic numbers placed at random. To date there is no authoritative information on the function of these marks and, therefore, they have been more or less ignored by collectors. Another small brushmark placed at random on many figurines has been reported by visitors to the Goebel Company to be the initial or other mark of the artist who painted the face of that particular piece. It has been reported that it is the mark of one of the master painters and used to indicate a quality check. In the illustrations, there is an exception in the case of model #154/1 which has the size not only incised, but also emphasized with black paint as well as the initials and a '62 date applied by brush.

Very seldom encountered is a scratchlike cut through the glaze over the mark or the number. There are also two opinions as to what this cut signifies. Some have the opinion that it represents a type of cancelation mark put on pieces sold to the employees so they would not resell them, but which are otherwise perfect pieces. Others feel that this cut mark was used to signify a piece that did not meet quality standards and which employees were allowed to buy at a discount, or were given. Whatever the reason, such pieces are known to exist and, if encountered, should be carefully scrutinized for imperfections.

To summarize graphically: a chart titled "M. I. Hummel" Base Shorthand with illustrations of the base of figurines #200/0, Little Goat Herder, and #387, Valentine Gift, is shown on page 27 with the name of each mark shown.

Other Adaptations of Hummel Art

M. I. Hummel porcelain figurines are only one adaptation of Sister Hummel's art. Other collectible adaptations are Hummel dolls, plates, prints, pictures, postcards, calendars, books, bells, boxes, and candles.

M. I. Hummel dolls are made exclusively by the W. Goebel Company and were added to the line in 1955. W. Goebel has been making other dolls since 1871, but the M. I. Hummel dolls can be identified by the facsimile signature M.J.Hummel®. These dolls are made of vinyl plastic. Doll collectors report that these dolls can be bought in the United States, but can be purchased for considerably less in Germany, where it seems the majority of Hummel dolls are sold.

M. I. Hummel plates entered the Goebel line in 1971 with their first limited edition annual (Christmas) plate. That same year Schmid Brothers, Inc., of Randolph, Massachusetts, introduced a Berta Hummel Christmas plate. Since that year both companies have continued to produce commemorative plates plus at least one limited edition each year. Schmid also introduced a limited edition Mother's Day plate in 1972 and has issued one each year since.

Paper prints, pictures, and postcards adapted from Sister Hummel's original paintings actually predate the production of figurines. Josef Müller and Emil Fink, both publishers, entered into separate agreements with Sister Hummel and her convent for the rights to reproduce her works in the early thirties. Paper calendars based on Hummel art are made by W. Goebel, Emil Fink, and Josef Müller.

Three books reproducing drawings and paintings of Sister Hummel are *The Hummel Book*, by Hummel and Seemann, copyrighted by Emil Fink Company in 1934, *The Hummel*, published and copyrighted by Josef Müller in 1939, and a rare, out-of-print biography by an American Franciscan nun entitled *Sketch Me*, publisher and date unknown.

Hummel bells, boxes, and candles for the most part are distributed by the Schmid Company using transfers or decoupages of reproductions of Sister Hummel's art. These adaptations can be identified in the same way as the reproduced Hummel prints, by the signature of Sister Hummel found in many forms. If the picture has been cropped, the collector must learn to recognize genuine Hummel adaptations, look for the Schmid name, or trust his dealer.

There are many Hummel-like products on the market of every type and form imaginable. The principal, authorized adaptations of Sister Hummel's can be identified by checking for the facsimile signature, the company, or by learning to recognize the distinctive style of Sister Hummel's art.

ANGEL TRIO (A) Hummel, III/38/39,/40.

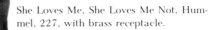

Figurines Calendar 1976

English issue M. I. Hummel 1976 calendar featuring Apple Tree Girl Annual Plate.

She Loves Me, She Loves Me Not, Hummel, 227, with brass receptacle.

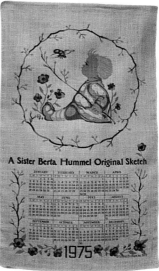

A Sister Berta Hummel Original Sketch

Sister Berta Hummel 1975 calendar towel by Schmid Brothers.

31

3.

Price Guides to Hummel Figurines

Price Guides Can Help

When Dale Carnegie wrote *How to Win Friends and Influence People*, he could not have had authors of price guides in mind. Having produced over ten price guides in the last fifteen years, this author is unaware of having won many friends. However, it appears from the many letters received that price guides do influence collectors, dealers, and appraisers. The people who use price guides most effectively view them as just one of four or five factors to be considered in any specific case. Unfortunately some readers select a price assuming it to be a quick and final answer. They use a book as a bible rather than a guide.

The prices listed in the tables of this price guide include new, old, rare, unusual, and scarce Hummels of all types. One nationally known collector commented, "Sure, you can issue price lists for new Hummel figurines easily, just take production costs and add a profit. But you can't publish a price guide of 'Old Hummels'; that's impossible." A sage once said, "The impossible only takes a little more time and a little more effort."

Hum. 50
VOLUNTEERS. Stamped *Low Bee* in blue in incised circle, TMK-2. Number/size 50/0-(6"), stamped in black "WESTERN GERMANY." No date, year, or copyright notice.

Publishing a price guide is not quick or easy. Data collected from hundreds of people, stacks of letters, many publications, and thousands of miles of travel must be compiled, sorted, and placed in meaningful order so that statistical methods can be applied. With many additional steps, including checking each figure with many experts, a guide price for each item is arrived at. What does that guide price mean? It is simply a price that applies for only one set of conditions. It is only a guide. It is not absolute. It is not exact.

It is a selected figure representing what might be a fair price in a number of instances. It is a starting point. From this price a figure to fit a particular situation can be determined with much greater accuracy. By modifying the listed figure for time, place, and circumstances, a price mutually satisfactory to the buyer and seller is more likely. The deal is made fairly and quickly.

For example: A collector no longer wants a Merry Wanderer, 7″ tall with an old Full Bee mark. By referring to Table II he will see a "guide price" of $367 listed. Does he expect to get this price? Only if he finds a collector who wants this exact model, size, and mark at the same time he wants to sell.

If he is in a hurry, he might offer the figurine to a dealer. What will be a fair price? The dealer may already have a large inventory of hundreds of items worth thousands of dollars. He is probably paying interest on a loan to the bank, as well as his rent, advertising, salaries, and other expenses. With these thoughts in mind, he offers the collector half the listed price or $183. When the dealer finally sells the item, he may end up with a small net profit of 5 percent to 10 percent of what he received. Was the $183 a fair price? In many cases it is. It is fair to the seller because he has his money at once with no expense or effort on his part and to the dealer because he is able to make a small net profit after expense on the transaction, which is why he is in business.

Another example of a sale might involve a collector who discovers from the price guide that he has an item with unusual size, color, and markings. According to the price guide only a few are known to exist and have sold from $900 to $1,400 when offered. While he's still undecided about what to do, a dealer calls to ask if he is interested in selling, having heard about the piece from a mutual acquaintance. The conversation might go something like this:

Dealer: "By any chance do you have an oversize Merry Wanderer with red shoes?"

Collector: "No, this one has green shoes, but otherwise it is just like the book says."

Dealer: "I have a good customer that's been waiting four years to find one like you describe. How much do you want for it?"

Collector: (After a moment's hesitation) "Fourteen hundred dollars."

Dealer: "All right, on one condition. I will send you a cashier's check for $1400 providing you give me five days to make sure the figurine is as you describe it."

Collector: "That's fine with me. I'll hold it if I get your check before next Tuesday."

What happened? Why was this dealer willing to pay more than some collectors had paid in the past? At least one good reason might have been that his customer had told him he would pay up to $1600 anytime for such an example. With little risk involved the dealer can make a fast, small profit. He's happy, his customer is happy, and the seller is ecstatic. In the seller's opinion the author of the price guide is a great fellow with conservative prices.

A final example of a possible sale might be as follows. The very same collector with the "$1400" figurine with green shoes might spend hours calling dealers and writing out-of-town ones listed in the Buyers' Guide. Finally, getting impatient and disgusted, he might give the piece to a commission auctioneer to sell who agrees to retain 25 percent of the proceeds as his commission. The auction is on a bad day. Only the mailman and a few hardy individuals are out. Nobody at the auction cares especially about the Hummel figurine or its value. It goes for only $50 on two bids. Now the collector is certain the author of the price guide knows nothing about pricing Hummel figurines. In both cases, although fictional and extreme, the price in the book was only a guide. The figure had to be modified by the conditions at the time of the sale.

CURRENT "M. I. HUMMEL" FIGURINES AND ADAPTATIONS

The following photographs are an alphabetical listing of Hummel figures currently being produced by Goebel. Figures not photographed are cross-referenced.

Figurines

1. A FAIR MEASURE
Hummel, 345

3. ADORATION
Hummel, 23

2. ACCORDION BOY
Hummel, 185

4. ADVENTURE BOUND
Hummel, 347

ANGEL DUET
Hum. 261.
See Angel Duet, Candleholder,
Hum. 193

ANGEL SERENADE
Hum. 214/D.
See Nativity Set for picture. Angel
Serenade (standing) Hum. 83 is
discontinued. See Section II, Table
II.

ANGEL TRIO (A)
Hum. III 38/0, 39/0, 40/0.
See Angel Trio (A) in
Candleholders.

ANGEL TRIO (B)
Hum. 238/A-C.
See Angel Trio (B) in Candleholders
for picture.

ANGEL WITH ACCORDION
Hum. 238/B.
See Angel Trio (B), in
Candleholders for picture.

ANGEL WITH LUTE
Hum. 238/8.
See Angel Trio (B), Candleholders,
for picture.

ANGELIC SLEEP
Hum. 25.
See Candleholders for picture.

36

5.   ANGELIC CARE
Hummel, 194

6.   ANGELIC SONG
Hummel, 144

7.   APPLE TREE BOY
Hummel, 142

8.   APPLE TREE GIRL
Hummel, 141

9.   ARTIST, THE
Hummel, 304

10.   AUF WIEDERSEHEN
Hummel, 153

11.   AUTUMN HARVEST
Hummel, 355

12.   BAKER
Hummel, 128

13.   BAND LEADER
Hummel, 129

14. BARNYARD HERO
Hummel, 195

15. BASHFUL
Hummel, 377

16. BE PATIENT
Hummel, 197

17. BEGGING HIS SHARE
Hummel, 9

18. BIG HOUSE-CLEANING
Hummel, 363

19. BIRD DUET
Hummel, 169

20. BIRTHDAY SERENADE
Hummel, 218

21. BLESSED EVENT
Hummel, 333

22. BOOK WORM
Hummel 3; Hummel 8

BOY WITH ACCORDION
Hum. 390.
See Children Trio (B) for picture.

BOY WITH HORSE
Hum. 117.
See Christmas Angels in
Candleholders for picture.

BOY WITH HORSE
Hum. 239/C.
See Children Trio (A) for picture.

23. BOOTS
Hummel, 143

24. BOY WITH TOOTHACHE
Hummel, 217

25. BROTHER
Hummel, 95

26. BUILDER, THE
Hummel, 305

27. BUSY STUDENT
Hummel, 367

28. CARNIVAL
Hummel, 328

29. CELESTIAL MUSICIAN
Hummel, 188

30. CHICK GIRL
Hummel, 57

31. CHICKEN-LICKEN
Hummel, 385

32. CHILDREN TRIO (A)
Hummel, 239/A, 239/B, 239/C

34. CHIMNEY SWEEP
Hummel, 12

33. CHILDREN TRIO (B)
Hummel, 389, 390, 391

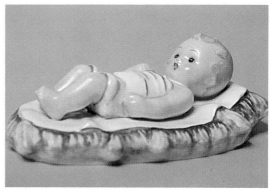

35. CHRIST CHILD
Hummel, 18

36. CINDERELLA
Hummel, 337

37. CLOSE HARMONY
Hummel, 336

38. CONFIDENTIALLY
Hummel, 314

39. CONGRATULATIONS
Hummel, 17

40. COQUETTES
Hummel, 179

41. CROSSROADS
Hummel, 331

42. CULPRITS
Hummel, 56/A

43. DOCTOR
Hummel, 127

44. DOLL BATH
Hummel, 319

45. DOLL MOTHER
Hummel, 67

46. DRUMMER
Hummel, 240

47. DUET
Hummel, 130

48. EASTER GREETINGS
Hummel, 378

49. EASTER TIME
Hummel, 384

EASTER PLAYMATES (secondary name for Hum. 384).

50. EVENTIDE
Hummel, 99

51. FAREWELL
Hummel, 65

52. FARM BOY
Hummel, 66

53. FAVORITE PET
Hummel, 361

54. FEATHERED FRIENDS
Hummel, 344

55. FEEDING TIME
Hummel, 199

58. FLOWER VENDOR
Hummel, 381

56. FESTIVAL HARMONY (MANDOLIN)
Hummel, 172

57. FESTIVAL HARMONY (FLUTE)
Hummel, 173

59. FLYING ANGEL
Hummel, 366

60. FOLLOW THE LEADER
Hummel, 369

61. FOR FATHER
Hummel, 87

62. FOR MOTHER
Hummel, 257

63. FRIENDS
Hummel, 136

64. GAY ADVENTURE
Hummel, 356

GIRL WITH DOLL
HUM. 239/B.
See Children Trio (A) for picture.

GIRL WITH FIR TREE
Hum. 116.
See Christmas Angels,
Candleholders.

GIRL WITH NOSEGAY
Hum. 115.
See Christmas Angels,
Candleholders.

GIRL WITH NOSEGAY
Hum. 239/A.
See Children Trio (A) for picture.

GIRL WITH SHEET OF MUSIC
Hum. 389.
See Children Trio (B) for picture.

GIRL WITH TRUMPET
Hum. 391.
See Children Trio (B) for picture.

65.   GLOBE TROTTER
Hummel, 79

66.   GOING TO GRANDMA'S
Hummel, 52

67.   GOOD FRIENDS
Hummel, 182

68.   GOOD HUNTING!
Hummel, 307

69.   GOOD NIGHT
Hummel, 214/C

70.   GOOD SHEPHERD
Hummel, 42

71.   GOOSE GIRL
Hummel, 47

72.   GUIDING ANGEL
Hummel, 357

73.   HAPPINESS
Hummel, 86

74.   HAPPY BIRTHDAY
Hummel, 176

77.   HAPPY TRAVELLER
Hummel, 109

HEAVENLY LULLABY
Hum. 262.
See Lullaby, Hum. 262 for picture.

75.   HAPPY DAYS
Hummel, 150

76.   HAPPY PASTIME
Hummel, 69

78.   HEAR YE, HEAR YE
Hummel, 15

79.   HEAVENLY ANGEL
Hummel, 21

80.   HEAVENLY PROTECTION
Hummel, 88

81. HELLO
Hummel, 124

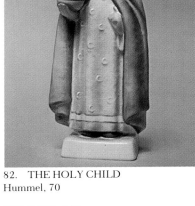

82. THE HOLY CHILD
Hummel, 70

83. HOME FROM MARKET
Hummel, 198

84. HOMEWARD BOUND
Hummel, 334

HOLY FAMILY
Hum. 214/A, 214/B.
See Nativity for picture.

85. INFANT JESUS
Hummel, 214/A/K

86. INFANT OF KRUMBAD
Hummel, 78/111

87. JOYFUL
Hummel, 53

JOYFUL ADVENTURE
Hum. 356. See Gay Adventure for picture.

88. JUST RESTING
Hummel, 112

89. KISS ME
Hummel, 311

90. KNITTING LESSON
Hummel, 256

91.   LATEST NEWS
Hummel, 184

92.   LET'S SING
Hummel, 110

93.   LETTER TO SANTA CLAUS
Hummel, 340

94.   LITTLE BAND (on base)
Hummel, 392

95.   LITTLE BOOKKEEPER
Hummel, 306

96.   LITTLE CELLIST
Hummel, 89

97.   LITTLE FIDDLER
Hummel 2—4

98.   LITTLE GABRIEL
Hummel, 32

99.   LITTLE GARDENER
Hummel, 74

100. LITTLE GOAT HERDER
Hummel, 200

101. LITTLE GUARDIAN
Hummel, 145

102. LITTLE HELPER
Hummel, 73

103. LITTLE HIKER
Hummel, 16

104. LITTLE PHARMACIST
Hummel, 322

105. LITTLE SCHOLAR
Hummel, 80

106. LITTLE SHOPPER
Hummel, 96

107. LITTLE SWEEPER
Hummel, 171

108. LITTLE TAILOR
Hummel, 308

109. LITTLE THRIFTY
Hummel, 118

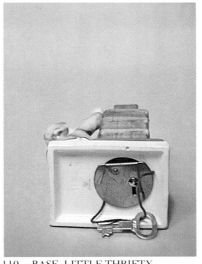

110. BASE, LITTLE THRIFTY
Showing door and key

111. LITTLE TOOTER
(Shepherd Kneeling with Flute)
Hummel, 214/H

112. LOST SHEEP, THE
Hummel, 68

113. LOST STOCKING
Hummel, 374

114. LULLABY
Hummel, 262

115. MAIL IS HERE
(Mail Coach)
Hummel, 226

116. MARCH WINDS
Hummel, 43

117. MAX AND MORITZ
Hummel, 123

118.   MEDITATION
Hummel, 13

119.   MERRY WANDERER
Hummel 7—11

120.   MISCHIEF MAKER
Hummel, 342

121.   MOTHER'S DARLING
Hummel, 175

122.   MOTHER'S HELPER
Hummel, 133

123.   MOUNTAINEER
Hummel, 315

124.   NOT FOR YOU!
Hummel, 317

125.   ON SECRET PATH
Hummel, 386

126.   OUT OF DANGER
Hummel, 56/B

127. PHOTOGRAPHER, THE
Hummel, 178

128. PLAYMATES
Hummel, 58

129. POSTMAN
Hummel, 119

130. PRAYER BEFORE BATTLE
Hummel, 20

131. PUPPY LOVE
Hummel, 1

132. RETREAT TO SAFETY
Hummel, 201

133. RIDE INTO CHRISTMAS
Hummel, 396

134. RING AROUND THE
ROSIE   Hummel, 348

135. RUNAWAY, THE
Hummel, 327

136. ST. GEORGE
Hummel, 55

137. ST. JOSEPH
Hummel, 214/B

138. SCHOOL BOY
Hummel, 82

139. SCHOOL BOYS
Hummel, 170

140. SCHOOL GIRL
Hummel, 81

141. SCHOOL GIRLS
Hummel, 177

142. SENSITIVE HUNTER
Hummel, 6

143. SERENADE
Hummel, 85

144. SHEPHERD'S BOY
Hummel, 64

145. SHE LOVES ME,
SHE LOVES ME NOT!
Hummel, 174

SHEPHERD KNEELING WITH
FLUTE
Hum. 214/H/II.
See Little Tooter.

146. SHINING LIGHT
Hummel, 358

147. SIGNS OF SPRING
Hummel, 203

148. SINGING LESSON
Hummel, 63

149. SISTER
Hummel, 98

150. SKIER
Hummel, 59

151. SMART LITTLE SISTER, THE
Hummel, 346

152. SOLDIER BOY
Hummel, 332

153. SOLOIST
Hummel, 135

154. SPRING CHEER
Hummel, 72

155. SPRING DANCE
Hummel, 353

156. STARGAZER
Hummel, 132

157. STITCH IN TIME, A
Hummel, 255

158. STORMY WEATHER
Hummel, 71

159. STREET SINGER
Hummel, 131

160. STROLLING ALONG
Hummel, 5

161. SURPRISE
Hummel, 94

162. SWEET MUSIC
Hummel, 186

163. TELLING HER SECRET
Hummel, 196

THE RUNAWAY
Hum. 327
See Runaway, The for picture.

164. TO MARKET
Hummel, 49

165. TRUMPET BOY
Hummel, 97

166. TUNEFUL ANGEL
Hummel, 359

167. UMBRELLA BOY
Hummel, 152/A

168. UMBRELLA GIRL
Hummel, 152/B

169. VALENTINE GIFT
Hummel, 387
(See Goebel Collectors' Club.)

170. VILLAGE BOY
Hummel, 51

171. VISITING AN INVALID
Hummel, 382

174. WASH DAY
Hummel, 321

172. VOLUNTEERS
Hummel, 50

173. WAITER
Hummel, 154

WATCHFUL ANGEL
Hum. 194. See Angelic Care.

175. WAYSIDE DEVOTION
Hummel, 28

176. WAYSIDE HARMONY
Hummel, 111

177. WEARY WANDERER
Hummel, 204

178. WE CONGRATULATE
Hummel, 220 (if no base # is 214/E)

179. WHICH HAND?
Hummel, 258

180. WHITSUNTIDE
Hummel, 163 (Discontinued)

Ashtrays

181. WORSHIP
Hummel, 84

182. BOY WITH BIRD
Hummel, 166

183. HAPPY PASTIME
Hummel, 62

184. JOYFUL
Hummel, 33

185. LET'S SING
Hummel, 114

186. SINGING LESSON
Hummel, 34

Bell

First Annual Hummel Bell. LET'S SING!
Hummel, 700.

Bookends

187. APPLE TREE BOY AND GIRL
Hummel, 252/A + B

188. BOOKWORM
Hummel, 14/A + B

189. GOOSE GIRL AND FARM BOY
Hummel, 60/A + B

190. LITTLE GOAT HERDER
AND FEEDING TIME
Hummel, 250/A + B

191. PLAYMATES AND CHICK GIRL
Hummel, 61/A + B

Candleholders

ADVENT CANDLESTICKS,
Hum. No's 115, 116, 117,
see Christmas Angels for pictures.

193.   ANGEL TRIO (A)
Hummel, III/40,/38,/39

194.   ANGEL TRIO (B)
Hummel, 238/A,/B,/C
Identical to ANGEL TRIO (A)
without candles.
Figure A is Angel with Mandolin,
Figure B is Angel with Accordian
and Figure C is Angel with Horn.

192.   ANGEL DUET
Hummel, 193

195.   ANGELIC SLEEP
Hummel, 25

196.   CANDLELIGHT
Hummel, 192

197.   CHRISTMAS ANGELS (SET)
Hummel, 117, 115, 116

198.   HERALD ANGELS
Hummel, 37

Candleholders

199.   LITTLE BAND
Hummel, 388

200.   LULLABY
Hummel, 24

201.   SILENT NIGHT
Hummel, 54

Candy Boxes

202.   CHICK GIRL
Hummel, III/57

203.   HAPPY PASTIME
Hummel, III/69

204.   JOYFUL
Hummel, III/53

Candy Boxes

205. LET'S SING
Hummel, III/110

206. PLAYMATES
Hummel, III/58

207. SINGING LESSON
Hummel, III/63

Fonts

208. ANGEL DUET
Hummel, 146

209. ANGELIC PRAYER
Hummel, 75

210. ANGEL AT PRAYER
Hummel, 91/A, /B

211. ANGEL WITH BIRD
Hummel, 167. (D'cont'd, 77)

212. ANGEL WITH BIRDS
Hummel, 22

213. ANGEL WITH FLOWERS
Hummel, 36

Fonts

214. CHILD JESUS
Hummel, 26

215. DEVOTION
Hummel, 147

216. GOOD SHEPHERD
Hummel, 35

217. HEAVENLY ANGEL
Hummel, 207

218. HOLY FAMILY
Hummel, 246

219. KNEELING ANGEL
Hummel, 248

220. MADONNA WITH CHILD
Hummel, 243. (D'cont'd, 77)

221. WORSHIP
Hummel, 164

Lamps

222. APPLE TREE GIRL
Hummel, 229

APPLE TREE BOY
Hummel, 230

223. CULPRITS
Hummel, 44/A

224. GOOD FRIENDS
Hummel, 228

225. JUST RESTING
Hummel, 225

SHE LOVES ME,
SHE LOVES ME NOT

Hummel, 227
See Rare and Unusual Section
for picture.

226. OUT OF DANGER, Hum. 44B.
Left, TMK-2, 9½", old style with brass
receptacle and switch in base. Right,
TMK-4, 9½", new-style socket with
switch in cord.

227. TO MARKET
Hummel, 223

228. WAYSIDE HARMONY
Hummel, 224

Madonnas

229. FLOWER MADONNA
Hummel, 10

MADONNA (Kneeling)
See Nativity Set 260, for picture.

230. MADONNA WITH HALO
Hummel, 45

231. MADONNA WITHOUT HALO
Hummel, 46

Music Boxes

232. LITTLE BAND (with candle)
Hummel, 388/M

233. LITTLE BAND
Hummel, 392/M

Nativity Sets

234. SMALL NATIVITY SET
Hummel, 214 A-0 + 366

235. LARGE NATIVITY SET
Hummel, 260 A-R

Plaques

236. BA-BEE RING
Hummel, 30/A

237. Back of ring
showing signature

238. CHILD IN BED
Hummel, 48

239. LITTLE FIDDLER
Hummel, 93

240. MADONNA
Hummel, 48

241. MAIL IS HERE (Mail Coach)
Hummel, 140

242. MERRY WANDERER
Hummel, 92
(Reinstated, 77)

243. M. I. HUMMEL DISPLAY
Hummel, 187/C

Plaques

244. QUARTET
Hummel, 134

245. RETREAT TO SAFETY
Hummel, 126

246. VACATION TIME
Hummel, 125

Annual Plates

247. ANNUAL PLATE—1971
Heavenly Angel, Hum. 264

248. ANNUAL PLATE—1972
Hear Ye, Hear Ye, Hum. 265

249. ANNUAL PLATE—1973
Globetrotter, Hum. 266

250. ANNUAL PLATE—1974
Goose Girl, Hum. 267

251. ANNUAL PLATE—1975
Ride into Christmas, Hum. 268

252. ANNUAL PLATE—1976
Apple Tree Girl, Hum. 269

253. ANNUAL PLATE—1977
Apple Tree Boy, Hum. 270

254. ANNUAL PLATE—1978
Happy Pastime, Hum. 271

255. ANNIVERSARY PLATE—1975
Stormy Weather, Hum. 280

Miscellaneous

256. M. I. HUMMEL BUST   (OLD)
Hummel, HU 1

257. SISTER M. I. HUMMEL BUST
Hummel, HU 2

258. Base of Hu I showing
sculptor's signature
(Skrobek) and date (1965)

Section I. Current Models and Prices

Table I, showing three different prices for new Hummel figurines, is designed principally for readers interested in buying and collecting new figures from normal outlets such as department stores and gift shops. Readers interested in previously owned examples with earlier trademarks or unlisted sizes should refer to Table II in Section II—Prices for "M. I. Hummel" Figurines with Old Marks, which contains answers and other related information. The examples found in Section II are not normally carried in gift shops or department stores. Section III lists very rare and unusual "M. I. Hummel" figurines. While a small percentage of readers are collectors of these items, the general reader might enjoy reading this section with the possibility that his collection might contain a rare or unique piece and, therefore, be quite valuable. Discovering a second example of a piece thought to be unique could prove to be better than winning the daily double at the nearest track.

Sections I, II, and III have all been arranged in alphabetical order for conveniently locating a model by name. The sequence and names have been assigned from the latest Goebel price list and may vary somewhat from the book, *Hummel*, by Eric Ehrmann. If you have the number of a piece but do not know the name, you can refer first to the Master Numerical List - Section IV and then use Section I for the price information you need. If you do not know the name or the number, refer to the 300 color illustrations for initial identification.

The first three columns are self-explanatory and use the English name assigned by the Goebel Company. The corresponding model number is in the second column, which also includes the size indicator code if more than one size has ever been produced. For those not conversant with this suffix after the Arabic number, the complete method of size coding is described in Chapter 2 under the heading, "How They Are Marked."

The third column shows the approximate size to the nearest ¼ inch plus or minus. The example you may buy at the present time may vary slightly from this figurine since these are handcrafted and also are subject to normal manufacturing variations. However, if the size should vary appreciably from the one that has been listed as the official size by the Goebel Company in the price list, some further checking is in order. First, look at the trademark on the bottom and compare it to the ones shown in this book. If it is not the one that was first used about 1971 and still in use (TMK-5, "V over G"), you may have an example that carries a premium price. Look up the price in Section II under the proper column for the mark on the back. If it has the current mark (#5), and the size is more than ¼ inch larger or smaller than the size indicator on the back suggests, you may also have a premium piece due to an unaccounted for variation in manufacturing. If it is other than #5 mark, use Table III.

The sizes listed in this third column do not always agree with the size for the same figures given in the book, *Hummel.* The assumption has been made that since this list was prepared by the Goebel Company after the book was published, that these figures are correct and take precedence over those in the other book. Some collectors have even taken the time to change their *Hummel* book sizes to agree with the official price list.

Any appreciable deviation from the standard manufacturing size can be an important premium factor in determining a fair value. So can the older mark. The greater the deviation in size or mark, the greater the premium it commands from Hummel collectors.

The column next to the last is headed "Retail Price." This is in U.S. dollars and is taken directly from the last "Suggested Retail Price List" that was published before this book went to press. All the prices are for an individual piece, except for some that are sold in sets and are so marked or indicated by more than one number. The Angel Trios and the two Children Trios are examples of this. The bookends are priced as pairs. The five- and eight-piece Orchestra groups are listed with the number of pieces, as are the various combinations of Nativity Sets.

The column to the left of the "Retail Price" column is headed "Low Price" and the one to the right is headed "High Price." The data for these two columns were obtained from numerous sources and represent thousands of individual prices that have been consolidated into one meaningful figure for each line. They came from ads in collectors' magazines, from dealers' shops visited on two different surveys, from auctions, private sales, overseas shops, and from Canada. The figures in the "Low Price" column are frequently the ones found in visiting overseas shops and from price lists and ads placed in American publications by foreign dealers. In fewer instances they represent the price received for new figurines sold at auction or by means of an advertised sale of someone liquidating a small collection.

The difference in the percentage of discount between the higher priced model and the less expensive ones is noticeable. The figurines with retail prices of several hundred dollars have the biggest discount from the retail price. This seems reasonable in view of the smaller market for such figures, and the actual dollar profit is equivalent to that of several lesser priced ones, combined. By and large, the discount from United States' prices average around 10 percent less. Of course, the percentage of figurines sold at these reduced prices is a very small fraction of the total quantities.

The figures listed in the "High Price" column were obtained to a great extent from dealers' shops in this country. Because of the scarcity of new figurines and the method by which they are allocated, dealers that maintain a very large inventory for their collectors are forced to buy from overseas, principally in Germany. The dealers' agents in Germany buy them from authorized Goebel dealers and pay the current local German retail price, which is somewhat less than that in the United States. By the time they arrive in this country they have to be marked up 10 percent in order for the American dealers to break even or to make a much smaller profit than they do on their own allocations. However, these few dealers render an invaluable service to their customers. Some of these dealers are listed in the back of the book under "Sources." Collectors finding themselves stymied in the search for a particular model might find help from these dealers. The ones specializing in mail orders are indicated for the convenience of buyers and collectors who do not have a nearby dealer.

Other prices in the "High" column are based on the prices charged by some Canadian dealers for reasons unknown. Since many Americans go to Canada on shopping trips or for vacations, they might find something they want there. In the "High" column there are some few examples that regular dealers charge for certain pieces because of excessive demand. The Ride into Christmas figurine is an example of such a premium price. The prices in these few cases are very unstable as the supply could increase at any time.

It is important to remember that while all of the prices shown here are based on actual transactions, they are also based on the circumstances at the time of the sale. These circumstances might not be the same at a later date. Since they are retail prices, they are higher than the individual can expect to receive if he is selling them to a dealer or at an auction. Such selling prices will vary widely and may be as much as 50 percent less than the retail prices shown here. For further information about this, see Chapter 8 entitled, "Where to Buy and Sell Hummel Art."

TABLE I.
ALPHABETICAL CURRENT PRICE GUIDE

Model	Number	Approx. Size Cm.	Inches	Low Retail	Retail Price	High Retail	Page No.
A Fair Measure	Hummel 345	14.0	5½"	57.00	63.00	69.00	36
Accordion Boy	Hummel 185	12.7	5"	35.00	39.00	43.00	36
Adoration	Hummel 23/I	15.9	6¼"	83.00	92.00	101.00	36
Adoration (Disc. in 78)	Hummel 23/III		9"	—	—	—	36
Adventure Bound	Hummel 347	21.0x19.1	8¼"x7½"	983.00	1,092.50	1,202.00	36
Angel Duet	Hummel 261	12.7	5"	50.00	55.50	61.00	36
Angel Serenade	Hummel 214/D/II	7.6	3"	18.00	19.50	21.00	36
Angel Trio (Candleholder)	Hummel 111/38, 39, 40	5.1	2"	38.00	42.00	46.00	36
Angel Trio	Hum 238/A-C	5.1	2"	38.00	42.00	46.00	36
Angelic Sleep	Hum 25/I	12.7x8.9	5"x3½"	46.00	51.50	57.00	36
Angelic Song	Hum 144	10.2	4"	38.00	42.00	46.00	37
Apple Tree Boy (Med.)	Hum 142/I	15.2	6"	44.00	60.50	67.00	37
Apple Tree Boy (Sm.)	Hum 142/3/0	10.2	4"	27.00	29.50	32.00	37
Apple Tree Boy (Lg.)	Hum 142/V	25.4	10"	300.00	333.50	367.00	37
Apple Tree Girl (Med.)	Hum 141/I	15.2	6"	54.00	60.50	67.00	37
Apple Tree Girl (Sm.)	Hum 141/3/0	10.2	4"	27.00	29.50	32.00	37
Apple Tree Girl (Lg.)	Hum 141/V	25.4	10"	300.00	333.50	367.00	37
Artist	Hum 304	14.0	5½"	44.00	49.00	54.00	37
Auf. Wiedersehen	Hum 153/0	12.7	5"	47.00	52.50	58.00	37
Autumn Harvest	Hum 355	12.1	4¾"	48.00	53.50	59.00	37
Baker	Hummel 128	12.1	4¾"	34.00	38.00	42.00	37
Band Leader	Hum 129	12.7	5"	40.50	45.00	49.50	37
Barnyard Hero	Hum 195/I	14.0	5½"	58.50	65.00	71.50	38
Barnyard Hero	Hum 195/2/0	10.2	4"	34.00	38.00	42.00	38
Bashful	Hum 377	12.1	4¾"	39.00	43.00	47.00	38
Be Patient	Hum 197/I	15.9	6¼"	52.00	57.50	63.00	38
Be Patient	Hum 197/2/0	10.8	4¼"	34.00	38.00	42.00	38
Begging His Share	Hum 9	14.0	5½"	40.00	44.50	49.00	38
Big Housecleaning	Hum 363	10.2	4"	61.00	67.50	74.00	38
Bird Duet	Hum 169	10.2	4"	35.00	39.00	43.00	38
Birthday Serenade	Hum 218/2/0	10.8	4¼"	39.00	43.50	48.00	38
Blessed Event	Hum 333	14.0	5½"	90.00	100.50	111.00	38
Bookworm	Hum 3/I	14.0	5½"	83.00	92.00	101.00	38
Bookworm	Hum 3/II	20.3	8"	362.00	402.50	443.00	38
Bookworm	Hum 8	10.2	4"	40.50	45.00	49.50	38
Boots	Hum 143/0	14.0	5½"	34.00	38.00	42.00	39
Boy With Toothache	Hum 217	14.0	5½"	37.00	41.50	46.00	39
Brother	Hum 95	12.1	4¾"	31.00	34.50	38.00	39
Builder	Hum 305	14.0	5½"	48.00	53.50	59.00	39
Busy Student	Hum 367	10.8	4¼"	35.00	38.50	42.00	39
Carnival	Hum 328	15.2	6"	35.00	39.00	43.00	39
Celestial Musician	Hum 188	17.8	7"	72.00	80.00	88.00	39
Chick Girl	Hum 57/0	8.9	3½"	31.00	34.50	38.00	39
Chick Girl	Hum 57/I	10.8	4½"	51.00	56.50	62.00	39
Chicken-Licken	Hum 385	12.1	4¾"	61.00	67.50	74.00	40
Children Trio	Hum 239/A-C	8.9	3½"	43.00	48.00	53.00	40
Children Trio	Hum 389-90-91	5.7	2¼"	54.00	60.00	66.00	40
Chimney Sweep	Hum 12/I	14.0	5½"	34.00	38.00	42.00	40
Chimney Sweep	Hum 12/2/0	10.2	4"	20.00	22.50	25.00	40
Christ Child	Hum 18	15.2x5.1	6"x2"	31.50	35.00	38.50	40
Cinderella	Hum 337	11.4	4½"	58.00	64.50	71.00	40
Close Harmony	Hum 336	14.0	5½"	62.00	68.50	75.00	40
Confidentially	Hum 314	14.0	5½"	48.00	53.50	59.00	41
Congratulations	Hum 17/0	15.2	6"	31.00	34.50	38.00	41
Coquettes	Hum 179	12.7	5"	54.00	60.50	67.00	41
Crossroads	Hum 331	17.1	6¾"	97.00	107.50	118.00	41
Culprits	Hum 56/A	15.9	6¼"	47.00	52.50	58.00	41
Doctor	Hum 127	12.1	4¾"	35.00	39.00	43.00	41
Doll Bath	Hum 319	12.7	5"	46.00	51.00	56.00	41
Doll Mother	Hum 67	12.1	4¾"	51.00	56.50	62.00	41
Drummer	Hum 240	10.8	4¼"	31.00	34.50	38.00	41
Duet	Hum 130	12.7	5"	54.00	60.50	67.00	42
Easter Greetings	Hum 378	13.3	5¼"	48.00	53.50	58.00	42
Easter Time	Hum 384	10.2	4"	57.00	63.00	69.00	42
Eventide	Hum 99	12.1x10.2	4¾"x4¼"	61.00	67.50	74.00	42
Farewell	Hum 65	12.1	4¾"	51.00	56.50	62.00	42
Farm Boy	Hum 66	12.7	5"	40.50	45.00	49.50	42

For more information see Tables II, III & IV

TABLE I.

Model	Number	Approx. Size Cm.	Inches	Low Retail	Retail Price	High Retail	Page No.
Favorite Pet	Hum 361	10.8	4¼"	48.00	53.50	59.00	42
Feathered Friends	Hum 344	12.1	4¾"	57.00	63.00	69.00	42
Feeding Time	Hum 199/0	10.8	4¼"	39.00	43.50	48.00	42
Feeding Time	Hum 199/I	14.0	5½"	48.00	53.50	59.00	42
Festival Harmony, w/mandolin	Hum 172/0	20.3	8"	69.00	76.50	84.00	43
Festival Harmony, w/mandolin	Hum 172/II	26.0	10¼"	134.00	149.00	164.00	43
Festival Harmony, w/flute	Hum 173/0	20.3	8"	69.00	76.50	84.00	43
Festival Harmony, w/horn	Hum 173/II	26.0	10¼"	134.00	149.00	164.00	43
Flower Vendor	Hum 381	13.3	5¼"	48.00	53.50	59.00	43
Follow The Leader	Hum 369	17.8	7"	253.00	281.50	310.00	43
For Father	Hum 87	14.0	5½"	39.00	43.50	48.00	43
For Mother	Hum 257	12.7	5"	31.00	34.50	38.00	43
Friends, Small	Hum 136/I	12.7	5"	31.00	43.50	48.00	43
Friends	Hum 136/V	27.3	10¾"	300.00	333.50	367.00	43
Gay Adventure	Hum 356	12.7	5"	48.00	53.50	59.00	43
Globe Trotter	Hum 79	12.7	5"	34.00	38.00	42.00	44
Going To Grandma's	Hum 52/0	12.1	4¾"	48.00	52.50	59.00	44
Good Friends	Hum 182	10.2	4"	37.00	41.50	46.00	44
Good Hunting	Hum 307	12.7	5"	48.00	53.50	59.00	44
Good Night	Hum 214/C/II	8.9	3½"	20.00	22.50	25.00	44
Good Shepherd	Hum 42	15.9	6¼"	38.00	42.00	46.00	44
Goose Girl	Hum 47/0	12.1	4¾"	44.00	49.00	54.00	44
Goose Girl	Hum 47/II	19.1	7½"	124.00	138.00	152.00	44
Goose Girl	Hum 47/3/0	10.2	4"	35.00	39.00	43.00	44
Guiding Angel	Hum 357	7.0	2¾"	23.00	26.00	29.00	45
Happiness	Hum 86	12.1	4¾"	27.00	30.50	34.00	45
Happy Birthday	Hum 176/0	14.0	5½"	47.00	52.50	58.00	45
Happy Days	Hum 150/2/0	10.8	4¼"	44.00	49.00	54.00	45
Happy Pastime	Hum 69	8.9	3½"	34.00	38.00	42.00	45
Happy Traveller	Hum 109/0	12.7	5"	28.00	31.50	35.00	45
Happy Traveller	Hum 109/II	19.1	7½"	114.00	126.50	139.00	45
Hear Ye! Hear Ye!	Hum 15/0	12.7	5"	40.00	44.50	49.00	45
Hear Ye! Hear Ye!	Hum 15/I	15.2	6"	57.00	63.00	69.00	45
Hear Ye! Hear Ye!	Hum 15/II	17.8	7"	110.00	122.00	134.00	45
Heavenly Angel	Hum 21/0	12.1	4¾"	26.00	29.00	32.00	45
Heavenly Angel	Hum 21/01/2	15.2	6"	40.00	44.00	48.00	45
Heavenly Angel	Hum 21/I	17.1	6¾"	51.00	57.00	63.00	45
Heavenly Angel	Hum 21/II	22.2	8¾"	104.00	115.50	127.00	45
Heavenly Lullaby	Hum 262	12.7x8.9	5x3½"	45.00	50.00	55.00	45
Heavenly Protection	Hum 88/I	17.1	6¾"	83.00	92.00	101.00	45
Heavenly Protection	Hum 88/II	22.9	9"	134.00	149.00	164.00	45
Hello	Hum 124/0	15.9	6¼"	34.00	38.00	42.00	46
Holy Child	Hum 70	17.1	6¾"	36.00	40.50	45.00	46
Holy Family, White	Hum 214/A+B/W	See Individual		68.00	75.50	83.00	46
Holy Family, Color	Hum 214/A+B/II	Item Listings		100.00	111.00	122.00	46
Home From Market	Hum 198/I	14.0	5½"	39.00	43.50	48.00	46
Home From Market	Hum 198/2/0	12.1	4¾"	31.00	34.50	38.00	46
Homeward Bound	Hum 334	13.3	5¼"	90.00	100..50	111.00	46
"Hummel" Display Plaque	Hum 187C	14.0x9.2	5½"x3⅝"	30.00	33.50	37.00	46
Infant Jesus, Color	Hum 214/A/K Child	8.9x3.8	3½"x1½"	14.00	16.00	18.00	46
Infant of Krumbad	Hum 78/1/II	6.4	2½"	13.00	14.00	15.00	46
Infant of Krumbad	Hum 78/11/III	8.9	3½"	17.00	18.50	20.00	46
Infant of Krumbad	Hum 78/111/II	11.4	4½"	22.00	24.50	27.00	46
Joyful	Hum 53	10.2	4"	21.00	23.00	25.00	46
Just Resting	Hum 112/I	12.7	5"	44.00	49.00	54.00	46
Just Resting	Hum 112/3/0	10.2	4"	27.00	30.50	34.00	46
Kiss Me	Hum 311	15.2	6"	47.00	52.50	58.00	46
Knitting Lesson	Hum 256	19.1	7½"	114.00	126.50	139.00	46
Latest News	Hum 184/O.S.	12.7	5"	54.00	60.50	67.00	47
Let's Sing	Hum 110/0	7.6	3"	31.00	34.50	38.00	47
Let's Sing	Hum 110/I	10.2	4"	37.00	41.50	46.00	47
Letter To Santa Claus	Hum 340	18.4	7¼"	72.00	80.50	89.00	47
Little Band	Hum 392	12.1x7.6	4¾"x3"	69.00	77.00	85.00	47
Little Bookkeeper	Hum 306	12.1	4¾"	63.00	70.50	78.00	47
Little Cellist	Hum 89/I	15.2	6"	40.50	45.00	49.50	47
Little Cellist	Hum 89/II	19.1	7½"	114.00	126.50	139.00	47
Little Fiddler	Hum 2/0	15.2	6"	44.00	49.00	54.00	47
Little Fiddler	Hum 2/I	19.1	7½"	114.00	126.50	139.00	47
Little Fiddler	Hum 2/II	27.3	10¾"	362.00	402.50	443.00	47
Little Fiddler	Hum 4	12.1	4¾"	34.00	38.00	42.00	47
Little Gabriel	Hum 32	12.7	5"	29.00	32.50	36.00	47
Little Gardener	Hum 74	10.2	4"	27.00	29.50	32.00	47
Little Goat Herder	Hum 200/0	12.1	4¾"	37.00	41.50	46.00	48
Little Goat Herder	Hum 200/I	14.0	5½"	48.00	53.50	59.00	48
Little Guardian	Hum 145	10.2	4"	38.00	42.00	46.00	48
Little Helper	Hum 73	10.8	4¼"	27.00	29.50	32.00	48
Little Hiker	Hum 16/I	15.2	6"	35.00	39.00	43.00	48
Little Hiker	Hum 16/2/0	11.4	4¼"	22.00	24.50	27.00	48
Little Pharmacist	Hum 322	15.2	6"	48.00	53.50	59.00	48
Little Scholar	Hum 80	14.0	5½"	34.00	38.00	42.00	48

Model	Number	Approx. Cm.	Size Model	Low Retail	Retail Price	High Retail	Page No.
Little Shopper	Hum 96	14.0	4½"	27.00	29.50	32.00	48
Little Sweeper	Hum 171	10.8	4¼"	27.00	29.50	32.00	48
Little Tailor	Hum 308	14.0	5½"	54.00	60.50	67.00	48
Little Thrifty	Hum 118	12.7	5"	37.00	41.50	46.00	49
Little Tooter	Hum 214/H/II	10.2	4"	27.00	30.00	33.00	49
Lost Sheep	Hum 68/0	14.0	5½"	35.00	39.00	43.00	49
Lost Sheep, Small	Hum 68/2/0	10.8	4¼"	39.00	43.00	47.00	49
Lost Stocking	Hum 374	10.8	4¼"	39.00	43.00	47.00	49
Mail Is Here	Hum 226	15.2x10.8	6"x4¼"	155.00	172.50	190.00	49
March Winds	Hum 43	12.7	5"	27.00	30.50	34.00	49
Max and Moritz	Hum 123	12.7	5"	38.00	42.50	47.00	49
Meditation	Hum 13/0	14.0	5½"	36.00	40.00	44.00	50
Meditation, Small	Hum 13/2/0	10.8	4¼"	27.00	29.50	32.00	50
Merry Wanderer	Hum 7/0	15.9	6¼"	54.00	60.50	67.00	50
Merry Wanderer	Hum 7/I	17.8	7"	103.00	115.00	126.50	50
Merry Wanderer	Hum 7/II	24.1	9½"	362.00	402.50	443.00	50
Merry Wanderer	Hum 11/0	12.1	4¾"	34.00	38.00	42.00	50
Merry Wanderer	Hum 11/2/0	10.8	4¼"	27.00	29.50	32.00	50
Mischief Maker	Hum 342	12.7	5"	58.00	64.50	71.00	50
Mother's Darling	Hum 175	14.0	5½"	40.50	45.00	49.50	50
Mother's Helper	Hum 133	12.7	5"	42.00	46.50	51.00	50
Mountaineer	Hum 315	12.7	5"	48.00	53.50	59.00	50
Not For You	Hum 317	15.2	6"	47.00	52.50	58.00	50
On Secret Path	Hum 386	13.3	5¼"	58.00	64.50	71.00	50
Orchestra 5 Pcs.	Hum 4, 85/0, 129, 185 & 186	RE: Indiv. Item		177.00	197.00	217.00	50
8 Pcs.	5PCs & 130, 131 & 135	Listings		290.00	322.50	355.00	50
Out of Danger	Hum 56/B	15.9	6¼"	47.00	52.50	58.00	50
Photographer	Hum 178	13.3	5¼"	52.00	57.50	63.00	51
Playmates	Hum 58/0	10.2	4"	39.00	34.50	38.00	51
Playmates	Hum 58/I	10.8	4¼"	51.00	56.50	62.00	51
Postman	Hum 119	12.7	5"	39.00	43.50	48.00	51
Prayer Before Battle	Hum 20	10.8	4¼"	40.50	45.00	49.50	51
Puppy Love	Hum 1	12.7	5"	37.00	41.50	46.00	51
Retreat to Safety	Hum 201/I	14.0	5½"	57.00	63.00	69.00	51
Retreat to Safety	Hum 201/2/0	10.2	4"	34.00	38.00	42.00	51
Ride into Christmas	Hum 396	14.6	5¾"	104.00	115.50	127.00	51
Ring Around The Rosie	Hum 348	17.1	6¾"	714.00	793.50	873.00	51
St. George	Hum 55	17.1	6¾"	86.00	96.00	106.00	52
St. Joseph, White	Hum 214/B/W	19.1	7½"	31.50	35.00	38.50	52
St. Joseph, Color	Hum 214/B/II	19.1	7½"	40.00	44.50	49.00	52
School Boy	Hum 82/0	12.7	5"	34.00	38.00	42.00	52
School Boy	Hum 82/2/0	10.2	4"	27.00	29.50	32.00	52
School Boys	Hum 170/I	19.1	7½"	300.00	333.50	367.00	52
School Boys	Hum 170/III	26.0	10¼"	766.00	851.00	936.00	52
School Girl	Hum 81/0	12.7	5"	34.00	38.00	42.00	52
School Girl	Hum 81/2/0	10.8	4¼"	27.00	29.50	32.00	52
School Girls	Hum 177/I	19.1	7½"	300.00	333.50	367.00	52
School Girls	Hum 177/III	24.1	9½"	766.00	851.00	936.00	52
Sensitive Hunter	Hum 6/0	12.1	4¾"	34.00	38.00	42.00	52
Sensitive Hunter	Hum 6/I	14.0	5½"	44.00	49.00	54.00	52
Sensitive Hunter	Hum 6/II	19.1	7½"	93.00	103.50	114.00	52
Serenade	Hum 85/0	12.1	4¾"	28.00	31.50	35.00	52
Serenade	Hum 82/II	19.1	7½"	114.00	126.50	139.00	52
She Loves Me, She Loves Me Not	Hum 174	10.8	4¼"	39.00	43.50	48.00	53
Shepherd's Boy	Hum 64	14.0	5½"	40.50	45.00	49.50	52
Shining Light	Hum 358	7.0	2¾"	23.00	26.00	29.00	53
Signs of Spring	Hum 203/I	14.0	5½"	47.00	52.50	58.00	53
Signs of Spring	Hum 203/2/0	10.2	5"	35.00	39.00	43.00	53
Singing Lesson	Hum 63	7.0	2¾"	27.00	30.50	34.00	53
Sister	Hum 98/0	14.0	5½"	31.00	34.50	38.00	53
Sister	Hum 98/2/0	12.1	4¾"	27.00	29.50	32.00	53
Skier	Hum 59	12.7	5"	38.00	42.50	47.00	53
Smart Little Sister	Hum 346	12.1	4¾"	48.00	53.50	59.00	53
Soldier Boy	Hum 332	15.2	6"	31.00	34.50	38.00	53
Soloist	Hum 135	12.1	4¾"	27.00	30.50	34.00	53
Spring Cheer	Hum 72	12.7	5"	27.00	29.50	32.00	54
Spring Dance	Hum 353/I	17.1	6¾"	145.00	161.00	177.00	54
Star Gazer	Hum 132	12.1	4¾"	40.50	45.00	49.50	54
Stitch In Time	Hum 255	17.1	6¾"	46.00	51.00	56.00	54
Stormy Weather	Hum 71	15.9	6¼"	124.00	138.00	152.00	54
Street Singer	Hum 131	12.7	5"	31.00	34.50	38.00	54
Strolling Along	Hum 5	12.1	4¾"	34.00	38.00	42.00	54
Surprise	Hum 94/I	14.0	5½"	47.00	52.50	58.00	54
Surprise	Hum 94/3/0	10.2	4"	39.00	34.50	38.00	54
Sweet Music	Hum 186	12.7	5"	31.00	43.50	48.00	54
Telling Her Secret	Hum 196/0	12.7	5"	58.50	65.00	71.50	55
The Run-a-Way	Hum 327	13.3	5¼"	61.00	67.50	74.00	51
To Market	Hum 49/0	14.0	5½"	57.00	63.00	69.00	55
To Market	Hum 49/3/0	10.2	4"	38.00	42.50	47.00	55
Trumpet Boy	Hum 97	12.1	4¾"	27.00	29.50	32.00	55

TABLE I.

Model	Number	Approx. Size Cm.	Inches	Low Retail	Retail Price	High Retail	Page No.
Tuneful Angel	Hum 359	7.0	2¾"	23.00	26.00	29.00	55
Umbrella Boy	Hum 152/A/0	12.1	4¾"	145.00	161.00	177.00	55
Umbrella Boy	Hum 152/A/II	20.3	8"	450.00	500.00	550.00	55
Umbrella Girl	Hum 152/B/0	12.1	4¾"	145.00	161.00	177.00	55
Umbrella Girl	Hum 152/B/II	20.3	8"	450.00	500.00	550.00	55
Village Boy	Hum 51/0	15.2	6"	38.00	42.00	46.00	55
Village Boy	Hum 51/2/0	12.7	5"	27.00	30.50	34.00	55
Village Boy	Hum 51/3/0	10.2	4"	21.00	23.00	25.00	55
Visiting an Invalid	Hum 382	12.7	5"	58.00	64.50	71.00	55
Volunteers	Hum 50/2/0	12.7	5"	54.00	60.50	67.00	56
Waiter	Hum 154/0	15.2	6"	40.50	45.00	49.50	56
Wash Day	Hum 321	15.2	6"	47.00	52.50	58.00	56
Watchful Angel	Hum. 194	17.1	6¾"	77.00	86.00	95.00	56
Wayside Devotion	Hum 28/II	19.1	7½"	91.00	101.50	112.00	56
Wayside Devotion	Hum 28/III	22.2	8¾"	137.00	152.50	168.00	56
Wayside Harmony	Hum III/I	12.7	5"	44.00	49.00	54.00	56
Wayside Harmony	Hum 111/3/0	10.2	4"	27.00	30.50	34.00	56
Weary Wanderer	Hum 204	15.2	6"	37.00	41.50	46.00	56
We Congratulate	Hum 214/E/II	8.9	3½"	33.00	37.00	41.00	56
We Congratulate	Hum 220	10.2	4"	35.00	39.00	43.00	56
Which Hand?	Hum 258	14.0	5½"	31.00	34.50	38.00	56
Worship	Hum 84/0	12.7	5"	41.00	45.50	50.00	57
Worship	Hum 84V	32.4	12¾"	405.00	450.50	496.00	57

ANNUAL BELL

Model	Number	Approx. Size Cm.	Inches	Low Retail	Retail Price	High Retail	Page No.
Let's Sing	Hum 700	10.2x8.9 x15.9	4"x3½"x 6¼"	45.00	50.00	55.00	57

ANNUAL PLATES

Model	Number	Approx. Size Cm.	Inches	Low Retail	Retail Price	High Retail	Page No.
1971 (Edition Complete)	Hum 264	19.1	7½"	*****	*****	*****	66
1972 (Edition Complete)	Hum 265	19.1	7½"	*****	*****	*****	
1973 (Edition Complete)	Hum 266	19.1	7½"	*****	*****	*****	
1974 (Edition Complete)	Hum 267	19.1	7½"	*****	*****	*****	
1975 (Edition Complete)	Hum 268	19.1	7½"	*****	*****	*****	
1976 (Edition Complete)	Hum 269	19.1	7½"	*****	*****	*****	66
1977 (Edition Complete)	Hum 270	19.1	7½"	*****	*****	*****	67
1978	Hum 271	19.1	7½"	58.50	65.00	71.50	67

ANNIVERSARY PLATE

Model	Number	Approx. Size Cm.	Inches	Low Retail	Retail Price	High Retail	Page No.
1975 (Edition Complete)	Hum 280	25.4	10"	*****	*****	*****	67

ASHTRAYS

Model	Number	Approx. Size Cm.	Inches	Low Retail	Retail Price	High Retail	Page No.
Boy With Bird	Hum 166	8.3x15.9	3¼"x6¼"	46.00	51.00	56.00	57
Happy Pastime	Hum 62	8.9x15.9	3½"x6¼"	39.00	43.00	47.00	57
Joyful	Hum 33	8.9x15.2	3½"x6"	33.00	37.00	41.00	57
Let's Sing	Hum 114	8.9x15.9	3½"x6¼"	39.00	43.00	47.00	57
Singing Lesson	Hum 34	8.9x15.9	3½"x6¼"	46.00	51.00	56.00	57

BOOKENDS

Model	Number	Approx. Size Cm.	Inches	Low Retail	Retail Price	High Retail	Page No.
Apple Tree Boy & Girl	Hum 252/A&B	12.7	5"	62.00	69.00	76.00	58
Bookworms	Hum 14/A&B	14.0	5½"	84.00	93.50	103.00	58
Good Friends, She Loves Me, She Loves Me Not	Hum 251/A&B	12.7	5"	84.00	93.50	103.00	58
Goose Girl & Farm Boy	Hum 60/A&B	12.1	4¾"	100.00	111.00	122.00	58
Little Goat Herder and Feeding Time	Hum 250/A&B	14.0	5½"	84.00	93.50	103.00	58
Playmates and Chick Girl	Hum 61/A&B	10.2	4"	100.00	111.00	122.00	58

CANDLEHOLDERS

Model	Number	Approx. Size Cm.	Inches	Low Retail	Retail Price	High Retail	Page No.
Angel Duet	Hum 193	12.7	5"	44.00	49.00	54.00	59
Angel-3 Ass't Sitting (w/candle)	Hum 111/38/0, 39/0, 40/0	5.1	2"	38.00	42.00	46.00	59
Watchful Angel	Hum 194	17.1	6¾"	77.00	86.00		59
Angelic Sleep	Hum 25/I	12.7x8.9	5"x3½"	46.00	51.50	57.00	59
Christmas Angels	Hum 115/115/117	8.9	3½"	43.00	48.00	53.00	59
Herald Angels	Hum 37	10.2x5.7	4"x2¼"	45.00	50.00	55.00	59
Little Band	Hum 388	12.1x7.6	4¾"x3"	69.00	77.00	85.00	60
Lullaby	Hum 24/I	12.7x8.9	5"x3½"	46.00	51.50	57.00	60
Silent Night	Hum 54	12.1x9.5	4¾"x3¾"	61.00	67.50	74.00	60

CANDY BOXES

Model	Number	Approx. Size Cm.	Inches	Low Retail	Retail Price	High Retail	Page No.
Joyful	Hum 111/53	15.9	6¼"	51.00	57.00	63.00	60
Chick Girl	Hum 111/57	15.9	6¼"	51.00	57.00	63.00	60
Playmates	Hum 111/58	15.9	6¼"	51.00	57.00	63.00	61
Singing Lesson	Hum 111/63	15.2	6"	51.00	57.00	63.00	61
Happy Pastime	Hum 111/69	15.2	6"	51.00	57.00	63.00	60
Let's Sing	Hum 111/II0	15.2	6"	51.00	57.00	63.00	61

*See Section II for current prices on closed editions 1971 thru 1976

Model	Number	Approx. Size Cm.	Inches	Low Retail	Retail Price	High Retail	Page No.
FONTS							
Angel Duet	Hum 146	8.3x12.1	3¼"x4¾"	13.00	14.50	16.00	61
Angelic Prayer	Hum 75	4.4x8.9	1¾"x3½"	10.00	11.00	12.00	61
Angels at Prayer	Hum 91/A&B	5.1x12.1	2"x4¾"	20.00	22.00	24.00	61
Angel with Birds	Hum 22/0	7.0x8.9	2¾"x3½"	10.00	11.00	12.00	61
Angel with Flowers	Hum 36/0	7.0x10.2	2¾"x4"	10.00	11.00	12.00	61
Child Jesus	Hum 26/0	3.8x12.7	1½"x5"	10.00	11.00	12.00	62
Devotion	Hum 147	7.6x12.7	3"x5"	13.00	14.50	16.00	62
Good Shepherd	Hum 35/0	5.7x12.1	2¼"x4¾"	10.00	11.00	12.00	62
Heavenly Angel	Hum 207	5.1x12.1	2"x4¾"	13.50	15.00	16.50	62
Holy Family	Hum 246	8.3x10.2	3¼"x4"	16.00	18.00	20.00	62
Kneeling Angel	Hum 248	5.7x14.0	2¼"x5½"	13.00	14.50	16.00	62
Worship	Hum 164	7.0x12.1	2¾"x4¾"	15.00	17.00	19.00	62
LAMP BASES (WIRED)							
Apple Tree Boy	Hum M/230	19.1	7½"	93.00	103.50	114.00	63
Apple Tree Girl	Hum M/229	19.1	7½"	93.00	103.50	114.00	63
Culprits	Hum M44/X	24.1	9½"	110.00	122.00	134.00	63
Good Friends	Hum M/228	19.1	7½"	93.00	103.50	114.00	63
Just Resting	Hum M/225/I	19.1	7½"	93.00	103.50	114.00	63
Out of Danger	Hum M/44/B	24.1	9½"	110.00	122.00	134.00	63
She Loves Me, She Loves Me Not	Hum M/227	19.1	7½"	93.00	103.50	114.00	63
To Market	Hum M223	24.1	9½"	127.00	141.00	155.00	63
Wayside Harmony	Hum M/224/I	19.1	7½"	93.00	103.50	114.00	63
MADONNAS							
Flower Madonna, Color	Hum 10/I/II	21.0	8¼"	69.00	77.00	85.00	64
Flower Madonna, White	Hum 10/I/W	21.0	8¼"	36.00	40.00	44.00	
Flower Madonna, Color	Hum 10/III/II	29.2	11½"	204.00	227.00	250.00	64
Flower Madonna, White	Hum 10/III/W	29.2	11½"	104.00	115.00	127.00	
Madonna	Hum 214/A/M/II	15.9	5¼"	45.00	50.50	56.00	
Madonna w/Child, 2 pcs., Color	Hum 214/A M&K	C8.9x3.8	C3½"x1½"	60.00	66.50	73.00	
Madonna w/Child 2 Pcs., White	Hum 214 AM&K/W	C8.9x3.8	C3½"x1½"	36.00	40.50	45.00	
Madonna w/Halo, Color	Hum 45/0/6	26.7	10½"	25.00	27.50	30.00	64
Madonna w/Halo, Color	Hum 45/I/6	30.5	12"	31.00	34.50	38.00	64
Madonna w/Halo, White	Hum 45/0/W	26.7	10½"	15.00	17.00	19.00	
Madonna w/Halo, White	Hum 45/I/W	30.5	12"	19.00	21.50	24.00	
Madonna, Praying							
Color	Hum 46/0/6	26.0	10¼"	25.00	27.50	30.00	64
Color	Hum 46/1/6	28.6	11¼"	31.00	34.50	38.00	64
White	Hum 46/0/W	26.0	10¼	15.00	17.00	19.00	
White	Hum 46/1/2	28.6	11¼"	19.00	21.50	24.00	
MUSIC BOXES							
Little Band	388M(w/Candle)	12.1x12.7	4¾"x5"	108.00	120.50	133.00	64
Little Band	392M(w/o Candle)	12.1x12.7	4¾"x5"	108.00	120.50	133.00	64
NATIVITY SETS							
Holy Family, 3 Pcs. Set, Color	Hum 214/A&B/II			100.00	111.00	122.00	
White	Hum 214/A&B/W	See Individual		68.00	75.50	83.00	
12 Piece set, figures only, Color	Hummel 214/A, B, F, G, J, K, L, M, N, O/II, 366	Component Size		360.00	400.50	441.00	64
16 Piece set, figures only, Color	Hummel 214/A, B, C, D, E, F, G, H, J, K, L, M, N, O/11, + 366			459.00	509.50	560.00	
16 Piece set, Large figures only, Color	Hummel 260 A – R			1,511.00	1,679.00	1,847.00	64
Stable Only, To Fit 12 or 16 Piece	Hum 214/SI						64
	Hum 214 Set			32.00	35.00	40.00	
Stable Only, To Fit 3 Pc. Hum 214 Set	Hummel 214/SII			18.00	19.50	21.00	
Stable only to fit 16 pc. Hum 260 set	Hum 260/S			172.00	191.50	211.00	64
NATIVITY SETS COMPONENTS							
Madonna & Child, 2 pcs., White	Hum 214 AM&K/W	M15.9	M-6¼"	36.00	40.50	45.00	
2 pcs., Color	Hum 214 AM&K	C-8.9x3.8	C-3½"x1½"	60.00	66.50	73.00	
Madonna	Hum 214/A/M/II	M-15.9	M-6¼"	45.00	50.50	56.00	
Infant Jesus Only	Hum 214/A/K	8.9x3.8	3½"x1½"	14.00	16.00	18.00	
St. Joseph, White	Hum 214B/W	19.1	7½"	31.50	35.00	38.50	
Color	Hum 214B/II	19.1	7½"	40.00	44.50	49.00	
Goodnight	Hum 214/C/II	8.9	3½"	20.00	22.50	25.00	
Angel Serenade	Hum 214/D/II	7.6	3"	18.00	19.50	21.00	
We Congratulate	Hum 214/E/II	8.9	3½"	33.00	37.00	41.00	
Shepherd w/Sheep-1 pc	Hum 214/F/II	17.8	7"	46.00	51.50	57.00	
Shepherd Boy	Hum 214/G/II	12.1	4¾"	29.00	32.00	35.00	
Little Tooter	Hum 214/H/II	10.2	4"	27.00	30.00	33.00	
Donkey	Hum 214/J/II		5"	16.00	18.00	20.00	
Cow	Hum 214/K/II	15.9x8.9	6½"x3½"	19.00	21.50	24.00	

Model	Number	Approx. Size Cm.	Inches	Low Retail	Retail Price	High Retail	Page No.
King (Standing)	Hum 214/L/II	21.0	8¼″	45.00	50.00	55.00	
King Kneeling on one Knee	Hum 214/M/II	14.0	5½″	40.50	45.00	49.50	
King, Kneeling on two knees	Hum 214/N/II	14.0	5½″	33.00	37.00	41.00	
Lamb	Hum 214/0/II	5.1x3.8	2″x1½″	4.00	4.50	5.00	
Camel	HX 306/0/6	21.0	8¼″	66.00	73.00	80.00	
Flying Angel/Color	Hum 366	8.9	3½″	27.00	30.00	33.00	
Flying Angel/White	Hum 366/W	8.9	3½″	10.00	11.50	13.00	
Madonna	Hum 260A	24.8	9¾″	143.00	158.50	174.00	
St. Joseph	Hum 260B	29.8	11¾″	148.00	164.00	180.00	
Infant Jesus	Hum 260C	14.6	5¾″	52.00	35.50	39.00	
Good Night	Hum 260D	13.3	5¼″	36.00	40.00	44.00	
Angel Serenade	Hum 260E	10.8	4¼″	32.00	35.50	39.00	
We Congratulate	Hum 260F	15.9	6¼″	98.00	109.00	120.00	
Shepherd, Standing	Hum 260G	29.8	11¾″	162.00	180.00	198.00	
Shep (Standing) w/Lamb	Hum 260H	9.5	3¾″	24.00	27.00	30.00	
Shepherd Boy, Kneeling	Hum 260J	17.8	7″	78.00	87.00	96.00	
Little Tooter	Hum 260K	13.0	5⅛″	37.00	41.50	46.00	
Donkey	Hum 260L	19.1	7½″	33.00	37.00	41.00	
Cow	Hum 260M	15.2x28.0	6″x11″	43.00	47.50	52.00	
Moorish King	Hum 260N	32.4	12¾″	168.00	187.00	206.00	
King, Standing	Hum 2600	30.5	12″	158.00	175.50	193.00	
King, Kneeling	Hum 260P	22.9	9″	135.00	149.40	164.00	
Sheep (Lying)	Hum 260R	8.3x10x2	3¼″x4″	12.00	13.00	14.00	
WALL PLAQUES							
Ba Bee Ring	Hum 30 A-B Set	12.1x12.7	4¾″x5″	48.00	53.50	58.00	65
Child in Bed	Hum 137	7.0x7.0	2¾″x2¾″	22.00	24.00	26.00	65
Display Plaque	Hum 187C	14.0x9.2	5½″x3⅝	30.00	33.50	37.00	65
Madonna	Hum 48/0	7.6x10.2	3″x4″	27.00	29.50	32.00	65
Mail Is Here	Hum 140	15.9x10.8	6¼″x4¼″	66.00	73.00	80.00	65
Merry Wanderer	Hum 92	12.1x12.7	4¾x5″	36.00	40.00	44.00	65
Retreat to Safety	Hum 126	12.1x12.1	4¾″x4″	52.00	57.50	63.00	66
Quartet	Hum 134	15.2x15.2	6″x6″	76.50	85.00	93.50	66
Vacation Time	Hum 125	10.2x12.1	4″x4¾″	55.00	61.00	67.00	66
MISCELLANEOUS							
M.I. Hummel Bust	Hum 2	14.6	5¾″	14.00	15.50	17.00	67

Section II.

"M. I. Hummel" Figurines with Old Marks and Size Variations

Section II contains values for those figurines that have old trademarks and compares them with the price of those which have the current trademark. In addition it also covers those examples which may not be the same size as the ones currently in production. It also suggests ways of determining guide prices for these pieces. It is a nearly complete alphabetical list of pieces that are both on and off the current price list. Included are ones that have been discontinued or that have had a number assigned but not yet available to the public.

Therefore, Section II is termed a Master Alphabetical List and was arranged in this form because many collectors prefer this method over the numerical listing. However, if only the number that is on the bottom of a figurine is known, the name can be found by referring to the Master Numerical List and then returning to this section to find the approximate value. If the reader only knows what the figure looks like, he should refer to the color illustrations.

Looking at the table itself, the first column contains letter abbreviations. These indicate whether the name and rest of the data refer to a figurine or one of the other groups of articles that Goebel produces such as lamps or fonts. The key to these abbreviations and others appears on page 81. The second column is the name assigned by the Goebel Company in the Suggested Retail Price List. In some cases these names vary from those used in Ehrmann's book, *Hummel*. Such differences have been cross-referenced to the official names. The third column gives the model number as listed in the latest price list and is combined with the "size indicator code" mark, if any. In column number four, the actual dimensions given in the same price list are used to the nearest ¼ inch. These sizes may vary somewhat from those listed in other publications but are the latest figures listed by Goebel.

As previously explained, the sizes of some of the models have varied over the years due to molding processes and perhaps for other reasons. In considering whether or not any size is a deviation from the current standard listed in column four, a minimum deviation of ¼ inch, plus or minus, has been assumed to be the least difference to have any significance. If the size deviates by this amount or more, that example may have a greater value as noted in the last column on the right, entitled, "Notes." The "Notes" column also shows references to Section III for further important information.

Opposite page. Very rare Hummel figurines dressed in Hungarian costume. From the Robert E. Miller collection.

Since "M. I. Hummel" figurines were first manufactured in 1935, there have been numerous changes in the trademarks used on the bottom. Five of these marks have been selected in order to group values into meaningful categories. Another reason for using these five choices is that they are already being used and accepted by collectors as being the most important marks. There are many more trademarks than are shown and discussed elsewhere in this book, but the five being used here simplify the separation of time periods and are easily identified and remembered.

Each of these five trademarks, representing an approximate span of years, is assigned one of the next five columns in the Section II table, numbered five to nine. Below that is the trademark that was in use at the start of the period. Below that is a very abbreviated description of the above mark. An elaboration of the five column headings is shown below.

Column No.	5	6	7	8	9
Trademark No.	1	2	3	4	5
Trademark				by W. Goebel © W. Germany	Goebel
First Used	1934	1950	1960	1968	1972
Trademark Name	Crown	Full Bee	Stylized Bee	Three Line	Vee Gee

The trademarks are an oversimplification of the variations and combinations used for over fifty years. More detailed information is given in the section of the book on marks for those interested. Pictures of the trademarks and other markings are on pages 22 through 28.

Many of the figurines have an incised date (year) on the underside near the trademark. This is normally the copyright date and does not always agree with the year the piece was first issued or cataloged for sale. An example is the figurine, Artist, which was first issued in 1971. The copyright date on the bottom of this piece is 1955. The trademark in such cases is more likely to agree with the year of issue and is a better guide for approximate dating than is the copyright date, since a copyright is good for many years after the year it was registered. Some older figurines, i.e. 1950s, carry no copyright notice or year. In these cases the trademark is the only apparent method of approximately dating the piece.

Below the headings in these five columns and horizontally opposite the name of the figurine are various figures and symbols. Where they are numbers, they represent the recommended guide price in dollars. These are the approximate selling prices for that model size with the mark shown at the top of the column and on the underside of the piece. This guide figure is what is says. It is the best estimate available at this time of what the piece should bring when being sold by a willing seller to a willing buyer. Consideration should be given to the many other factors that may justify an entirely different price at another time, at another place, and with another individual. This is fully discussed in the section titled "Price Guides Can Help." It is suggested that be read before making use of this section and the one following.

Many of the figures in these columns are representative of what similar pieces have sold for on many previous occasions. Other figures, perhaps the majority, represent the best estimate of the probable selling prices using mathematical projections. The backup of the remaining ones falls somewhere in between these two extremes. A well-known figurine such as Little Fiddler #4 that was among the first figures issued in 1935 is an example of a piece that may be found with all the different marks shown in the five columns. These dollar figures are $147, $111, $74, $49, and $38 in the retail column. These figures are based on many actual sales at different times and places and, therefore, should be quite representative of actual conditions. For Little Fiddler #2/I - 7½" high, there were no actual figures to fall back on. The figures shown of $379.50, $253, $158, and $126.50 were calculated by using mathematical ratio charts and, therefore, represent what should be close to a fair price in relation to others.

Changes in sizes from the intended standard have happened over the years. Some of these differences are important to collectors and will affect the guide price. Many small deviations are practically meaningless, but significant differences on some models can be quite important. The range of size variations is almost infinite. To give collectors some idea that size can be an important element in determining the selling price, a notation in the "Notes" column has been added where appropriate and is expressed as a percentage to be added for variations of listed size.

Using Apple Tree Boy, 142/I - 6", as an example, the last column says, "Oversize — add 30%." This means that if the piece at hand were 6½" tall instead of the standard 6" and had a Crown mark, the guide price would be $316 instead of $242. The $316 figure being arrived at by adding 30 percent to the $242 base price. This example and the use of 30 percent is an oversimplification of the problem. A list of every possible deviation in size and the best percentage to use for each possibility would make the table so voluminous as to make it useless. Another reason to simplify is actual knowledge of all the variations is very limited, as is the frequency with which they occur. The figure of 30 percent is placed in the "Notes" as a reminder and convenience. It says in essence, "some deviations are known to be worth a premium of 30 percent; some are worth more than this; and some are worth less." Size, therefore, may be a valuable attribute and should be given some weight, perhaps 30 percent, plus or minus, when arriving at the guide price.

In various parts of Section II there are no guide prices shown. Instead of a numerical figure there may be one of two symbols. One of these is a dash (—) mark. It is used to indicate that in all probability the mark at the top of the column was not used for this combination of model number and size code. In other words, the likelihood of finding an example of this specific piece with that mark is very remote. The dash is used to be conservative. If the work sheets showed no record of this trademark being used, a dash was probably placed in the block so as not to mislead the collector. It definitely does not mean that in all cases such pieces with that trademark may not exist. The tendency in preparing these tables was to use the dash until more facts were available.

The second symbol that appears in some of the spaces is the question mark(?). This one is easy to explain. It means just what it indicates, the author has a question about how applicable an estimated value would be and whether or not collectors would waste time looking for something that they might not find. There is a further slight shading in the use of this mark. That is the question mark that is used after some of the dollar figures. This is intended as more assurance that such a mark exists but there is still a reasonable doubt that it does, and if it does, that the value assigned is realistic. Another interpretation is that it is a caution sign in arriving at the selling price. Undue emphasis should not be placed on guide price figures followed by question marks.

The last column on the right, headed "Notes," is more or less self-explanatory. The most important note that appears a number of times is "See Section III." This is to warn the reader that this particular model and size has been found with additional variations that are of importance to collectors and in setting a selling price. Section II is limited to the variations in trademarks and sizes while Section III covers other important and valuable characteristics that are occasionally found. These may be extremely rare or even unique (one of a kind) and command a four-digit-figure guide price (from $1,000 to $10,000). They may also refer to something much less exciting, such as a small color change that may not be of much importance. Hopefully such a note will produce enough feeling of suspense to encourage readers to compare their examples with other possible variations.

The general idea of the "Notes" column has been to record anything which may be of assistance in the way of interesting information or something that has a bearing on the arriving at a fair asking price. It is anticipated that as future editions of this book appear that the "Notes" column will be considerably amplified with further contributions and suggestions from those persons who have used this book. There is much left to be recorded.

TABLE II.
ALPHABETICAL PRICE GUIDE FOR FIGURINES
WITH OLD MARK AND SIZE VARIATIONS

Key to Symbols

Abbreviations: F-Figurine; BE-Bookends; CAN-Candleholder; HWF-Holy Water Font; PLQ-Plaque;PLT-Plate; LMP-Table Lamp Base; MBX-Music Box; AT-Ashtray; MAD-Madonna; CBX-Candybox; NAT-Nativity Set or Part; WVS-Wall Vase.

Prices in columns 5-9 are for old marks only. For additional size variations add 20-40% to price. For variations in DESIGN, COLOR, RARE and UNUSUAL VARIATIONS refer to Section III.

a. Insufficient data to date.
b. No record of examples.
c. Date discontinued unknown.
d. Reissue of this expected in 1977 or later.
?   Availability with this trademark not verified.
A   Assigned
____ Unlikely to find with this trademark.
D. Discontinued. Removed from English catalog.
P. Being produced but not cataloged.
R. Reissued or expected to be at a later date.

1	2	3	4	5	6	7	8	9	10
					FULL	STYL.	THREE		
		MODEL	DIMEN-	CROWN	BEE	BEE	LINE	VEE/G	
CLASS	NAME	& SIZE #	SIONS	TMK-1	TMK-2	TMK-3	TMK-4	TMK-5	DESCRIPTION
F	A FAIR MEASURE	345	5½"	____	____	?	85	63	
F	ACCORDION BOY	185	5"	146	110	73	49	39	
F	ADORATION	23/I	6¼"	445	259	186	104	92	
F	ADORATION	23/III	9"	____	____	200	160	132	In '66 P. L. Discont'd? Reissued in 1977
F	ADORATION W/BIRD	105	?						Reported as un-used number. Example found in 1977. See Sec. III
BE	Adoration/Wayside Devotion	90A & 90B	Unk.					D	See Section III; Discontinued
CAN	Advent Group with Candle	31	Unk.					D	See Section III; Discontinued
F	ADVENTURE BOUND	347	8¼"x7½"	____	____	1824	1453	1,092.50	
F	ANGEL AND BASKETS	301	?					A	May be released in 1978 or later
HWF	Angel Cloud	206	2¼"x4¾"					D	Reported produced in 1949? b
CAN	Angel Duet	193	5"					D	
F	ANGEL DUET	261	5"	____	____	____	146	55.50	Without mug (candle socket) called "Angelic Song" in *HUMMEL* book
HWF	Angel Duet	146	3¼"x4¾"	60	42	30	19	14.50	
HWF	Angel Guardian	39	2½"x5¾"					D	
CAN	Angel, Joyous News	See ANGEL TRIO B, 38, 39, & 40							Called Angel Trio in set of 3. III/38/39&/40 and sold as set in 1977 catalog for $33. The prefix III refers to the diam. of the candle.

TABLE II.

1	2	3	4	5	6	7	8	9	10
CLASS	NAME	MODEL & SIZE #	DIMEN-SIONS	CROWN TMK-1	FULL BEE TMK-2	STYL. BEE TMK-3	THREE LINE TMK-4	VEE/G TMK-5	DESCRIPTION
HWF	Angel at Prayer, faces left	91A	2″x4¾″					22	
HWF	Angel at Prayer, faces right	91B	2″x4¾″	43	31	18	33	the pair	
F	ANGEL SERENADE	83	5½″	?	?	____	____	D/R	Discontinued. Will be reissued in 1978 or later. See Section III. Superceded by 214/D (Kneeling). Illus. p. 98
F	ANGEL SERENADE	214/D	3″	85	61	43	27	19.50	
F	ANGEL SERENADE	260/E	4½″	____	____	____	____	____	Nativity Set (large size) component
F	ANGEL STANDING	See Goodnight #214/C/II-NATIVITY SET COMPONENT							
HWF	Angel with Bird	167	3″x3¾″	50	40	30	20	D	
HWF	Angel with Birds	22/0	2¾″x3½″	35	25	18	12	D	Discontinued in 1977
HWF	Angel with Birds	22/I	3¼″x4″	?	90	60	?	D	Also referred to as Sitting Angel
HWF	Angel w/Flowers	36/0	2¾″x4″	35	25	18	12	9	
HWF	Angel with Flowers	36/I	3½″x4½″	60	50	40	25	D	
HWF	Angel with Yellow Bird	167	?	?	?	?	?	D	No examples reported
CAN	Angel w/Nosegay (child)	115	3½″					48	
CAN	Angel w/Fir Tree (child)	116	3½″	185	148	92	75	the set	3 piece set called "Christmas Angels" in 1977 catalog
CAN	Angel w/Horse (child)	117	3½″						
CAN	ANGEL TRIO (A)	III/38 [1]	2″					42	
CAN	ANGEL TRIO (A)	III/39 [1]	2″	159	127	76	57	the set	3 piece set
CAN	ANGEL TRIO (A)	III/40 [1]	2″						
F	ANGEL TRIO (B) (Standing)	238/ABC	2″	____	108	60	48	42	
F	ANGEL, TUNEFUL	See TUNEFUL ANGEL #359							
F	ANGELIC CARE with Candle	194	6½″	240	170	125	80	60	In 1950 catalog under this name and 6¼. 1″ oversize known w/ design changes w/TMK-2. Not in 1966 catalog. See Sect. III & illus. p. 98
HWF	Angelic Prayer	75	1¾″x3½″	43	31	22	15	11	
F	ANGELIC SLEEP With Candle	25/I	5″x3½″	222	174	111	70	51.50	
F	ANGELIC SONG	144	4″	159	116	72	51	42	Kneeling figure also known with blue flowers in headband. Add 25%
PLQ	Anniversary Plate 1975	280	10″	____	____	____	____	100	Ed. closed in 1976. Price $150
PLT	Annual Plate 1971	264	7½″	____	____	____	____	25	$1,000
	Annual Plate 1972	265	7½″	____	____	____	____	38	90
	Annual Plate 1973	266	7½″	____	____	____	____	40	180
	Annual Plate 1974	267	7½″	____	____	____	____	46	90 Approximate current value.
	Annual Plate 1975	268	7½″	____	____	____	____	50	75
	Annual Plate 1976	269	7½″	____	____	____	____	50	70
	Annual Plate 1977	270	7½″	____	____	____	____	53	60
	Annual Plate 1978	271	7½″	____	____	____	____	65	Year of issue
F	APPLE TREE BOY	142/3/0	4″	117	86	55	37	29.50	
F	APPLE TREE BOY	142/I	6″	242	181.50	121	85	60.50	Oversize-add 30%. Variations in design since 1950
F	APPLE TREE BOY	142/V	10½″	____	____	____	300	275	
F	APPLE TREE BOY	142/X	29″	____	____	____	____	P	Very limited availability. Reports of sales at $6,500-$8,000
F	APPLE TREE GIRL	141/3/0	4″	123	92	61	37	29.50	This size has no bird in branch. (See illus. p. 93)

1 Prefix I & III denote different candle diameters

TABLE II.

CLASS	NAME	MODEL & SIZE #	DIMEN-SIONS	CROWN TMK-1	FULL BEE TMK-2	STYL. BEE TMK-3	THREE LINE TMK-4	VEE/G TMK-5	DESCRIPTION
1	2	3	4	5	6	7	8	9	10
F	APPLE TREE GIRL	141/I	6"	242	181.50	121	85	60.50	Oversize-add 30%. Variations in design found
F	APPLE TREE GIRL	141/V	10"	——	——	——	364	333.50	
F	APPLE TREE GIRL	141/X	29"	——	——	——	——	P	Very limited availability. Reports of sales at $6,500-$8,000
LMP	Apple Tree Boy	230	7½"	——	304	207	146	103.50	
LMP	Apple Tree Girl	229	7½"	——	304	207	146	103.50	
BE	Apple Tree Boy & Girl	252/A&B	5"/ea.	——	266	181	128	69.00	
F	ART CRITIC	318	?					A	May be released in 1978 or later
F	ARTIST	304	5½"	——	?	?	68	49	
F	AUF WIEDERSEHEN	153/0	5"	214	159	110	73.50	52.50	Rare examples w/hat. Also see Section III for variations.
F	AUF WIEDERSEHEN	153/I	7"	750	650	550	——	D/R	Discontinued. May be reissued in 1978 or later
F	AUTUMN HARVEST	355	4¾"	——	——	——	73	53.50	
PLQ	Ba-Bee Rings (2)	30 A & B	4¾"x5"	195	152	97	61	53.50	Set of 2
F	BAKER	128	4¾"	153	110	74	49	38	Add 30% for oversize
F	BANDLEADER	129	5"	170	134	73	55	45	Not scarce
MBX	Band, Little	See LITTLE BAND #392M							
F	BARNYARD HERO	195/2/0	4"	135	104	61	49	38	Not scarce
F	BARNYARD HERO	195/I	5½"	240.50	168	120	84.50	65	Add 30% for oversize
F	BASHFUL	377	4¾"	——	——	——	60	43	
F	BE PATIENT	197/2/0	4¼"	?	110	74	49	38	Not scarce
F	BE PATIENT	197/I	6¼"	?	214	122	74	57.50	See Section III for unusual example & higher price
F	BEGGING HIS SHARE	9	5½"	1	1	1	60	44.50	See Section III for rare & higher priced version with TMK-1, 2, or 3. (Illus. on page 98)
F	BIG HOUSECLEANING	363	4"	——	——	?	92	67.50	
F	BIRD DUET	169	4"	158	116	79	55	39	
F	BIRD WATCHER	300	?					A	May be released in 1978 or later
F	BIRTHDAY PRESENT	341	?					A	May be released in 1978 or later
F	BIRTHDAY SERENADE	218/2/0	4¼"	?	?	90	60	43.50	d-See Section III for earlier reverse mold & higher price
F	BIRTHDAY SERENADE	218/0	5¼"	?	?	100	65	D	
LMP	Birthday Serenade	231	9¾"	?	?	?	?	D	See Section III for estimated price
LMP	Birthday Serenade	234	7¾"	?	?	?	?	D	
F	BIRTHDAY WISH	338	?					A	May be released in 1978 or later
F	BLESSED EVENT	333	5½"	——	?	194	134	100.50	
F	BLESSED MADONNA & CHILD	364	?					A	May be released in 1978 or later
	Bookkeeper, Little	See LITTLE BOOKKEEPER #306							
F	BOOKWORM	3/I	5½"	359	269	179	120	92	
F	BOOKWORM	3/II	8"	?	733	672	487	402.50	
F	BOOKWORM	3/III	9"	——	——	*	?	D/R	Discontinued; will be reissued in 1978 or later. *See Section III for TMK-3 price
F	BOOKWORM	8	4"	182	134	91		45	Add 30% for oversize
BE	Bookworms (a pair)	14/A&B	5½"/ea	319	255	159	117	93.50	See Section III for variations
F	BOOTS	143/0	5½"	153	116	61	49	38	
F	BOOTS	143/I	6½"	——	——	——	——	D	See Section III for more information and prices
F	BOY W/ACCORDION	390	2½"	——	——	?	20		See Little Band ex: Children Trio
	Boy w/Horse 239C See CHILDREN TRIO #239 A&B									
AT	Boy w/Bird	166	3¼"x6¼"	194	146	97	67	51	
F	BOY W/HORSE	239C-	3½"	——	36	24	16	13	

CLASS	NAME	MODEL & SIZE #	DIMEN-SIONS	CROWN TMK-1	FULL BEE TMK-2	STYL. BEE TMK-3	THREE LINE TMK-4	VEE/G TMK-5	DESCRIPTION
F	BOY W/TOOTHACHE	217	5½"	?	134	73	55	41.50	
F	BROTHER	95	4¾"	131	92	59	43	34.50	
F	BUILDER	305	5½"	——	?	110	61	53.50	
F	BUSY STUDENT	367	4¼"	——		78	50	38.50	
PLQ	Butterfly & Boy	See: FLITTING BUTTERFLY #139							
CAN	Candlelight	192	6¾"	?	?	?	50	D/R	Discontinued. Reported reissued at $39. See Section III for old prices
F	CARNIVAL	328	6"	——	——	——	49	39	
F	CELESTIAL MUSICIAN	188	7"	327	233	160	102	80	
	Cellist, Little	See: LITTLE CELLIST #89/I&89/II							
	Chef, Hello	See: HELLO #124/0							
F	CHICK GIRL	57/0	3½"	131	92	59	43	34.50	
F	CHICK GIRL	57/I	4¼"	221	160	105	73	56.50	
CB	Chick Girl	III/57	6¼"	230	164	109	79	57	
BE	Chick Girl (#57) & Playmates (#58)	61/A&B	4"	317	238	169	132	111	Pair 61/A&B(#57 & #58 figurines)
F	CHICKEN LICKEN	385	4¾"	——	——	——	92	67.50	
PLQ	Child in Bed	137	2¾"x2¾"	180	150	72	36	24	Reported marked 137A, 137B. If found add 30%
HWF	Child Jesus	26/I	2½"x6"	?	75	50	30	D	Estimated price if found with old mark
	Child Jesus	26/0	1½"x5"	41	30	21	14	11	
F	CHILDREN TRIO (A)	239ABC	3½"/ea	——	?	?	?	48	Price is for set of 3
	CHILDREN TRIO (B)	389/90-91	2½"					54	Price is for set of 3
F	CHIMNEY SWEEP	12/2/0	4"	95	71	47	30	22.50	
F	CHIMNEY SWEEP	12/I 12. 12/II	5½" 6¼" 7¼"	221 —— ——	147	74	43	38 —— ——	See Section III for reported 12/2-7¼" size and 12.-6¼" size
F	CHRIST CHILD	18	6"x2"	133	98	63	42	35	
CAN	Christmas Angels	115 116 117	3½"	?	?	?	?	48 3 pcs.	Also called: ADVENT CANDLESTICKS, also see Children Trio(A) #239A, B, & C
F	CINDERELLA	337	4½"	——	——	——	85	64.50	
F	CLOSE HARMONY	336	5½"	——	——	——	86	68.50	
F	CONFIDENTIALLY	314	5½"	——	*	*	73	53.50	*See Section III for variation with TMK-2 & 3
F	CONGRATULATIONS	17/0	6"	?	107	71	48	34.50	See Section III for variation in prices
F	CONGRATULATIONS	17/2	8"	a	?	?	?	D	Size discontinued. See Section III
F	COQUETTES	179	5"	247	185	123	80	60.50	See Section III for variations
F	CROSSROADS	331	6¾"	——	——	——	153	107.50	
F	CULPRITS	56/A	6¼"	?	146	104	67	52.50	
LMP	Culprits	44/A	9½"	?	366	244	159	122	See illus. on pg. 63 for old and new style lamp bases
HWF	Devotion	147	3"x5"	60	43.50	30	18	14.50	Also called Angel Shrine and Angelic Devotion
F	DOCTOR	127	4¾"	158	122	79	51	39	
F	DOLL BATH	319	5"	——	——	109	67	51	
F	DOLL MOTHER	67	4¾"	246	184	123	80	56.50	
BE	Doll Mother & Prayer Before Battle	76A&B	Unk.	?	?	?	——	D	Discontinued. Rare if found. See Section III
F	DRUMMER	240	4¼"	?	119	83	48	34.50	Also called LITTLE DRUMMER
F	DUET	130	5"	242	181.50	109	79	60.50	
F	EASTER GREETINGS	378	5¼"	——	——	——	73	53.50	
F	EASTER TIME	384	4"	——	——	——	79	63	
F	EVENTIDE	99	4¾"x4¼"	270	196	123	86	67.50	
F	FAREWELL	65	4¾"	246	185	123	73	56.50	See Section III for variation & higher price

1	2	3	4	5	6	7	8	9	10
CLASS	NAME	MODEL & SIZE #	DIMEN-SIONS	CROWN TMK-1	FULL BEE TMK-2	STYL. BEE TMK-3	THREE LINE TMK-4	VEE/G TMK-5	DESCRIPTION
LMP	Farewell	103		?	?	—	—	D	Discontinued. Very rare, if found See Section III
F	FARM BOY	66	5″	268	182	91	61	45	
BE	Farm Boy & Goose Girl	60/A&B	4¾″	423	317	211	138	111.00	
F	FAVORITE PET	361	4¼″	—	—	—	73	53.50	
F	FEATHERED FRIENDS	344	4¾″	—	—	—	79	63	
F	FEEDING TIME	199/0	4¼″	?	135	90	60	43.50	See Section III for variation & price
F	FEEDING TIME	199/I	5½″	?	243	170	73	53.50	
F	FESTIVAL HARMONY W/MANDOLIN	172/0	8″	?	220	147	88	76.50	
F	FESTIVAL HARMONY W/MANDOLIN	172/II	10¼″	*	358	268	194	149	*See Section III for design variation with TMK-1 & illus. on p. 99
F	FESTIVAL HARMONY W/FLUTE	173/0	8″	?	220	147	88	76.50	
F	FESTIVAL HARMONY W/FLUTE	173/II	10¼″	*	358	268	194	149	*Design changes. See Section III for higher prices
F	FIDDLER	See LITTLE FIDDLER #2							
PLQ	Flitting Butterfly	139	2½″x2½″	?	*	*	?	D/R	*Discontinued. Reissue announced in 78 or later. See Section III for prices with TMK-2 & 3
F	FLOWER LOVER	349	?					A	May be released in 1978 or later
MAD	Flower Madonna	10/I/W	8¼″	242	182	121	61	40	
MAD	Flower Madonna	10/I/11	8¼″	?	244	183	98	77	See Section III for design variations and higher price. See illus. on p. 104
MAD	Flower Madonna	10/III/W	11½″	?	316	246	141	115.50	
MAD	Flower Madonna	10/III/II	11½″	550	586	379	275	227	
F	FLOWER VENDOR	381	5½″	—	—	—	73	53.50	
F	FLYING ANGEL	366	3½″	—	—	50	35	25?	
F	FLYING ANGEL	366/W	3½″	—	—	18	12	10?	
F	FOLLOW THE LEADER	369	7″	—	—	—	318	281.50	
F	FOREST SHRINE	183	9″	—	*	*	*	D/R	*Very Rare. Discontinued. Reissue expected in '78 or later. See Section III for prices with TMK-1, 2, or 3. See illus. on pg. 99
F	FOR FATHER	87	5½″	169	121	84	54	43.50	Father's Joy 5¼″ in 1950 catalog
F	FOR MOTHER	257	5″	—	—	66	48	34.50	
F	FRIENDS	136/I	5″	?	103	79	60	43.50	
F	FRIENDS	136/V	10¾″	*	*	*	424	333.50	*See Section III for more detail on Arabic size code. See illus. on p. 99
BE	Friends, Good	See: GOOD FRIENDS #251A&B, also							
	Gabriel	See: LITTLE GABRIEL #32							
	Gardener	See: LITTLE GARDENER #74							
F	GAY ADVENTURE	356	5″	—	—	—	73	53.50	Also referred to as Joyful Adventure
F	GIRL WITH FROG	219/2/0	?	—	*	—	—		Recently discovered. Number had been classified as never used. *See Sect. III for price
F	GIRL W/NOSEGAY	239A	3½″	—	—			38	
F	GIRL W/DOLL	239B	3½″	—	?	80	50	the	Called Children Trio A. Set of 3 standing figures
F	BOY W/HORSE	239C	3½″	—				set	
F	GIRL W/SHEET MUSIC	389	2½″	—	—	—			

TABLE II.

CLASS	NAME	MODEL & SIZE #	DIMEN- SIONS	CROWN TMK-1	FULL BEE TMK-2	STYL. BEE TMK-3	THREE LINE TMK-4	VEE/G TMK-5	DESCRIPTION
F	GIRL W/TRUMPET Also,	391	2½"					53 the set	Called Children Trio B. Set of 3 seated figures
F	BOY W/ACCORDION	390	2½"	___	___	___			
F	GLOBETROTTER	79	5"	147	110	74	51	38	See Section III for design change and higher price
BE	Goat Herder/Feeding Time	250A&B	5½"/ea.	___	223	186	127	93.50/pair	1977 catalog adds word "Little"
	Goat Herder	See: LITTLE GOAT HERDER							
F	GOING TO GRANDMA'S	52/0	4¼"	243	182	116	73	53.50	
F	GOING TO GRANDMA'S	52/I	6"	*	*	*	___	D	*See Section III for more information & prices with TMK-1, 2, & 3
F	GOOD FRIENDS	182	4"	?	122	85	55	41.50	
LMP	Good Friends	M228	7½"	___	?	207	140	103.50	
BE	Good Friends & She Loves Me	251/A & B	5"/ea.	___	?	192	127	93.50	1977 catalog calls this "Friends". Set of 2
F	GOOD HUNTING	307	5"	___	?	110	73	53.50	
F	GOOD NIGHT	214C	3½"	___	71	47	30	22.50	Nativity piece has also been referred to as Angel Standing
F	GOOD SHEPHERD	42	6¼"	?	123	80	58	42	See Section III—eyes & size. Discontinued in 1950
F	GOOD SHEPHERD	42/I	8"					D	
HWF	Good Shepherd	35/0	2¼"x4¾"	44	33	22	15	11	
	Good Shepherd	35/I	2¾"x5¾"					D	Discontinued. Date unknown. See Section III for information & prices
F	GOOSE GIRL	47/3/0	4"	?	122	79	49	39	See illus. on p. 44
F	GOOSE GIRL	47/0	4¾"	245	171.50	110	68	49	Oversize add 30%. Known in size 47 (only)
F	GOOSE GIRL	47/II	7½"	476	352	251	175	138	May be some Arabic size indicators. When found, add 25%
BE	Goose Girl & Farm Boy	60/A&B	See: FARM BOY & GOOSE GIRL						
F	GREETINGS FROM	309	?					A	May be released in 1978 or later
F	GROUP OF CHILDREN	392	See: LITTLE BAND						

Key to Symbols

Abbreviations: F-Figurine; BE-Bookends; CAN-Candleholder; HWF-Holy Water Font; PLQ-Plaque; PLT-Plate; LMP-Table Lamp Base; MBX-Music Box; AT-Ashtray; MAD-Madonna; CBX-Candybox; NAT-Nativity Set or Part; WVS-Wall Vase.

Prices in columns 5-9 are for old marks only. For additional size variations add 20-40% to price. For variations in DESIGN, COLOR, RARE and UNUSUAL VARIATIONS refer to Section III.

a. Insufficient data to date.
b. No record of examples.
c. Date discontinued unknown.
d. Reissue of this expected in 1977 or later.
? Availability with this trademark not verified.
A Assigned
____ Unlikely to find with this trademark.
D. Discontinued. Removed from English catalog.
P. Being produced but not cataloged.
R. Reissued or expected to be at a later date.

TABLE II.

1 CLASS	2 NAME	3 MODEL & SIZE #	4 DIMEN-SIONS	5 CROWN TMK-1	6 FULL BEE TMK-2	7 STYL. BEE TMK-3	8 THREE LINE TMK-4	9 VEE/G TMK-5	10 DESCRIPTION
HWF	Guardian Angel	29	2½x5¾″	a				D	Discontinued date unknown. See Section III for estimated price, if found. Redesigned and renamed Kneeling Angel #248.
F	GUIDING ANGEL	357	2¾″	?	?	47	35	26	
	Guardian, Little	See: LITTLE GUARDIAN							
F	HAPPINESS	86	4¾″	146	110	73	43	30.50	
F	HAPPY BIRTHDAY	176/0	5½″	214	159	110	67	52.50	
F	HAPPY BIRTHDAY	176.	6″x6¼″	?	?	?	?	D/R	Discontinued date unknown. Reissue expected in 1978 or later. See Section III for price, if found
PLQ	Happy Bugler	180	5″ x4¾″ See new name — Tuneful Goodnight						
F	HAPPY DAYS	150/2/0	4¼″	196	147	73.50	61	49	
F	HAPPY DAYS	150/0	5¼″	?	*	*	?	D/R	*Discontinued date unknown. Reissue expected in 1978 or later. See Section III for price; see illus. p. 100
F	HAPPY DAYS	150/I	6¼″	*	*		?	D/R	*Discontinued date unknown. Reissue expected in 1978 or later. See Section III for price; see illus. p. 100
LMP	Happy Days	232	9¾″	a				D/R	Discontinued date unknown. Reissue expected in 1978 or later. See Section III for price; see illus. p. 100
LMP	Happy Days	235	7¾″	a				D/R	Discontinued date unknown. Reissue expected in 1978 or later. See Section III for price; see illus. p. 100
F	HAPPY PASTIME	69	3½″	153	123	74	49	38	
CBX	Happy Pastime	III/69	6″	218	158	109	73	57	
AT	Happy Pastime	62	3½″x6¼″	167	120	83	54	43	
F	HAPPY TRAVELLER	109/0	5″	122	91	49	39	31.50	
F	HAPPY TRAVELLER	109/II	7½″	?	?	253	158	126.50	
F	HEAR YE, HEAR YE	15/0	5″	150	110	90	60	44.50	
F	HEAR YE, HEAR YE	15/I	6″	243	181	121	79	63	
F	HEAR YE, HEAR YE	15/II	7″	?	?	244	152.50	122	
F	HEAVENLY ANGEL	21/0	4¾″	106	79	53	36	29	
F	HEAVENLY ANGEL	21/0/½	6″	165	124	83	55	44	
F	HEAVENLY ANGEL	21/1	6¾″	250	188	125	76	57	
F	HEAVENLY ANGEL	21/11	8¾″	468	299	203	136	115.50	
HWF	Heavenly Angel	207	2″x4¾″	58	40	29	18	15	
	Heavenly Lullaby	262	3½″x5″	See: LULLABY					
F	HEAVENLY PROTECTION	88/I	6¾″	356	267	178	119	92	
F	HEAVENLY PROTECTION	88/II	9″	542	407	271	176	149	In 1950 catalog was called Guardian Angel. Original number 88 (only) was 9″ high. See illus. p. 100. Discontinued. Reissue expected in 1978 or later. Also see Section III
CAN	Heavenly Song	113	3½″x4¾″	a				D/R	(See SILENT NIGHT #54 for similar group) See Sec. III
F	HELLO	124/0	6¼″	147	110	74	49	38	See Section III—color change and prices
F	HELLO	124/I	7″	b				D	Discontinued date unknown. See Sec. III for estimated price
	Helper, Little	See: LITTLE HELPER							
CAN	Herald Angels	37	4″x2¼″	195	146.50	97.50	61	50	

1 CLASS	2 NAME	3 MODEL & SIZE #	4 DIMEN-SIONS	5 CROWN TMK-1	6 FULL BEE TMK-2	7 STYL. BEE TMK-3	8 THREE LINE TMK-4	9 VEE/G TMK-5	10 DESCRIPTION
	Hiker	See: LITTLE HIKER							
F	HOLIDAY SHOPPER	350	?					A	May be released in 1978 or later
F	HOLY CHILD	70	6¾"	168	126	70	56	40.50	
HWF	Holy Family	246	3¼"x4"	____	54	36	24	18	
NAT	Holy Family (c)	214 A&B/II	3 pc.	?	?	229	157	111	White. Discontinued in 1978
	Holy Water Font	36/0	See: ANGELS W/FLOWERS						
F	HOME FROM MARKET	198/2/0	4¾"	119	89	59	42	34.50	See illus. p. 100 for "traditional" and "modern" look
F	HOME FROM MARKET	198/I	5½"	193	151	97	60	43.50	See Section III for variation
F	HOMEWARD BOUND	334	5¼"	____	____	?	121	100.50	See Section III for design change
PLQ	Hummel Display Plaques	187c	5½"x3⁵/₈"	____	____	____	?	33.50	See illustrations on p. 104. Restyled 1972 w/o Bee. English
		187	English						All these Display Plaques are old style with "BEE" on top & discontinued. Superceded by restyled 187c for English. Are found with variations in color & printing. See Section III for more information & estimated prices
		205	German						
		208	French						
		209	Swedish						
		210	English						
		211	English						
		212	Schmid						
		213	Spanish						
MIS	"Hummel" Bust	H-1	12 +"	____	?	?	150	D	Large bisque bust of Sister Hummel
	"Hummel" Bust	HU-2	5¾"	____	____	____	____	15.50	New issue in 1977
F	INFANT, JESUS, Color	214/A/K	3½"x1½"	62	46	31	20	16	
F	INFANT OF KRUMBAD	78/0/11	2"	a				D	In 1950 catalog. Discontinued
F	INFANT OF KRUMBAD	78/I/11	2½"	____	____	28	17	14	
F	INFANT OF KRUMBAD	78/II/11	3½"	____	____	37	21	18.50	
F	INFANT OF KRUMBAD	78/III/11	4½"	____	____	49	33	24.50	
F	INFANT OF KRUMBAD	78/V/11	7¾"	a				D	
F	INFANT OF KRUMBAD	78/VI/11	10"	a				D	
F	INFANT OF KRUMBAD	78/III/11	13½"	a				D	Ones not in present catalog
F	INFANT OF KRUMBAD	78/I/83	2½"	a				D	probably discontinued. Made in color — 11 and flesh tones —
F	INFANT OF KRUMBAD	78/II/83	3½"	a				D	83. Flesh bisque has been reported as in production. More
F	INFANT OF KRUMBAD	78/III/83	5½"	a				D	facts needed before speculating on paying premium prices
F	INFANT OF KRUMBAD	78/V/83	7¾"	a				D	
F	INFANT OF KRUMBAD	78/VI/83	10"	150	125	?	?	D	In early 50s price list
F	INFANT OF KRUMBAD	78/VIII/83	13¼"	200	175	?	?	D	In early 50s price list
F	JAM POT	312	?					A	May be released in 1978 or later
F	JOYFUL	53	4"	97	73	49	30	23	See Section III for larger variation and higher prices
	JOYFUL ADVENTURE — See GAY ADVENTURE #356								
CBX	Joyful	III/53	6¼"	?	?	109	67	57	See Section III for design and price change
AT	Joyful	33	3½"x6"	?	111	74	49	37	
F	JOYFUL & LET'S SING on Wood Base	120	Unk.						Discontinued. See Section III for estimated price b
CAN	Joyous News	See: ANGEL TRIO, [1]III38/0, [1]III39/0, & [1]III40/0							
F	JOYOUS NEWS	27/III	4¼"x4¾"	a				D	Discontinued. Rare; see Section III for information and prices

1 Prefix I & III denote different candle diameters

1	2	3	4	5	6	7	8	9	10
CLASS	NAME	MODEL & SIZE #	DIMEN-SIONS	CROWN TMK-1	FULL BEE TMK-2	STYL. BEE TMK-3	THREE LINE TMK-4	VEE/G TMK-5	DESCRIPTION
F	JUST RESTING	112/3/0	4″	122	91.50	61	37	30.50	
F	JUST RESTING	112/I	5″	196	147	98	61	49	
LMP	Just Resting	M225/I	7½″	——	292	195	134	103.50	
LMP	Just Resting	M225/II	9½″	——	?	?	?	D/R	Date unknown. Reissue expected in 1978 or later
F	KISS ME	311	6″	——	——	104	67	52.50	W/o socks. See Section III for earlier examples of doll with socks. See illus. on p. 100
F	KNEADING DOUGH	330	?					A	May be released in 1978 or later
HWF	Kneeling Angel	248	2¼″x5½″	——	46	30	18	14.50	
F	KINDERGARTEN ROMANCE	329	?					A	May be released in 1978 or later
F	KNITTING LESSON	256	7½″	——	——	?	157	126.50	
F	KNIT ONE, PURL ONE	302	?					A	May be released in 1978 or later
F	LATEST NEWS	184/0	5″	266	194	121	79	60.50	See Section III for variation & higher prices
F	LET'S SING	110/0	3″	131	95	66	42	34.50	
F	LET'S SING	110/I	4″	?	?	?	?	41.50	Size added and priced in 1977
CBX	Let's Sing	III/110	6″	?	?	109	67	57	
AT	Let's Sing	114	3½″x6¼″	?	?	83	54	43	See Section III for variations
F	LETTER TO SANTA	340	7¼″	——	——	——	104	80.50	
F	LITTLE BAND	392	4¾″x3″	——	——	——		77	
CAN	Little Band	388	3″x4¾″	——	——	——		a	Assigned (?) but not priced
MBX	Little Band w/Candle	388M	4¾″x5″	——	——	——	146	120.50	
MBX	Little Band w/oCandle	392M	4¾″x5″	——	——	——	146	120.50	
F	LITTLE BOOKKEEPER	306	4¾″	——	——	?	91	70.50	
F	LITTLE CELLIST	89/I	6″	194	146	97	61	45	
F	LITTLE CELLIST	89/III	7½″	——	——	253	158	126.50	See Section III for variation and higher prices
F	LITTLE DRUMMER		See: DRUMMER, #240						
F	LITTLE FIDDLER	2/0	6″	196	147	98	61	49	For oversize add 30%
F	LITTLE FIDDLER	2/I	7½″	?	379.50	253	158	126.50	
F	LITTLE FIDDLER	2/II	11½″	?	875	672	460	402.50	
F	LITTLE FIDDLER	2/III	12¼″	——	?	1			[1]See Section III for detail with rare TMK-3
F	LITTLE FIDDLER	4	4¾″	147	111	74	49	38	
PLQ	Little Fiddler	93	5″x5½″	——	——	——	——	——	See Section III
PLQ	Little Fiddler	107	Unk.	——	——	——	——	——	See Section III
F	LITTLE GABRIEL	32	5″	136	108	68	41	32.50	
F	LITTLE GARDENER	74	4″	123	98	61	37	29.50	
F	LITTLE GOAT HERDER	200/0	4¾″	?	122	85	49	41.50	
F	LITTLE GOAT HERDER	200/I	5½″	?	152	110	73	53.50	See illus. on p. 100; size variation add 30%
F	LITTLE GUARDIAN	145	4″	159	116	80	51	42.00	
F	LITTLE HELPER	73	4¼″	123	92	62	37	29.50	Base variations reported to exist. Add 20% if found
F	LITTLE HIKER	16/2/0	4½″	93	70	47	29	24.50	
F	LITTLE HIKER	16/I	6″	158	116	79	49	39	
F	LITTLE PHARMACIST	322	6″	——	?	?	73	53.50	With Rizinsal on bottle. See Section III for others
F	LITTLE SCHOLAR	80	5½″	147	110	74	49	38	
F	LITTLE SHOPPER	96	5½″	123	92	61	43	29.50	
F	LITTLE SWEEPER	171	4¼″	123	92	61	43	29.50	
F	LITTLE TAILOR	308	5½″	——	?	121	79	60.50	Design change in 1972
F	LITTLE THRIFTY	118	5″	305	171	98	55	41.50	Scarce and premium price shown for TMK-1
F	LITTLE TOOTER	214/H/11	4″		90	60	36	30	Nativity piece, small set
F	LITTLE TOOTER	260/K	5″		——	——	——	——	Nativity piece, large set
F	LOST SHEEP	68/2/0	4¼″	123	92	61	43	29.50	

1 Refers to diameter of candle.

TABLE II.

CLASS	NAME	MODEL & SIZE #	DIMEN-SIONS	CROWN TMK-1	FULL BEE TMK-2	STYL. BEE TMK-3	THREE LINE TMK-4	VEE/G TMK-5	DESCRIPTION
F	LOST SHEEP	68/0	5½"	*158	122	85	49	39	Many sizes, marks, and color
F	LOST SHEEP	68	5½"					D	deviations reported. These prices may vary. *See Section
F	LOST SHEEP	68	6¼"	300	240	?	?	D	III for variation and higher price. 1950 catalog lists as Shepherd Boy, 19 cm. See Sec. III
F	LOST STOCKING	374	4¼"	___	___	83	54	43	
F	LULLABY	262	3¼"x5"	___	?	65	45	36	Similar to candleholder 24/I
CAN	Lullaby	24/I	5"x3½"	209	153	97	70	51.50	
CAN	Lullaby	24/III	6¼"x8¾"	*	*	?	?	D	Discontinued date unknown. Reissue expected in 1978 or later. *Rare; see Section III for higher prices with TMK-1 or 2 when found. See illus. on p. 101
MAD	Madonna	151/W	11½"	?	?	___	___	D/R	Discontinued; to be reissued in 1978 or later. See Section III for information and price
MAD	Madonna	151/II	11½"					D/R	
MAD	Madonna, Flower	See: FLOWER MADONNA #10							
HWF	Madonna w/Child	243	3"x4"	___	___	?			Not in U.S. catalog or price list
MAD	Madonna	214/A/M/11	6¼"	___	?	103	62	50.50	Madonna w/o child—color
MAD	Madonna w/Child	214/AM&/K	3½"x1½"	___	?	120	80	66.50	Madonna w/child — color
MAD	Madonna w/Child	214/AM& K/W	6½"	___	?	60	35	D	Discontinued in 1977, white
MAD	Madonna w/Halo	45/0/6	10½"	___	?	55	36	27.50	Color
MAD	Madonna w/Halo	45/0/13	10½"	___	?	70	50	D	Color variation; discontinued
MAD	Madonna w/Halo	45/0/W	10½"	___	?	33	21	17	White
MAD	Madonna w/Halo	45/I/6	11½"	?	50?	38	25	D	Discontinued c
MAD	Madonna w/Halo	45/I/13	11½"	___	a___			D	Discontinued c. Color variation
MAD	Madonna w/Halo	45/I/W	11½"	___	a___			17	Reinstated in 1977
MAD	Madonna w/Halo	45/III/6	16¾"	___	a___			D	Discontinued
MAD	Madonna w/Halo	45/III/13	16¾"	___	a___			D/R	Discontinued. Will be reissued in 1978 or later
MAD	Madonna w/Halo	45/III/W	16¾"	___	a___			D/R	Discontinued. Will be reissued in 1978 or later
MAD	Madonna w/o Halo	46/0/6	10¼"	___	___	55	36	27.50	Color
MAD	Madonna w/o Halo	46/0/13	10½"	___	?	70	50	D	Discontinued; color variation
MAD	Madonna w/o Halo	46/0/W	10¼"	___	___	33	21	17	White
MAD	Madonna w/o Halo	46/I/6	11¼"					34.50	Reinstated in 1978
MAD	Madonna w/o Halo	46/I/13	11½"					D	Discontinued date unknown
MAD	Madonna w/o Halo	46/I/W	11¼"	___	57	38	32	21.50	Reinstated in 1978
MAD	Madonna w/o Halo	46/III/6	16¾"	___	a___			D/R	Discontinued. Reissue expected in 1978 or later
MAD	Madonna w/o Halo	46/III/13	16¾"	___	a___			D	Discontinued
MAD	Madonna w/o Halo	46/III/W	16¾"	___	a___			D/R	Discontinued. Reissue expected in 1978 or later
PLQ	Madonna w/Child	48/0	3"x4"	123	92	61	37	29.50	Madonna in Red w/metal frame
PLQ	Madonna w/Child	48/II	4¾"x6"	a___				D/R	Discontinued. Reissue expected in 1978 or later
PLQ	Madonna w/Child	48/V	8½"x10½"	___	?			D	See Section III for comment and price. Madonna in Red
PLQ	Madonna	222	4"x5"	___	a___			D/R	Discontinued. Reissue expected in 1978 or later. See Section III for comment and price. Madonna in Red w/metal frame
F	MAIL IS HERE	226	6"x4¼"	___	362	266	210	172.50	
PLQ	Mail Is Here	140	6¼"x4¼"	?	219	122	97	73	In 1950 catalog
F	MARCH WINDS	43	5"	183	91.50	61	39	30.50	
F	MAX & MORITZ	123	5"	?	133	91	55	42.50	
F	MEDITATION	13/2/0	4¼"	?	?	61	39	29.50	
F	MEDITATION	13/0	5½"	?	242	73	48	40	For size variation, add 30%. Premium price for TMK-2

1	2	3	4	5	6	7	8	9	10
CLASS	NAME	MODEL & SIZE #	DIMEN-SIONS	CROWN TMK-1	FULL BEE TMK-2	STYL. BEE TMK-3	THREE LINE TMK-4	VEE/G TMK-5	DESCRIPTION
F	MEDITATION	13/II	7"	a——				D/R	Discontinued. Reissue expected in 1978 or later. See Section III for more information & prices
F	MEDITATION	13/V	13¾"	——	——	?		D/R	Discontinued. d Reissue expected in 1978 or later. See Section III for more information and prices
F	MERRY CHRISTMAS	323	?					A	May be released in 1978 or later
F	MERRY WANDERER	7/0	6¼"	212	139	91	79	60.50	1950 example had lower eyelashes, no upper and six, not five buttons on vest
F	MERRY WANDERER	7/I	7"	490	367	245	147	115	See Section III for design changes and higher prices. See illus. on p. 101 for variation
F	MERRY WANDERER	7/II	9½"	1465	1099	733	459	402.50	
F	MERRY WANDERER	7/III	11¼"	a——				D/R	Discontinued. See Section III
F	MERRY WANDERER	7/X	29"					P	See illus. p. 101. Limited availability. Sales reported from $6,500 to $8,000
F	MERRY WANDERER	11/2/0	4¼"	123	92	61	43	29.50	Oversize, add 30%. 1950 catalog lists as 3¾"- high
F	MERRY WANDERER	11/0	4¾"	153	116	80	49	38	Oversize, add 30%. Many size variations
F	MERRY WANDERER	11	5½"	200	150	?	——	D	Examples without size marker reported
PLQ	Merry Wanderer	92	4¾"x5"	a——				40	Added to 1977 price list
PLQ	Merry Wanderer	106	Unk.	a				D	See Section III for comment. Re-introduced in 1977
PLQ	Merry Wanderer	263	4"x5¾"	a——				D	See Section III for comment
PLQ	"M. I. Hummel" Plaques - See: HUMMEL DISPLAY PLAQUES								
F	MISCHIEF MAKER	342	5"	——	——	122	85	64.50	
F	MOTHER'S AID	325	?					A	May be released in 1978 or later
F	MOTHER'S DARLING	175	5½"	194	134	85	55	45	See Section III — color variation & higher price. See illus. p. 101
F	MOTHER'S HELPER	133	5"	196	147	98	61	46.50	
F	MOUNTAINEER	315	5"	——	?	110	73	53.50	
F	MUSICAL GOOD MORNING	352	?					A	May be released in 1978 or later
NAT	Nativity Set (12)	214	Sml.	——	?	?	?	400.50	
NAT	Nativity Set (16)	214	Sml.	——	?	?	?	509.50	
NAT	Nativity Set (17)	260	Lrg.	——	——	?	2183	1679	
F	NIGHTLY RITUAL	316	?					A	May be released in 1978 or later
F	NOT FOR YOU	317	6"	——	——	104	67	52.50	Oversize-add 30%
F	NAUGHTY BOY	326	?					A	May be released in 1978 or later
F	ON SECRET PATH	386	5¼"	——	——	——	92	64.50	Issued 1971. On Schmid 1977 M. D. Plate
F	OTHER SIDE OF FENCE	324	?					A	May be released in 1978 or later
F	ORCHESTRA-5 pieces			a——				162	
F	ORCHESTRA-8 pieces			a——				265	
F	OUT OF DANGER	56B	6¼"	214	159	104	67	52.50	Oversize — add 30%
LMP	Out of Danger	M44B	9½"	488	366	244	152.50	122	In 1950 catalog. Earlier ones had switch on base. When found, add 25%
	Pharmacist	See: LITTLE PHARMACIST							
F	PHOTOGRAPHER	178	5¼"	——	183	110	74	57.50	In 1950 catalog. Some with 1948 date. If found, add 25%
F	PLAYMATES	58/0	4"	149	107	77	48	34.50	Oversize—add 30%
F	PLAYMATES	58/I	4¼"	?	154	111	73	56.50	
CBX	Playmates	III/58	6¼"	?	?	109	73	57	
F	POSTMAN	119	5"	181	121	73	54	43.50	
F	PRAYER BEFORE BATTLE	20	4¼"	182	121.50	73	55	45	

TABLE II.

CLASS	NAME	MODEL & SIZE #	DIMENSIONS	CROWN TMK-1	FULL BEE TMK-2	STYL. BEE TMK-3	THREE LINE TMK-4	VEE/G TMK-5	DESCRIPTION
F	PUPPY LOVE	1	5"	183	134	92	55	41.50	Oversize—add 25%
F	PUPPY LOVE, & SERENADE HAPPINESS (on wood base)	122	Unk.	a____				D	No record of having been produced. See Section III for estimated price
PLQ	Quartet	134	6"x6"	?	?	152	103	85	
F	REMEMBERING	351	?					A	May be released in 1978 or later
F	RETREAT TO SAFETY	201/2/0	4"	?	110	74	49	38	
F	RETREAT TO SAFETY	201/I	5½"	243	181	121	79	63	Oversize—add 30%
F	RETREAT TO SAFETY	201.	5½"	250	180	?	____	____	Reported with decimal marker
PLQ	Retreat to Safety	126	4¾"x4¾"	?	?	?	60	A	No old marks recorded. Not in 1977 catalog
F	RIDE INTO CHRISTMAS	396	5¾"	____	____		365	115.50	Price variable. Scarce. Premium price for TMK-4
F	RING AROUND THE ROSIE	348	6¾"	____	____	1468	1285	793.50	Scarce and extra premium with TMK-3 or 4 when found
F	Run-Away, The	See: THE RUN-AWAY #327							
F	ST. GEORGE	55	6¾"	275	233	151	116	96	Old marks uncertain
F	ST. JOSEPH—Color	214/B/11	7½"	?	?	97	63	44.50	
F	ST. JOSEPH—White	214/B/W	7¾"	?	?	50	35	D	White discontinued in 1977
	Scholar, Little	See: LITTLE SCHOLAR #80							
F	SCHOOL BOY	82/2/0	4"	123	92	61	37	29.50	
F	SCHOOL BOY	82/0	5"	153	110	74	49	38	
F	SCHOOL BOY	82/II	7½"	?	*	?	?	D/R	Discontinued. Reissue expected in 1978. *See Section III for rarity w/TMK-2
F	SCHOOL BOYS	170/I	7½"	____	____	607	394	333.50	
F	SCHOOL BOYS	170/III	10¼"	____	?	1217	911	851	Limited production since early 1970s.
F	SCHOOL GIRL	81/2/0	4¼"	123	92	61	37	29.50	See Sec. III for unusual decimal mark (81.-4¼") and price
F	SCHOOL GIRL	81/0	5"	153	110	74	49	38	
F	SCHOOL GIRL	81/II	7½"	a____	____	?	?	D	
F	SCHOOL GIRLS	177/I	7½"	____	____	607	387	333.50	
F	SCHOOL GIRLS	177/III	9½"	____	____	1217	911	851	Limited production since early 1970s
F	SCHOOL LESSON	303	?					A	May be released in 1978 or later
F	SEARCHING ANGEL	310	?					A	May be released in 1978 or later
F	SENSITIVE HUNTER	6/0	4¾"	184	123	74	43	38	Older models had parallel suspender straps in back. See Section III
F	SENSITIVE HUNTER	6/I	5½"	196	147	98	61	49	Older models had parallel suspender straps in back. See Section III
F	SENSITIVE HUNTER	6/II	7½"	365	274	182	134	103.50	
	Shepherd, Good	See: GOOD SHEPHERD #42 and also HWF #35							
F	SERENADE	85/0	4¾"	121	91	60	43	31.50	Oversize — add 30%
F	SERENADE	85/II	7½"	____	?	253	152	126.50	If found with Arabic 2 marker, add 30%
	Sheep, Lost	See: LOST SHEEP							
F	SHE LOVES ME . . . SHE LOVES ME NOT	174	4¼"	175	133	84	54	43.50	See Section III. Eyes open — add 30%
LMP	She Loves Me	M227	7½"	____	?	195	122	103.50	
NAT	Shepherd w/Sheep	214/F	7"	?	?	102	60	51.50	Nativity component
F	SHEPHERD'S BOY	64	5½"	219	164	109	61	45	Oversize—add 30%
NAT	Shepherd Boy	214/G	4¾"	?	?	59	42	32	Kneeling—Nativity component

CLASS	NAME	MODEL & SIZE #	DIMEN-SIONS	CROWN TMK-1	FULL BEE TMK-2	STYL. BEE TMK-3	THREE LINE TMK-4	VEE/G TMK-5	DESCRIPTION
F	SHINING LIGHT	358	2¾"	——	——	52	32.50	26	
	Shopper, Little	See: LITTLE SHOPPER #96							
LMP	Shrine	100	7½"	a				D	Examples are rare. See Sec. III
F	SIGNS OF SPRING	203/2/0	4"	153	110	79	49	39	See Section III for design variation and prices
F	SIGNS OF SPRING	203/I	5½"	207	159	104	67	52.50	
CAN	Silent Night	54	4¾"x3¾"	?	?	130	78	67.50	See illus. on p. 102. See Section III for very rare variation
F	SINGING ANGEL See Heavenly Song 113 (child has halo)	343						A	May be released in 1978 or later
F	SINGING LESSON	63	2¾"	?	91.50	61	37	30.50	Oversize—add 30%
CBX	Singing Lesson	III/63	6"	?	?	109	73	57	
AT	Singing Lesson	34	3½"x6¾"	?	97	85	61	51	
F	SISTER	98/2/0	4¾"	123	92	61	39	29.50	Oversize—add 30%
F	SISTER	98/0	5½"	143	107	71	48	34.50	For decimal marking add 50%
F	SKIER	59	5"	——	152	85	55	42.50	Current model w/metal poles. See Section III for variation and prices. See illus. p. 102
F	SMART LITTLE SISTER	346	4¾"	——	——	97	67	53.50	
F	SOLDIER BOY	332	6"	——	——	66	48	34.50	
F	SOLOIST	135	4¾"	?	91.50	61	39	30.50	
F	SPRING CHEER	72	5"	——	184	123	39	29.50	For present model with flowers & green dress. See Section III for early design.
F	SPRING DANCE	353/0	5¼"	——	——	?		D/R	Discontinued. Reissue expected in 1978 or later.
F	SPRING DANCE	353/I	6¾"	——	——	304	195	161	
PLQ	Standing Boy	168	5¾"x5¾"	a				D/R	Discontinued. Reissue expected in 1978 or later. See Section III for rare examples
F	STAR GAZER	132	4¾"	182	134	91	56	45	With purple shirt. For old blue shirt, see Section III
F	STITCH IN TIME	255	6¾"	?	?	?	61	51	
F	STORMY WEATHER	71	6¼"	502	377	251	170	138	Oversize or color — add 30%. See. illus. on p. 102
F	STREET SINGER	131	5"	143	107	71	42	34.50	
F	STROLLING ALONG	5	4¾"	153	110	74	43	38	
F	SURPRISE	94/3/0	4"	?	?	71	42	34.50	
F	SURPRISE	94/2/0	4½"	——	——	70	?	D	See Sec. III for price on 94/2/0 & 94/0, both discontinued. See illus. p. 102
F	SURPRISE	94/I	5½"	214	134	110	67	52.50	Add 20-30% for variations
PLQ	Swaying Lullaby	165	5¼"x5¼"		*	*	?	D	Rare. *See Section III for information and prices with TMK-2 or 3
	Sweeper	See: LITTLE SWEEPER #171							
F	SWEET MUSIC	186	5"	?	139	73	48	43.50	
	Tailor	See: LITTLE TAILOR #308							
F	TELLING HER SECRET	196/0	5"	?	181	120	78	65	See illus. on p. 102
F	TELLING HER SECRET	196.	5¼"	——	200	?	——	D	This price for 196 or 196. (w/decimal). Discontinued. Reissue expected in 1977 or later.
F	TELLING HER SECRET	196/I	6¾"	——	*	*	?	D/R	*See Sec. III for TMK-2 or 3. Illus. on p. 102
F	THE PROFESSOR	320	?					A	May be released in 1978 or later
F	THE RUN-AWAY	327	5¼"	——	——	123	80	67.50	See Section III for more information

TABLE II.

1	2	3	4	5	6	7	8	9	10
CLASS	NAME	MODEL & SIZE #	DIMEN-SIONS	CROWN TMK-1	FULL BEE TMK-2	STYL. BEE TMK-3	THREE LINE TMK-4	VEE/G TMK-5	DESCRIPTION
F	Thoughtful	362	?					A	May be released in 1978 or later
	Thrifty, Little, See:	LITTLE THRIFTY							
F	TO MARKET	49/3/0	4″	?	122	73	51	42.50	
F	TO MARKET	49/0	5½″	243	169	109	72	63	
F	TO MARKET	49/I	6¼″	a				D/R	Discontinued. Reissue expected in 1978 or later. See Section III
LMP	To Market	M101	7½″	a				D	See Section III. Example found in 1977
LMP	To Market	M223	9½″	——	?	305	171	141	
	Tooter, Little	See: LITTLE TOOTER							
F	TRUMPET BOY	97	4¾″	123	92	61	37	29.50	Oversize—add 30%
F	TUNEFUL ANGEL	359	2¾″	——	——	52	32.50	26	
PLQ	Tuneful Goodnight (Happy Bugler)	180	5″x4¾″	a				D/R	Rare. Discontinued. Reissue expected in 1978 or later. See Section III
F	UMBRELLA BOY	152/A/O	4¾″	?	?	309	185	161	
F	UMBRELLA BOY	152/A/II	8″	?	?	855	580	500	
F	UMBRELLA GIRL	152/B/0	4¾″	?	?	309	185	161	
F	UMBRELLA GIRL	152/B/II	8″	?	?	855	580	500	
PLQ	Vacation Time	125	4″x4¾″	244	183	122	73	61	See illus. p. 103. Also Sec. III
F	Valentine Gift	387	4½″	——	——	——	——	43	Limited Edition. Available only to members of Goebel Collectors' Club $40±. Issued in 1977
F	VILLAGE BOY	51/3/0	4″	97	73	42	30	23	
F	VILLAGE BOY	51/2/0	5″	122	91.50	61	37	36.50	
F	VILLAGE BOY	51/0	6″	180	138	90	54	42	
F	VILLAGE BOY	51/I	6½″	*	*	*	——	D/R	Discontinued. Reissue expected in 1978 or later. *See Section III for information and price with TMK-1, 2 or 3
F	VISITING AN INVALID	382	5″	——	——	?	79	64.50	
F	VOLUNTEERS	50/2/0	5″	?	181.50	97	73	60.50	See illus. p. 103. Discontinued Reissue expected in 1978 or later. See Section III
F	VOLUNTEERS	50/0	5½″	a				D/R	Discontinued. Reissue expected in 1978 or later. See Section III & illus. on p. 103
F	VOLUNTEERS	50/I	6½″	a				D/R	Discontinued. Reissue expected in 1978 or later. See Section III & illus. on p. 103
LMP	Volunteers	102	7½″	b				D/R	Discontinued. Reissue expected in 1978 or later. See Section III
F	WAITER	154/0	6″	182	140	91	55	45	Add 40% for different name
F	WAITER	154	6½″	a				D/R	Discontinued. Reissue expected in 1978 or later. See Section III for information & prices. See illus. on p. 103
F	WAITER	154/1	7″	a				D	See Section III for information & prices. See illus. on p. 103
F	WALKING HER DOG	339	?					A	May be released in 1978 or later
WVS	Wall Vase, Boy & Girl	360/A	4½″x6¼″	a				D/R	Discontinued. To be reissued in 1978 or later. See Section III
WVS	Wall Vase, Boy	360/B	4½″x6¼″	a				D/R	To be reissued in 1978 or later. See Section III
WVS	Wall Vase, Girl	360/C	4½″x6¼″	a				D/R	To be reissued in 1978 or later. See Section III
F	WASH DAY	321	6″	——	?	104	67	52.50	
CAN	Watchful Angel w/Candle	194 See: ANGELIC CARE	6½″					?	Reported to have been listed by this name
F	WAYSIDE DEVOTION	28/II	7½″	507.50	319	217	131	101.50	Add 30% for Arabic 2, if found. In 1950 catalog.
F	WAYSIDE DEVOTION	28/III	8¾″	555	416	278	194	152.50	In early 1950s catalog

TABLE II.

1	2	3	4	5	6	7	8	9	10
					FULL BEE	STYL. BEE	THREE LINE	VEE/G	
CLASS	NAME	MODEL & SIZE #	DIMEN-SIONS	CROWN TMK-1	TMK-2	TMK-3	TMK-4	TMK-5	DESCRIPTION
BE	Wayside Devotion & Adoration	90/A&B	?	b___				___	If found, price in mid 4 figs.
LMP	Wayside Devotion	104	7½"	b___				D	See Section III for information & price
F	WAYSIDE HARMONY	III/3/0	4"	122	91.50	61	43	30.50	Add 30% for variations. See Section III for information & price
F	WAYSIDE HARMONY	III/I	5"	196	147	98	61	49	Oversize—add 30%
F	WAYSIDE HARMONY & JUST RESTING	121		b___				D	Both on a wooden base. See Section III
LMP	Wayside Harmony	M224/I	7½"	___	?	195	122	103.50	
LMP	Wayside Harmony	M224/II	9½"	b___				D/R	To be reissued? See Section III
F	WE CONGRATULATE	220	4"			73	49	39	Reissued in 1959 catalog as 220-3½" — added to 1977 catalog
NAT	We Congratulate	214/E/11	3½"	___	99	74	44	37	Nativity component—similar to 220 but w/o base
F	WEE ANGEL	365	?					A	May be released in 1978 or later
F	WEARY WANDERER	204	6"	207.50	128	73	49	41.50	
F	WHICH HAND	258	5½"	___	95	66	43	34.50	
F	WHITSUNTIDE ("Christmas" - old name)	163	7"	a				D/R	Discontinued. Reissue expected in 1978 or later. See Section III. See illus. on p. 103
F	WORSHIP	84/0	5"	183	132	88	53	45.50	Listed in 1950 catalog
F	WORSHIP	84/V	12¾"	a				450.50	Issued in 1978 catalog. See Section III for information & prices
HWF	Worship	164	2¾"x4¾"	?	?	36	22	17	

note:

In Section II there are over four thousand entries of suggested guide prices or indications of availability of a mark or size. The possibility that all of these entries are absolutely accurate is exactly zero. As discussed, the assurance and experience behind some of them is very high and ranges from there downward. The question marks are at the low end of the assurance range. If the information is used in the manner intended, there should be little doubt that the user will be far better off having made use of what is available than resorting to flipping a coin or using a crystal ball.

Recently discovered GIRL WITH FROG, 219/2/0, TMK-2. May be unique; is unlisted in Goebel records or books.

Section III.
Rare and Unusual Figurines

Section III of the Price Guide has been included for the advanced collector who is looking for new worlds to explore—and conquer. Collecting these rare and unusual figurines has as much challenge to offer collectors as any other type of collectible. There is so much to do and so much to be found that "Horizons Unlimited" could be an alternate title for this section. Like oil wells, new areas and fields of rare and unusual Hummels are being discovered almost daily. Some are gushers; some are dry. New oil wells take a lot of drilling to make a strike; finding rarities like some of the ones listed in Section III also takes a lot of digging. Fortunately, the expense of digging for Hummels is not as high as that of drilling for oil wells.

Table III lists about one hundred and twenty discoveries, ranging from major to minor. Some items are well documented and authenticated, while there are many about which the information is incomplete and uncertain. This wide range of confidence is expressed in Table III by various symbols to alert the reader where doubts still exist concerning price or comments. The format of this table is similar to that of Table II, which includes many references to this table.

The five columns relating to the suggested prices, one for each of the five trademarks, contain caution signs of several kinds. If the guide price shows as an actual dollar figure, the suggested price is supported by evidence of actual offers and sales. In cases in which experience is more limited the dollar figure is followed by either a question mark(?) or a plus and minus sign(±). Both notations indicate that there has been insufficient activity and knowledge to establish a firmer guide price. Also, there are many situations in which the dates of actual production of a particular model/size number are not known. For these items the price is shown with a plus or minus sign (±) in the Description column and other symbols, such as questions marks(?), are entered in the trademark columns to show the extent of existing knowledge.

Where no price is shown for a model/size number, some columns will have a question mark(?) in them and others will have a dash(—). Such an example is the figurine Angel Serenade #83 (5½″ high). Known examples have been found with the Crown mark (TMK-1) and sold for around $750. The same is true for the Full Bee mark (TMK-2) except the price would be lower, about $600. Because the date this model was discontinued is not accurately known, the Stylized Bee (TMK-3) column shows a question mark(?), indicating that at present collectors do not know of sales of any examples with this mark. The fourth column of the Three Line mark (TMK-4) also shows a question mark(?) for the same reason. In column five the dash mark(—) indicates the very remote possibility of ever finding this model with the V over G (TMK-5), which has been used from 1972. The date a model was discontinued has been determined by examining company catalogs to find the years in which it was offered for sale, or from collectors and dealers who have done similar research.

The descriptive phrases printed across the columns are self-explanatory. These are "Insufficient Data to Date," "No Record of Any Examples," and "Date Discontinued Unknown." In many instances it is almost a certainty that no examples will be found, as the only piece known was probably a prototype or special order of some kind. For example, it appears extremely unlikely that the table lamp Birthday Serenade, #231 (9¾″ high) was ever made. It was listed as a "Closed Edition" in *Hummel*, but no one has been able to locate one to date. If one is ever located, the estimated price is probably in the high four digit figures.

Some models are listed because of evidence or rumor that such a piece exists. A very interesting story illustrating a success-ful follow-up of such a rumor appeared in the March, 1977 issue of *Acquire* magazine. In this article Robert E. Miller tells how he started a hunt based on hearing a rumor of special Hummel figurines made in Hungarian costume. He managed to trace the rumor down and finally bought the figurines in Hungary. He now owns the rarest related set of figurines known.

A table like Section III published five years ago would have contained many more questionable and doubtful statements and a fraction of the number of pieces. During the past five years much has been done to substitute fact for fiction and reality with esti-mates. Five years from now it seems likely that many more blank spaces will be filled in with prices, and the comment will be writ-ten more authoritatively. This section is where the challenge lies; so start looking. We welcome reports of any successes you may have. Perhaps your finds will be included in the next revision of this book. Good hunting!

RARE AND UNUSUAL
M. I. HUMMEL FIGURINES

1. ADORATION, 23.
TMK-2, 7¾″, 23/2 previously unlisted size, also rare Arabic size mark.

2. ADORATION WITH BIRD, 105.
Factory lists this number as never having been used. Discovered in 1977. See Adoration, 23 for comparison.

3. ANGEL SERENADE, 83, (Standing Angel). TMK-3, 5¾″ or 6″. Rare, discontinued, superceded by 214/D/22, Angel Serenade or Kneeling Angel.

4. ANGELIC CARE, 194.
Left, TMK-5, 6¾″. Right, TMK-2, 7¼″. (Note design changes since 1950.)

5. APPLE TREE GIRL, 141.
Left, TMK-1, 141/V. Center, TMK-4, 141/I. Right, TMK-4, 141/3/0. Left base and trunk merge. Center, no dots in dress, "modern face." Birds in top of these two. Right, raised dots in dress. No bird is included in this small size.

6. BEGGING HIS SHARE, 9.
Left, TMK-4, 5½″, solid cake (no candle socket). Right, rare oversize, 7″, with hollow cake or candleholder socket.

7. BOOTS, 143.
Right, TMK-1, 143/I, 6½″, (but oversize) scarce, discontinued size. Left, TMK-5, 143/0, 5½″.

8. CONFIDENTIALLY, 314.
TMK-5, 5½″. Left, new model with step in stand and red bow tie. Right, TMK-2, old model—no step and no tie. Note hair difference. Rare.

9. FESTIVAL HARMONY, 172A. TMK-1. Old style has flowers in front and bird on top.

10. FESTIVAL HARMONY, 172B. TMK-5. New style has no flowers and bird on mandolin. Note hairline difference and shinier finish on new one.

11. FOREST SHRINE, 183.
TMK-2, 9″. Discontinued and very rare. In 1959 catalog. See Section III.

12. FRIENDS, 136A.
136/I, 5″ tall, TMK-5.

13. FRIENDS, 136B.
136/V, 11½″, TMK-3, scarce. Note difference in design, color, and rows of spots.

14. GIRL WITH FROG, 219/2/0.
Unlisted in Goebel records or books. Picture of only recorded piece. Recently discovered. May be unique. Extremely rare if found. Found with TMK-2.

15. GOOSE GIRL, 47.
Left, 47/II. Left center, 47. Right center, 47/0. Right, 47/3/0. Left center 47, was

original old size before 1950. Discontinued—scarce. Note changes in base bump and coloring.

16. HAPPY DAYS, 150.
TMK-2, 150/0, 5¾" high (½" oversize).
This has both printed and incised Full
Bee on back. "Traditional look" and
flower on base.

17. HEAVENLY ANGEL, 21.
This figurine known with
"Musterzimmer" on left side of base.
"Musterzimmer" translates as showroom.

18. HEAVENLY PROTECTION, 88.
(Guardian Angel in 1950 catalog.)
TMK-2, 9". (See Trademark section for
illustration of bottom.) Original standard
size, no ridge inside basket. Present 88/II
is now 9" high.

19. HOME FROM MARKET, 198.
Left, TMK-3, 198/I, 5½". "Traditional
face." Right, TMK-5, 198/0, 4¾", with
"modern face."

20. INFANT JESUS, 214/A/K.
Eyes open, with bed. Similar to Infant of
Krumbad 78, eyes closed, but without
bed.

21. KISS ME, 311.
Left, TMK-5 (new mark), doll has no
socks. Right, TMK-3, doll has socks.
More detail in hair and ribbon.

22. LITTLE GOAT HERDER, 200.
Left, TMK-4, 200/I, 5½". Right, TMK-2,
200 (original standard size), 6¼" (should
be smaller than 200/I). Note hump
behind lamb in right figure.

23. LITTLE FIDDLER, 2/1.
TMK-3, 8″. Note differences with current TMK-5 model.

24. LITTLE THRIFTY, 118.
This piece is a bank. See picture of bottom with metal lock and key in Main Photo Section.

25. LULLABY CANDLEHOLDER, 24.
TMK-2, 24/3, 6″x8″. Rare large size with Arabic size mark. (See Trademark section for illustration of base. Compare with Lullaby Candleholder, 24 in Main Photo Section for differences.)

26. MERRY WANDERER, 7A.
TMK-1 (Crown). 7/1. (decimal) unusual size mark and double-tiered base.

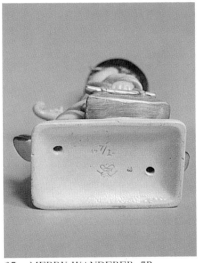

27. MERRY WANDERER, 7B.
Shows Crown trademark and unusual number/size mark.

28. MERRY WANDERER, 7.
TMK-5, 7/X, 29″. First issued in 1976, not cataloged. Note new type textured finish. When found, $6,500—$8,000.

29. MOTHER'S DARLING, 175.
Left, TMK-3, 5½″, regular coloring. Right, TMK-3, 6″ (½″ oversize). Note colored kerchief in each hand and gold center in polka dots on dress.

30. SHEPHERD'S BOY, 64.
Left, TMK-2, 5½″, (1″ oversize). Note traditional face and coloring. Right, TMK-5, 4½″. Note modern look and face coloring.

31. SILENT NIGHT, 54.
Listed in 1977 catalog as a candleholder. Rare example known with black child at left. (See *Antique Trader*, 3/2/77, page 25.) Similar to 113, Heavenly Song, except Christ Child in 113 has halo.

32. SKIER, 59.
TMK-3, 5¼″, (¼″ oversize). Note wooden poles and fiber discs. Currently made (TMK-5) with metal poles and discs. Other variations known.

33. STORMY WEATHER, 71.
Left, TMK-3, oversize with traditional look and matt finish. Right, TMK-5, standard 6¼″ high with modern look and shinier finish. Different expression on faces than Anniversary Plate—1975.

34. SURPRISE, 94.
Left, TMK-3, 94/2/0 (unlisted), base round. Right, TMK-3, 94/0 (unlisted) with rectangular base and chamfered corners.

35. TELLING HER SECRET, 196.
Left, TMK-3, 196/I, 6½″, with traditional look. Right, TMK-5, 196/0, 5¼″, (¼″ oversize). Note raised black polka dots on left figure.

36. TO MARKET (Lamp), 101.
Factory lists this as a "closed edition."
Found in 1977. See lamp To Market,
223, for comparison.

37. VACATION TIME, 125. This
plaque also known with six uprights in
fence.

38. VOLUNTEERS, 50. Left, TMK-2,
50/0, 6½″, (discontinued), drummer has
tie. Right, TMK-3, 196/2/0, 5½″.
"Modern look" but has no tie on drummer.

39. WAITER, 154.
Left, TMK-2, 154/I, 7″, (discontinued).
Traditional look, matt finish. Right,
TMK-5, 154/0, 6″, current model with
modern look, shiny finish and
difference in hair.

40. WHITSUNTIDE, 163
TMK-2, 7″, (discontinued). Very rare.
TMK-1 and 2 may have red, yellow, or
no candle held by bottom figure. TMK-3
found only with red candle to date.

GUARDIAN ANGEL (Font), 29.
Discontinued; has been redesigned to
strengthen wings. See Kneeling Angel
248, for stronger version.

41. LET'S SING (Candy Box), III/110.
Left is old-style box with rounded bottom
and inset top. (Scarce.) Right is current
model with straight sides and overlapped
top.

42. FLOWER MADONNA, 10A.
Left, TMK-2, 10/III/II, 12¼″ (¾″ oversize). Doughnut-type halo. Note bird with tail up. Right, TMK-4, 10/III/II, 11½″, has halo with no hole, and bird has tail down.

43. FLOWER MADONNA, 10B.
Left, 10/III/II, 12½″, showing hole in halo. (Has no model number shown on bottom.) Right, 10/III/II, 11½″, showing solid halo. Note more sculptured hair.

44. SHE LOVES ME, SHE LOVES ME NOT
Hummel, 227

45. ANNUAL PLATE—1971,
Heavenly Angel, 264.
Special edition, 7½″ in diameter. Each Goebel Company employee received one of these with special inscription of appreciation.

45A. Obverse of first edition 1971 Annual Plate showing inscription, "1871-1971. IN COMMEMORATION OF THE 100TH ANNIVERSARY OF W. GOEBEL-HUMMELWERK, W. Germany."

46. HUMMEL DISPLAY PLAQUE, 187.
With TMK-2, English, old-style design with bee on top. Differs in coloring from one in *Hummel*, page 137, which is 187C, and from 211 on page 147 which has all black letters. 212 is the same except for Schmid Bros. printed on bag.

47. HUMMEL DISPLAY PLAQUE, 205.
Old-style German; differs from 205 on page 145 of *Hummel* as only capital letters are orange.

48. HUMMEL DISPLAY PLAQUE, 208.
Old-style French; differs from 208 on page 146 of *Hummel* as only lower word is in orange.

49. BUSTS OF SISTER M. I. HUMMEL,
HU-2, HU-1.
On left is new HU-2, 5¾″, compared to
discontinued one marked HU-1.

50. World's rarest Hungarian-costumed
Hummel figurines. Owned by Robert
Miller, Eaton, Ohio.

51. More Hungarian-costumed figurines
from the collection of Robert Miller,
Eaton, Ohio.

52. Madonna, seated with child,
Hummel 151. Extremely rare figur-
ines in brown, blue and white.
Exhibited by Robert Miller, Eaton,
Ohio.

TABLE III.
PRICE GUIDE FOR RARE AND UNUSUAL FIGURINES

Key to Symbols
Abbreviations: F-Figurine; BE-Bookends-pair; CAN-Candleholder; HWF-Holy Water Font; PLT-Plate; PLQ-Plaque; CBX-Candybox; TLP-Lamp Base; ATR-Ashtray; NAT-Nativity Set or part; WVS-Wall Vase

a	Insufficient data to date
b	No record of examples to date
c	Date discontinued unknown
d	To be reissued in 1978 or later
____	Unlikely to find with this trademark
?	Availability with this trademark not verified
D	Discontinued
P	Being produced but not cataloged
R	Reissued or expected to be reissued in 1977 or later
Unk	Unknown
Unb	Unnumbered

1	2	3	4	5	6	7	8	9	10
CLASS	NAME	MODEL & SIZE #	DIMEN-SIONS	CROWN TMK-1	FULL BEE TMK-2	STYL. BEE TMK-3	THREE LINE TMK-4	VEE/G TMK-5	DESCRIPTION
BE	Adoration & Wayside Devotion	90A&B	Unk.						Discontinued. Rare. Estimated price, mid four digit figures.
F	ADORATION W/BIRD	105	Unk.						Example discovered in 1977, number previously cataloged as unused. Estimated price if found, high four-digit numbers.
CAN	Advent Groups w/Candle	31	Unk.						Discontinued. Three known. Estimated , mid four digit figures.
HWF	Angel Cloud	206	2¼"	500	400	300	?		Discontinued. Rare.
HWF	Angel at Prayer, Left	91A	2¼x4¾"						Design change. Present models
	Angel at Prayer, Right	91B	2¼x4¾"	?	100	?	?	19/pr.	have halos; prices of ones without, in Column 6.
F	ANGEL SERENADE	83	5½"	750	600	?	?	____	Discontinued. Rare; plans to reissue in 1977 or later (standing angel with banjo)
HWF	Angel with Birds	22/I	3¾x4"	?	75	60	?	____	Discontinued; reissued with color and size changes
HWF	Angel with Flowers	361	3½x4½"					D	Discontinued size, scarce; estimated price $200±
HWF	Angel with Yellow Bird	167	?					D	If found $400±
PLT	Annual Plate 1971	264	7½"	____	____	____	____	1000±	Edition closed; only with TMK-5
PLT	Annual Plate 1971	264S	7½"	____	____	____	____	1250±	Special employees' inscription.
F	AUF WIEDERSEHEN	153	5¼"	____	1800	____	____		Size and design variation. Very rare, with hat.
F	AUF WIEDERSEHEN	153/I	7"	1000	750	500	?	____	Discontinued size. No hat, rare
F	BE PATIENT	197.	6¼"	200	150	?	?	____	Mark unusual; with decimal point
F	BEGGING HIS SHARE	9	5½-6"	400	300	200	150	____	Design variation; prices are for examples with hollow cake which served as a candle receptacle
TLP	Birthday Serenade	234	7¾"						Discontinued. Rare; estimated price mid four digit figures
TLP	Birthday Serenade	231	9¾"						Discontinued. Rare; estimated price mid four digit figures
F	BIRTHDAY SERENADE	218/2/0	4¼"	200	150	?	?	____	Design reversed with boy playing horn and girl with accordion; current model opposite.

TABLE III.

CLASS	NAME	MODEL & SIZE #	DIMEN-SIONS	CROWN TMK-1	FULL BEE TMK-2	STYL. BEE TMK-3	THREE LINE TMK-4	VEE/G TMK-5	DESCRIPTION
F	BIRTHDAY SERENADE	218/0	5¼″	?	?	350	?	———	Design reversed with boy playing horn and girl with accordion; current model is opposite
F	BOOKWORM	3/III	9″	?	?	?	?	———	Discontinued size; date unknown. Estimated price $2,500 ±
BE	Bookworm	14 A&B	5½″	300	200	?	?	———	Design and color variation reported. If found, estimated price $300 ±
F	BOOTS	143/I	6½″	650	450	350	?	———	Discontinued size, date uncertain
CAN	Candlelight	192	6¾″	600	500	400	?	———	Discontinued; prices shown are for models with long candle passing through the hands. Other models have candle socket in hands. Estimated 50% ± of prices shown
F	CONFIDENTIALLY	314	5½″		500	?	?	———	Redesigned, date uncertain. Older models without bow tie and smaller pedestal under cactus with TMK-2
F	CONGRATULATIONS	17/0	6″	400	300	?	?	———	Redesigned, probably in 1971, socks added, hair waved. Without socks
F	CONGRATULATIONS	17/II	8¼″	*	?	?	?	———	*Discontinued size. Two known. Estimated price in mid four digit figures.
F	COQUETTES	179	5½″	200	?	?	?	———	Price for model with dark blue dress and carrying flowers
BE	Doll Mother & Prayer Before Battle	76 A&B	Unk.	?	?			———	Discontinued. Rare; estimated price in mid four digit figures.
F	FAREWELL	65.	5″	600	?	?			Decimal mark unusual
TLP	Farewell	103	Unk.						Discontinued. Rare; estimated price in mid four digit figures.
F	FEEDING TIME	199.	5½″	?	?	?			Decimal mark unusual. Estimated price $400 ±
F	FESTIVAL HARMONY/ MANDOLIN	172/II	10¼″	750 ±	?	———	———	———	Redesigned after 1950 (date unknown), spray of flowers removed from front of figure. Bird moved from flowers to mandolin. See picture page 99.
F	FESTIVAL HARMONY/ HORN	173/II	10¼″	750 ±	?	———	———	———	Redesigned after 1950 (date unknown), spray of flowers removed from front of figure
PLQ	Flitting Butterfly	139	2½x2½″	250	150	125	?	?	Discontinued; scarce with TMK-1, 2, & 3
MAD	Flower Madonna	10/I/II	8¼″						Design variation; early examples known with open halo. Late ones are solid. Estimated price $150-$250. Also known with golden color and also in light brown color instead of regular blue-lavender color. Estimated price mid four-digit figures
F	FOREST SHRINE	183	9″	2400	2000	1600	———	———	Discontinued. Dates unknown. Very rare
F	FRIENDS	136/5	11½″	1000	700	400	?	———	Size mark unusual; price shown for Arabic 5 only
F	GIRL WITH FROG	219/2/0	4″						This number originally listed in *HUMMEL* book as never used and never would be. Two examples discovered in 1977. Mid four-digit figure estimated price
F	GLOBETROTTER	79	5¼″	200	150	75	?	———	Redesigned, date unknown, with double over and under weave. Original design was single.

CLASS	NAME	MODEL & SIZE #	DIMEN-SIONS	CROWN TMK-1	FULL BEE TMK-2	STYL. BEE TMK-3	THREE LINE TMK-4	VEE/G TMK-5	DESCRIPTION
F	GOING TO GRANDMA'S	52/0	4¾"	?	?			——	Price for examples found without flowers in cone and square bases. Estimated price $300 ±
F	GOING TO GRANDMA'S	52/I	6"	?	650	550	?	——	Discontinued size. Date uncertain. Considered rare
F	GOOD SHEPHERD	42/I	7½"						Discontinued size. Listed in early 1950s price list. Rare. Estimated, low four digit figures
HWF	Good Shepherd	35/I	2¾x5¾"						Discontinued on unknown date. Scarce. Estimated price when found $200 ±
HWF	Guardian Angel	29	2½x5¾"						Discontinued. Restyled as #248 (Kneeling Angel) stronger wings. Estimate price $1000 ±
F	HAPPY BIRTHDAY	176	6"						Unusual decimal mark size 176(.) Reissue in 1978 or later. Estimated price $250 ±
F	HAPPY DAYS	150/0	5¼"	?	300	200	?	——	Discontinued. To be reissued in 1978 or later. Rare
F	HAPPY DAYS	150/I	6½"	600	500	400	?	——	Discontinued. To be reissued in 1978 or later. Rare
TLP	Happy Days	232	9¾"						Discontinued. Rare; estimated price if found $1,000 ±
TLP	Happy Days	235	7¾"			750	?	a	Discontinued. Rare
CAN	Heavenly Song	113	3½x4¾"					a	Design discontinued before 1950. RARE, if found. One known. Estimated price in high four digit figures
F	HELLO	124/0	6¼"	?	200	150	?	——	Redesigned, date uncertain. Newer design is smaller with medium dark brown trousers. Older design has lighter greenish tone trousers. Estimated price for old version $250 ±
F	HELLO	124/I	7"					b	Discontinued; RARE. Estimated price when found. $600 ±
F	HOME FROM MARKET	198	5½"					a	Unusual decimal mark instead of 198 (listed in early 1950s). When found, add 50% to 5½" prices in Section II
F	HOMEWARD BOUND	334	5"	——	?	?	130	——	Design change c. 1970; removed support under goat
PLQ	Hummel (M.I.) Display Plaques	187c 205 208 209 210 211 212 213	3½x5" 3½x5" 3½x5" 3½x5" 3½x5" 3½x5" 3½x5" 3½x5"	a				28	See illustrations on page 104. 187 was issued between 1948-1950. Redesigned in 1972 without "Bee" as 187c in English. Other numbers were issued early in the 1950s and superceded by 187 with suffix. Old designs are rare especially with older marks. Estimated price from $400 to $900 depending on variation in designs. #212 is reported to be marked "Schmid Bros." on bag. Estimated price, mid four-digit figure
F	JOYFUL	53	3½"	250	150	?	?		Oversize; scarce with premium, shown for larger versions 4-4¼" high
CBX	Joyful	III/53	6"	a					Design change; newer models have cap-type top and straight sides. If older, flush lid tops found, add 50% to Section II prices. See picture page 60
F	JOYFUL & LET'S SING (on wood base)	120	——					b	Discontinued; extremely RARE; if found, estimated price low four-digit figure.

1	2	3	4	5	6	7	8	9	10
CLASS	NAME	MODEL & SIZE #	DIMEN-SIONS	CROWN TMK-1	FULL BEE TMK-2	STYL. BEE TMK-3	THREE LINE TMK-4	VEE/G TMK-5	DESCRIPTION
F	JOYOUS NEWS	27/III	4¼x4¾"	2500	200	1500	——	——	Discontinued; was in 1950 catalog, possibly replaced by 238/c (Angel with Horn). Reported to have been made with Arabic 3. VERY RARE. Estimated price when found low four-digit figure
F	KISS ME (w/socks)	311	6"	200	170	140	——	——	Redesigned, date unknown. Example with TMK-1, 2 & 3 have socks on. Current ones do not. See illus. on page 100.
F	LATEST NEWS	184/0	5¼"	a				——	Design variation; found with numerous names on newspaper which brings premium up to 20% over Section II prices
AT	Let's Sing	114	3½x6¼"	a				——	Design variation; early examples reported with boy on right. If found, add 50% to Section II prices
F	LITTLE CELLIST	89/III	8"					a	Reported with eyes up, if found add 25% to Section II prices
F	LITTLE FIDDLER	2/III	12¼"					a	Discontinued size; RARE. Price of examples when found may be in low four-digit figures
PLQ	Little Fiddler	107	Unk.					b	Discontinued; RARE. Estimated price, $750±
F	LITTLE PHARMACIST	322	6"					a	Design variation; with "Vitamins" on label add 30%
F	LOST SHEEP	68	5½"	a				——	Design variation. Older brown command premium. Discontinued size; RARE, estimated price $300±
F	LOST SHEEP	68.	6¼"	a				——	Discontinued size; RARE, estimated price $400
CAN	Lullaby	24/III	8¾"	*	*	?	?	D/R	*Discontinued size. Plans for reissue in 78 or later. Listed in 1950 catalog. Very rare with estimated price in low four-digit figure for TMK-1 or 2 see illus. on pg. 101.
MAD	Madonna	151/II	11½"					a	Discontinued. May be reissued -color unknown. Known examples with very rare blue or brown cloak with estimated price in low four-digit figures.
MAD	Madonna	151/W	11½"					a	White example also low four digit figures
PLQ	Madonna in Red w/child	222	4x5"					a	Discontinued. Rare when found in wire frame, similar to 48/0. Estimated price $800±
PLQ	Madonna in Red w/Child in Metal Frame	48/II	4¾x6"	350	250	150		——	Discontinued size. Date unknown. In catalogs 1950-1966. Estimated prices as shown at left
PLQ	Madonna in Red w/Child in Metal Frame	48/V	8½x10"	800	700	?	?	——	Discontinued size. RARE!
F	MEDITATION	13/II	7"	2500	?	?	?	$750	Discontinued size. VERY RARE in this size, may have Arabic 2 size marker and basket partially filled with flowers
F	MEDITATION	13/V	13¾"	——	?	3000	?	$1500	Discontinued size, extremely RARE with Arabic 5 size marker and basket filled with flowers
F	MERRY WANDERER	7/I	7"	a				——	Design variation; known to have been made with two-tier base in this size. Also known with G-button vest and only lower eyelashes. Estimated price $500±. See illus. on page 101

Key to Symbols

Abbreviations: F-Figurine; BE-Bookends-pair; CAN-Candleholder; HWF-Holy Water Font; PLT-Plate; PLQ-Plaque; CBX-Candybox; TLP-Lamp Base; ATR-Ashtray; NAT-Nativity Set or part; WVS-Wall Vase

a   Insufficient data to date
b   No record of examples to date
c   Date discontinued unknown
d   To be reissued in 1978 or later
____ Unlikely to find with this trademark
?   Availability with this trademark not verified
D   Discontinued
P   Being produced but not cataloged
R   Reissued or expected to be reissued in 1977 or later
Unk Unknown
Unb Unnumbered

1	2	3	4	5	6	7	8	9	10
				CROWN	FULL BEE	STYL. BEE	THREE LINE	VEE/G	
CLASS	NAME	MODEL & SIZE #	DIMEN-SIONS	TMK-1	TMK-2	TMK-3	TMK-4	TMK-5	DESCRIPTION
F	MERRY WANDERER	7/III	11¼"					a	Discontinued size, date uncertain. When found, size may vary. Estimated price for TMK-3 $1,500±
F	MERRY WANDERER	7/X	29"	—	—	—	—	P	Produced in 1976. Not cataloged in 1977. When found $6,500-$8,000. See illus. on page 101
PLQ	Merry Wanderer	106	Unk.					b	No records showing this was ever produced. Not to be confused with #92 reintroduced in 1977. If found and verified, would be extremely rare; possibly unique. Estimated price, low to mid four-digit figure
PLQ	Merry Wanderer	263	4x5¾"					b	Discontinued. Rare if found. Estimated price in low four-digit figure
F	MOTHER'S DARLING	175	5½"					a	Color variation in two kerchief bundles known to have distinct blue and pink color. See illustration on page 101. Estimated price $400±
F	PUPPY LOVE SERENADE, HAPPINESS (on wood base)	122	Unk.					b	Discontinued. VERY RARE. No record of this model **ever** existing. If found, estimated price in low to mid four-digit figure
F	RUNAWAY, THE — (SEE THE RUNAWAY)								
F	SCHOOL BOY	82/II	7½"	2000	1500	?	—	—	Discontinued size was listed in early 1950s price list as 182/2-7¼". VERY RARE
F	SCHOOL GIRL	81.	4¼"					a	Reported with unusual decimal mark. Estimated price $400±.
F	SENSITIVE HUNTER	6/0	4¾"	150+	100+	?	—	—	Design variation, restyled; early models made with parallel suspender straps in back. Current models have "X" straps in back; mark #1 and #2 prices are for parallel straps
F	SHE LOVES ME . . . SHE LOVES ME NOT	174	4¼"	—	?	90	?	—	*Design variation. Premium price shown for eyes open
TLP	Shrine	100	7½"	2000	—	—	—	—	Discontinued. VERY RARE. If found, estimated price with TMK-1 only
F	SIGNS OF SPRING	203/2/0	4"	a				—	Design variation. Premium for examples found with a shoe on each foot, 50% above Section II prices

TABLE III.

111

CLASS	NAME	MODEL & SIZE #	DIMEN-SIONS	CROWN TMK-1	FULL BEE TMK-2	STYL. BEE TMK-3	THREE LINE TMK-4	VEE/G TMK-5	DESCRIPTION
F	SIGNS OF SPRING	203/I	5½"	a				43-	Design variation. Premium for examples found with a shoe on each foot, 50% above Section II prices
CAN	Silent Night	54	5½x4¾"					——	See illus. on page 102. Color variation. EXTREMELY RARE example found with black child as left figure in scene. Estimated price in mid four-digit figures
F	SKIER	59	5¼"	?	*130	100?	55?	——	*Design variation. 20% premium for older models found with wooden ski poles. See illus. on page 102
F	SPRING CHEER	72	5"	300	200	100	?	——	Design and color variation; older model shows yellow dress with no flowers in right hand; newer model shows green dress and flowers in right hand
F	SPRING DANCE	353/0	5¼"	——	?	*	?	——	*Discontinued size, probably during 1960s. Plans to reissue in 1977 or later. Very RARE in small size. Estimated price in low four digit figures
PLQ	Standing Boy	168	5¾"	1800	1200	100	——	——	Discontinued, date uncertain. RARE; known with TMK-1,2,3 only
F	STAR GAZER	132	4¾"	a				37	Color variation; date uncertain; older models with blue shirt, newer models have purple shirt.
F	SURPRISE	94/2/0	4½"	——	——	300	?	D	Add 20% to Section II prices for blue shirt
F	SURPRISE	94/0	5"	——	——	300	?	D	See illus. on page 102. Both discontinued 94/2/0 on oval base and 94/0 on rectangular base with clipped corners. Scarce
PLQ	Swaying Lullaby	165	5¼x5¼"	1800	1200	1000	——	——	Discontinued, date uncertain. RARE; estimated prices with TMK-1,2,&3
F	TELLING HER SECRET	196/I	6¾"	?	400	300	?	——	Discontinued size between 1950 and 1966. Estimated price when found with TMK-2 or 3
F	THE RUNAWAY	327	5¼"	——	?	?	*	55	*Redesigned, date uncertain. Objects removed from basket and shirt now blue. Estimated price for old model $75±
F	TO MARKET	49.	Unk.	a				——	Reported with decimal after 49. Examples when found $200±
F	TO MARKET	49/I	6¼"	a				——	Discontinued size between 1950 and 1959. Plans to reissue in 1978 or later. Estimated price when found $500±
TLP	To Market	101	7½"		?	*	——	——	Discontinued. First example found in 1977 with TMK-3. Estimated value in low four-digit figures
PLQ	Tuneful Goodnight	180	5"	850	700	600	——	——	Discontinued between 1950 and 1959 catalogs, date uncertain. RARE, when found at prices shown at left. Old name "Happy Bugler"
PLQ	Vacation Time	125	4x4¾"	a					Some have one more fencepost (6). Add 30% to Sec. II prices. See illus. on pg. 103
F	VILLAGE BOY	51/I	7¼"	600	500	400	——	——	Discontinued between early 1950s price list and 1959 catalog. RARE, when found at prices shown at left
F	VOLUNTEERS	50/0	5½"	500±	400±	?	?	——	Discontinued size before 1966, date uncertain. Plans to reissue in 1978 or later. Very scarce. Estimated price when found shown at left

1	2	3	4	5	6	7	8	9	10
		MODEL &	DIMEN-	CROWN	FULL BEE	STYL. BEE	THREE LINE	VEE/G	
CLASS	NAME	SIZE #	SIONS	TMK-1	TMK-2	TMK-3	TMK-4	TMK-5	DESCRIPTION
F	VOLUNTEERS	50/I	6½″	800±	700±	?	———	———	Discontinued size before 1959, date uncertain. Plans to reissue in 1978 or later. Very scarce. Estimated prices when found shown at left. See illus. on page 103.
TLP	Volunteers	102	7½″					b	Discontinued (not in 1950 catalog). RARE. Estimated price in high four digit figures
F	WAITER	154/?	4½″	?	300±			———	Discontinued. Listed in E&R catalog of 1959 and not in 1966. Estimated price if found shown at left
F	WAITER	154	6½″	*				———	*Discontinued. Listed in 1950 catalog. Estimated price $400±.Reissue expected in 1978 or later
F	WAITER	154/I	7″	———	600	500	———	———	Discontinued size, dates uncertain. Estimated price when found shown with TMK-2&3. See illus. on page 103
WV	Wall Vase, Boy and Girl	360A	4½x6″					a	Discontinued. Copyright registered in 1959 but not listed in 1966 catalog. Production dates uncertain. Example known and considered VERY RARE. Estimated price $600±
WV	Wall Vase Boy (only)	360B	4½x6″					a	Discontinued. Copyright registered in 1959 but not listed in 1966 catalog. Production dates uncertain. Example known and considered VERY RARE. Estimated price if found $500±
WV	Wall Vase Girl (only)	360C	4½x6″					a	Discontinued. Copyright registered in 1959 but not listed in 1966 catalog. Production dates uncertain. Example known and considered VERY RARE. Estimated price if found $500±
TLP	Wayside Devotion	104	7½″	*	?	———	———		*Discontinued, probably before 1950, date uncertain. RARE, if found. *Estimated price $1,500
F	WAYSIDE HARMONY	III/3/0	4″	?	150	80	?	———	Known with yellow shirt and with 1938 (copyright?) date incised. Estimated price as indicated at left
F	WAYSIDE HARMONY & JUST RESTING	121	Unk.	b				———	Discontinued. Both mounted on wooden base. Not in available catalogs. VERY RARE, if found. Estimated price in low four-digit figures
TLP	Wayside Harmony	224/II	9½″	b				———	Discontinued. Plans to reissue in 1978 or later date uncertain. Estimated price, if found, $600±
F	WHITSUNTIDE (Christmas - old name)	163	7″	*	*	*	———	———	*Discontinued. Plans to reissue in 1978 or later. VERY RARE; listed in 1950 catalog. Early 1950 price list showed size as 17.50 cm (6.88″). Not in 1959 catalog; reported with and without candle held by angel on base. *Estimated price in low to mid four-digit figures. See illus. on page 103
F	WORSHIP	84V	12¾″	a				347	Discontinued and reissued in 1977 catalog. In early 1950s price list reported in Arabic 5 size marker. Early examples were $800-$1,000 before reintroduction in 1977. Price may be affected by reissue.

TABLE III.

Section IV.
Master Numerical List
of Hummel Figurines

Section IV is a Master Numerical listing of "M. I. Hummel" figurines. If only the number of an item is known, this table should be the starting place for information. For the whole story on the piece, the reader should check all four tables.

Section IV is the most comprehensive table of them all. First, it includes a translation of the German name of each figurine. This translation is listed in parentheses just underneath the English catalog name, and in many instances, they are essentially the same. In others, the English name and the English translation of the German name are not the same. This fact may explain the confusion existing with some figurines. An example of such confusion is #124, "Hello" in English. The German word "Chef" was combined with Hello and published as "Chef, Hello" in *HUMMEL*. In addition to the translated name, entirely different names have been or are currently being applied to the same figurine. These alternate names have been shown, where possible, as a further clarification. Some examples of name changes are taken from a 1950 catalog which list #12 Smoky, #141 Spring, and #142 Fall. The present names of these figurines are Chimney Sweep, Apple Tree Girl, and Apple Tree Boy, respectively.

Table IV lists more size code marks than any other list. Many of these additional size code marks have been reported as having been seen or are owned by collectors and dealers. Others were added as a result of research of old catalogs. Still others were added even though no known examples exist. Such unknowns were included when it seemed reasonable to expect that they had once been produced and had been discontinued, perhaps with very limited production. If they eventually surface the space will be there to accommodate them. In the meantime, the listing may serve as a clue for "Want Lists." For example, Apple Tree Girl #141, is presently not issued in 141/0 size. It seems likely that at one time it may have also been produced with the similar marking of 141 or 141. (decimal). For this reason, it is listed here as a possibility. However, size codes between 141V and 141X are not listed because it is known that these were bypassed last year when the 141X was first produced in the 29″ size.

This table also provides three columns for listing the copyright date, the date of first issue, and if discontinued, that date. A glance at these columns will show how much information is still needed, especially in the lower numbers. The information presently and potentially available should be of major interest to collectors and dealers in determining the earliest date a figurine could have been made and the date after which it was not produced. Another column shows the page number where an illustration of the piece can be found.

The prices shown in the Class/Price column are those taken from the latest company "Suggested Retail Price List" of "M. I. Hummel" Figurines. In those instances where no price is shown, other useful information showing current production status is included.

Production Status Code Letters

There are a number of tables in this book, including the "Master Numerical List," that present essential information with respect to most all of the "M. I. Hummel" figurines produced by the W. Goebel Company since 1935. In order to accomplish this, these compact tabulations make use of code letters, numbers, and symbols. The set of code letters described below is designed to show the production status, as of this time, of each of the numbers, 1 through 400, allotted to these figurines and included in the "Master List" which follows.

P-PRODUCED

If a figurine is currently being produced, priced, and published in the current Goebel catalog, the price is shown in Column 5 on the line for that number in U.S. dollars. In case it is known to have been produced but not published in the current catalog or price list, the letter "P" is substituted instead of a dollar figure. Examples at this time are Apple Tree Girl and Boy, #141 and #142, in size X, 29″ high, and the Merry Wanderer, #7, also in size X, 29″ high. These were produced and sold in very limited quantities in 1976, but are not yet in either the 1976 or 1977 catalogs.

D-DISCONTINUED

Some of the items cataloged in past years have been removed and are not currently available. Twenty-eight of these are listed in *HUMMEL*, as "Closed Edition." There are now a great many more line items that this. Where research has established that a given number was once produced but no longer cataloged, the letter "D", for discontinued, is entered into the "Class/Price" Column 5 on the Master Numerical List opposite the model number. When there may be some doubt as to whether or not the piece was discontinued, the "D" is followed by a small question mark (?) indicating uncertainty.

CANCELLED

There are a considerable quantity of numbers that supposedly have not been used to date. Thirty-eight of these have been published in *HUMMEL* as a "number that has not been used and will not be used to identify M. I. Hummel figurines." In Column 6 and any other references, these are designated in this book by the letter "C" which stands for the number being cancelled. It would be unlikely to find any examples of these thirty-eight numbers although one, #219/2/0 has been reported and illustrated. If any of these do surface in years to come, they should be very attractive rarities.

A-ASSIGNED

Remaining in the three digit series are many that are unaccounted for. They are not in the catalog. They have not been discontinued or canceled. Some of these have been allocated, assigned, or approved for new models to be released at some undetermined date in the future, if all goes well. In other words, models may be in any one of a number of pre-production stages from conception to prototype. The *HUMMEL* book groups these along with the ones actually in production. Many collectors have been confused by a single classification for two different stages in the figurine "life cycle." To eliminate this, the letter "A" has been entered in Column 5 when it is believed that the number has been allocated for some advanced plans.

R-REISSUED

This classification was included to identify figurines which were originally cataloged and which authoritative sources have indicated will be reissued in the future. About fifty figurines are included in this plan. Whether or not the reissued numbers will be identical to the ones that were orginally cataloged has not been made known at this time. Since some of these numbers have been discontinued they have become high-priced rarities. What effect reinstating them will have on the prices of the old ones remains to be determined and will probably depend to some extent on whether the reissues are identical with the old ones.

CODE LETTER OMITTED

Where there is no price or letter code used in the Class/Price Column 5 for any Hummel model or size, there is insufficient information at this time to make a meaningful and accurate assignment. As noted, the use of a question mark following one of the classification letters indicates that there may be some evidence or indication that this is the proper class. However, this is still questionable and should not be fully relied on at this time. It is certainly expected that with assistance from Goebel, collectors, and dealers, that it will be possible to fill in most of the blanks and remove a large majority of the question marks in future editions.

This table was compiled with the assistance of many collectors and dealers. Numerous catalogs and price lists were studied. The book *Hummel*, published in 1976 by Portfolio Press was also a very valuable source of information. A glance at the table will indicate how much is still to be accounted for. It is earnestly requested that any corrections or additional information be sent to the author to be included in the next edition for the benefit of all readers.

O-OPEN

This leaves as unaccounted for, in the 1-396 series set aside for Hummel figurines, about 71 numbers which have been identified in research conducted for the book *HUMMEL* as being "not used" and which have been designated by the letters "ON" for Open Number. These can be considered as open for assignment in the future for designs and plans not yet formulated. For purposes of this book, the opportunity to use "O" on this occasion for OPEN seems like an outstanding and obvious out.

TABLE IV.
MASTER NUMERICAL LIST

Key to Symbols
A-Assigned
C-Cancelled
D-Discontinued
O-Open
P-Produced
R-Reissued

No.	Size Mk.	a. English / Name b. German	Size Inches	$ Price/ Status	Illus. on Page No.	Date of Copyr't.	Date of Issue	Date Discont'd.	Remarks
1	—	PUPPY LOVE (Little Fiddler with Dog)	4½	41.50	51		1935		
2	12/0	LITTLE FIDDLER (Little Fiddler w/o Dog)	6	49.00	47		1935		Called "Violinist" at one time
	/0		?	D?			1950-		Insufficient data to date
	—		?	D?					Insufficient data to date
	/I		7½	126.50	101		1950-		
	/II		10¾	402.50		R1972			Reregistered in 1972
	/III		?	D/R				1965 ±	Insufficient data to date
3	—	BOOKWORM (The Bookworm)	?	D?	38		1935		Same as #8
	/I		5½	92.00			1950-		
	/II		8	402.50		R1972			Reregistered in 1972
	/III		?	D/R					Insufficient data to date. See Sec. II & III
4	—	LITTLE FIDDLER (Little Fiddler w/o Dog)	4¾	38.00	47		1935		
5	—	STROLLING ALONG (Wanderer (Boy) with Dog)	4¾	38.00	54		1935		
6	—	SENSITIVE HUNTER (Little Hunter)	?	D?	52		1935		Insufficient data to date
	/0		4¾	38.00			1950-		
	/I		5½	49.00					
	/II		7½	103.50					
7	—	MERRY WANDERER (Wanderer (Boy) w/o Dog)	?	D?	50		1935		An early model had six button vest and lower eyelashes
	/0		6¼	60.50			1950-		
	/I		7	115.00	101				
	/II		9½	402.50		R1972			Reregistered in 1972 - See Sec. III
	/III		11¼	D/R					Insufficient data to date See Sec. III
	/V		?	?					Insufficient data to date
	/X		29	(8000)	101		1976		Price unofficial; Examples sold in 1976
8		BOOKWORM (The Bookworm)	4	45.00	38		1935		Similar to #3, except for size
9		BEGGING HIS SHARE (The Well-Wisher)	5½	44.50	38		1935		Old models rare, see Sec. III
10	—	FLOWER MADONNA (Flower Madonna W/Child)	?	D?	64				Insufficient data to date
	/I/11		8¼	77.00			1950-		Refer to Sec. III for more information
	/I/W		8¼	40.00					
	/II/11		?	D?					Insufficient data to date
	/II/W		?	D?					Insufficient data to date
	/III/11		11½	227.00	104		1950-		
	/III/W		11½	115.50					
11	/2/0	MERRY WANDERER (Wanderer [Boy] w/o Dog)	4¼	29.50	50				1950 catalog lists as 3¾" h.
	/0		4¾	38.00	175				
	—		?	D?					Insufficient data to date

1	2	3 a. English b. German	4	5	6	7	8	9	10
No.	Size Mk.	Name	Size Inches	$ Price/ Status	Illus. on Page No.	Date of Copyr't.	Date of Issue	Date Discont'd.	Remarks
12	/2/0	CHIMNEY SWEEP	4	22.50	40		1950-		Called "Smoky" in 1950 catalog
	/0	("I bring good luck")	?	D?					Insufficient data to date
	—	(Chimney Sweep)	?	D?					Example known 12. and 6¼" h.
	/I		5½	38.00			1950-		
	II		7	D					
13	/2/0	MEDITATION	4¼	29.50	50	1963			
	/0	(The Well-Wisher)	5½	40.00			1950-		
	—		?	D?		1957			Insufficient data to date
	/I		?	D?					Insufficient data to date
	/II		7	D/R				?	Date discontinued unknown
	/III		?	D?					Insufficient data to date
	/IV		?	D?					Insufficient data to date
	/V		13¾	D/R		1957		?	Date discontinued unknown
14	/A&B	Bookends—BOOKWORMS	5½	93.50	58				Book leaves not colored. Also see Sec. III
		(The Bookworm, Boy & Girl)							
15	—	HEAR YE, HEAR YE	?	D?	45		1940-?		Insufficient data to date
	/0	("Hear Ye" Nightwatchman)	5	44.50					
	/I		6	63.00					
	/II		8¾	P					
16	/2/0	LITTLE HIKER	4½	24.50	48		1950-		
	/0	(Hans in Fortune)	?	D?				?	To be reissued in '78 or later
	—		?	D?			1940-	?	Insufficient data to date
	/I		6	39.00					
17	—	CONGRATULATIONS	6	D	41		1940-	?	Date discontinued unknown
	/0	(I Congratulate You)	6	34.50		R1971			
	/I		?	D?					Insufficient data to date
	/2		8	D				?	See Sec. III - Rare, only 2 known
18		CHRIST CHILD	6x2	35.00	40		1940-		Called "Christmas Night" in 1950 catalog
		(Silent Night, Baby Jesus)							
19		(UNKNOWN)		C					No record of example to date
20		PRAYER BEFORE BATTLE	4¼	45.00	51		1940-		
		(The Pious Horseman)							
21	/0	HEAVENLY ANGEL	4¾	29.00	45		1950-		Called "Little Guardian" in 1950
	/0/½	(The Little Christ Child)	6	44.00			1950-		
	—		?	D?			1940-		Insufficient data to date
	/I		6¾	57.00					
	/II		8¾	115.50					
22	—	Font: Angel with Birds	?	D	61				Insufficient data to date
	/0	(Sitting Angel)	2¾x3½	D					Discontinued in 1977
	/I		3¼x4	D					Date discontinued unknown
23	—	ADORATION	?	D?	36		1940-	?	Insufficient data to date
	/I	(At Mother Maria's)	6¼	92.00			1950-		Called "Cradle Song" in 1950 catalog
	/II		?	D?	98			?	Insufficient data to date
	/III	(Discontinued in 1978)	9	132			1966-	1966+	Reissued in 1977
24	—	Candleholder: Lullaby	?	D?	60			?	Insufficient data to date
		(Cradle Song, Lullaby)							
	/I	Lullaby	5x3½	51.50					
	/II		?	D?					Insufficient data to date
	/III		6x8	D/R	100		1950-		Date discontinued unknown Rare, see Sec. III
25	—	ANGELIC SLEEP	3½x5	D	59		1940-	?	
	/I	(Silent Night)	5x3½	51.50					Added to 1977 Price List
26	/0	Font: Child Jesus Holy Water	1½x5	11.00	62				
	—	Holy Water Font (Child Jesus)	?	D?					Insufficient data to date
	/I		2½x6	P					Insufficient data to date
27	—	JOYOUS NEWS	?	D?					Insufficient data to date
	/I	("Oh, You Joyful One")	?	D?			1950-		Insufficient data to date
	/II		?	D?					Insufficient data to date
	/III		4¼x4¾	D					See Sec. III. Rare. Like 238C
28	—	WAYSIDE DEVOTION	?	D?	56			?	Insufficient data to date
	/I	(Evening Song)	?	D?				?	Insufficient data to date
	/II		7½	101.50			1950-		Known in Arabic 2 mark
	/III		8¾	152.50			1955-		
29	—	Font: Guardian Angel	2½x5¾	D					
	/0	(Holy Water Font)	2½x6	D					

TABLE IV.

1 No.	2 Size Mk.	3 Name a. English b. German	4 Size Inches	5 $ Price/ Status	6 Illus. on Page No.	7 Date of Copyr't.	8 Date of Issue	Date Discont'd.	9 10 Remarks
30	/A&B	Plq.: Ba-Bee Ring (Oh, The Bee, Wall Ring)	4¾x5	53.50	65		1950-		
31	—	CAN.: Advent Group w/Candle (Advent Group w/Candle)	Unk	D				?	
32	—	LITTLE GABRIEL (Oh, You Joyful One. Angel)	5	32.50	47		1940-		
33		Ashtray: Joyful (AT: Singing Rehearsal)	3½x6	37.00	57				
34		Ashtray: Singing Lesson (It's Not Right)	3½x6¼	51.00	57		1950-		
35	/0	Font: The Good Shepherd (The Good Shepherd)	2¼x4¾	11.00	62				
	—		?	D?				?	Insufficient data to date
	/I		2¾x5¾	D				?	See Sec. III. Scarce
36	/0	Font: Angel with Flowers (Sitting Angel)	2¾x4	11.00	61				
	—		?	D?			1940-	?	
	/I		3½x4½	P					Insufficient data to date
37		Candleholder: Herald Angels (Adv. Cndhldr. w/3 Angels)	4x2¼	50.00	59				
38	III/38/0	Candleholder: Angels, Joyous News w/Lute	2	42.00*	59		1950-		Candleholder, Angel Trio (A) 1 of 3 (3 ass't. sitting w/candle) sold as set for $42. See 238 A, B, & C called "Angel Trio" B, not candleholders
	I/38/0	(C: Little Advent-Angel w/Lute)	2¾	D			1950-		
			?	D?					
39	III/39/0	Candleholder: Angel, Joyous News w/Accordion	2	42.00*	59		1950-		*Price for set of 3
	I/39/0		2¾	D				?	
		(Little Advent-Angels w/ (Concertina)	?	D?					Insufficient data to date
40	III/40/0	Candleholder: Angel, Joyous News w/Trumpet	2	42.00*	59		1950-		
	I/40/0	(Little Advent Angel w/Trumpet	2¾	D				?	
			?	D					Insufficient data to date
41	—	(UNKNOWN)		C					No examples reported to date
42	—	GOOD SHEPHERD	6¼	42.00	44		1950-		In 1950 catalog as 42/0
	/I	(The Good Shepherd)	6¼or8?	D					This size listed in 1950 catalog as 18 cm.
43	—	MARCH WINDS (Rascal)	5	30.50	49		1950-		
44	/A	LB: Culprits (Applethief (boy)	9½	122.00	63	1950	1950?		At one time these were called "Out on a Limb." See illus. in Sec. III
	B	LB: Out of Danger (In Safety (girl) (Safe)	9½	122.00	63	1950	1950?		
45	/0/6	MADONNA WITH HALO (Color) (Madonna with Halo)	10½	27.50	64				Called "Holy Virgin" in early catalog
	/0/W	(White)	10½	17.00					
	—		?	D?				?	Insufficient data to date. Also reported in color 13 in addition to 6, various sizes
	/I/6		?	D?			?		Insufficient data to date
	/I/W		12"	21.50					Added to catalog in 1977
	/II/6		?	D?				?	Insufficient data to date
	/II/W		?	D?				?	Insufficient data to date
	/III/6		16¾	P?					Date discontinued unknown
	/III/W		16¾	P?					Date discontinued unknown
46	/0/6	MADONNA, PRAYING (Madonna)	10¼	27.50	64				No halo - /6 is color. /W is white. Color /13 discontinued
	/0/W								
	—		?	0?					Insufficient data to date
	/I/6		11¼	34.50					
	/I/W		11¼	21.50					
	/II/6		?	D?					Insufficient data to date
	/II/W		?	D?					Insufficient data to date
	/III/6		16¼	D/R				?	Expected to be reissued in 1978 or later

No.	Size Mk.	Name a. English b. German	Size Inches	$ Price/Status	Illus. on Page No.	Date of Copyr't.	Date of Issue	Date Discont'd.	Remarks
	/III/W		16¼	D/R				?	Expected to be reissued in 1978 or later
47	/3/0	GOOSE GIRL	4	39.00	44		1950-		Known w/Arabic size marks
	/2/0	(Goose Liesl)	?	?			?-		
	/0		4¾	49.00	99		1950-		
	—		?	D?				?	Insufficient data to date
	/I		?	D?				?	Insufficient data to date
	/II		7½	138.00	99		1950-		
48	/0	Plaque: Madonna (Madonna Picture)	3x4	29.50	65	1950-	1959+		Also "Virgin w/Child" earlier Madonna in Red
	—		?	D?					Insufficient data to date
	/I		?	D?					Insufficient data to date
	/II		4¾x6	D/R		1950-		?	Reissue expected in 1978 or later
	/V		8½x10	D				?	See Sec. III
49	/3/0	TO MARKET	4	42.50	55	1950-			
	12/0	(Little Brother and Sister)	5½	52.00					
	/0		?	D?		1950-			
	/I		6¼	D/R		1950-		?	Reissue expected in 1978 or later. See Sec. III
50	/2/0	VOLUNTEERS	5	60.50	56				
	/0	(Playing Soldiers)	?	D/R	103	1950-		?	Reissue expected in 1978 or later
	—		?	D?					Insufficient data to date
	/I		6½	D/R					Reissue expected in 1978 or later. See Sec. III
51	/3/0	VILLAGE BOY	4	23.00	55				
	/2/0	(Village Boy)	5¼	30.50		1961			
	/0		6	42.00			1950-		
	—		?	D?					Insufficient data to date
	/I		7¼	D/R				?	Reissue expected in 1978 or later. See Sec. III
52	/0	GOING TO GRANDMA'S (Little Housemother)	4¾	53.50	44		1950-		
	—		?	D?					Insufficient data to date
	/I		6	D				?	See Sec. III on TMK-1, 2 & 3. Called "Banjo Betty" in 1950
53		JOYFUL	4	23.00	46				See Sec. III for variation
III/53		Candy Box: Joyful (Singing Rehearsal, Audition)	6¼	57.00					See Sec. III for design change
54		Candleholder: Silent Night (Silent Night, Manger)	4¾x3¾	67.50	60		1950-		See Sec. III for rare variation. (Similar to 113)
55		SAINT GEORGE (Knight Saint George)	6¾	96.00	52				Not in 1950 catalog
56	/A	CULPRITS (Apple Thief, Boy)	6¼	52.50	41				
	/B	OUT OF DANGER (In Safety, Girl)	6¼	52.50	50				Listed as 56 (only) in 1950 catalog
57	/0	CHICK GIRL	3½	34.50	39		1950-		"Little" Chick Girl in 1950
	—	(Little Chick Mother)	?	D?				?	Insufficient data to date
	/I		4¼	56.50					
III/57		CBX-Chick Girl	6¼	57.00	60				
58	/0	PLAYMATES	4	34.50	51		1950-		
	—	(Rabbit Father)	?	D?				?	Insufficient data to date
	/I		4¼	56.50					
III/58		CBX-Playmates	6¼	57.00	61				
59		SKIER (Hail, Skiing)	5	42.50	53		1950-		Current model has metal poles - old (?) ones had wooden poles
60	A	Bookends: Farm Boy (Swineherd)	4¾	111.00	58		1950-		Sold by the pair
	B	Bookends: Goose Girl (Liesl)	4¾						
61	A	Bookends: Playmates (Rabbit Father)	4	111.00	58		1950-		Sold by the pair
	B	Bookends: Chick Girl (Chick Mother)	4						
62		Ashtray: Happy Pastime (Knitting Liesl)	3½x6¼	43.00	57		1950-		Called "Knitter" in 1950 catalog"
63		SINGING LESSON	2¾	30.50	53				Called "Duet" in 1950 catalog

TABLE IV.

1 No.	2 Size Mk.	3 Name a. English b. German	4 Size Inches	5 $ Price/ Status	6 Illus. on Page No.	7 Date of Copyr't.	8 Date of Issue	9 Date Discont'd.	10 Remarks
	III/63	CBX-Singing Lesson (It's Not Right)	6	57.00	61				
64		SHEPHERD'S BOY (Shepherd Boy)	5½	45.00	52		1950-		Oversize examples known
65		FAREWELL (Til We Meet Again)	4¾	56.50	42		1950-		Called "Goodbye" in 1950 catalog. Called "Three Pals" in 1960.
66		FARM BOY (Swineherd)	5	45.00	42		1950-		See Section III for variation
67		DOLL MOTHER (Little Doll Mother)	4¾	56.50	41		1950-		"Little" Doll Mother in 1950
68	/2/0 /0	LOST SHEEP (Shepherd Boy)	4¼ 5½	29.50 39.00	49	R1963	1950-		"Shepherd's Boy" in 1950. Many variation known in marks. See Section III for TMK-1
	—		?	D?					Insufficient data to date
69		HAPPY PASTIME (Knitting Liesl)	3½	38.00	45		1950-		
III/69		CBX-Happy Pastime	6	57.00	60				
70		HOLY CHILD (Little Jesus)	6¾	40.50	46		1950-		
71		STORMY WEATHER (Under One Roof)	6¼	138.00	54		1950-		"Under One Roof" in 1950 catalog. Oversize and color variations reported
72		SPRING CHEER (It's Spring)	5	29.50	54		1950-		See Section III for early design and prices
73		LITTLE HELPER (Busy Little Liesl)	4¼	29.50	48		1950-		"Diligent Betsy" in 1950. Base variations reported. See Sec. II for pricing
74		LITTLE GARDENER (The Little Gardener)	4	29.50	47		1950-		
75		HWF., Angelic Prayer (White Angel)	1¾x3½	11.00	61				Called "White" Angel in *HUMMEL* book
76	A&B	BE - Doll Mother & Prayer Before Battle	UNK.	D				?	Rare if found see Sec. III for price. Not in 1950 catalog
77		(UNKNOWN)		C					No example known to date
78		INFANT OF KRUMBAD			46		1950-		w. gown - no halo - no bed
/I/II		(Baby Jesus, Lying)	2½	14.00			1960?		Called "In the Crib" in 1950
	/II/11		3½	18.50			1960?		
	/III/11		4½	24.50			1950-		
	/IV/11		?	D?				?	
	/V/11		7¾	D?		1966		?	
78	/VI/11		?	D?				?	Insufficient data tŏ date
	/VII/11		?	D?				?	Insufficient data to date
	/VIII/11		13½	D?				?	Insufficient data to date
	/0								
78	/I/83		2½	D?				?	#83 is reported to be bisque
	II/83		3½	D?				?	white finish. Not verified
	III/83		4¼	D?				?	
	IV/83		—						Insufficient data to date
	V/83		7¾	D		1966		?	
	VI/83		?						Insufficient data to date
	VII/83		?						Insufficient data to date
	VIII/83		13½	D?					
79		GLOBE TROTTER (Out into the Distance)	5	38.00	44		1950-		"Happy Traveler" in 1950 See Section III for changes in basket design & prices
80		LITTLE SCHOLAR (First Trip to School, Boy)	5½	38.00	48		1950-		
81	/2/0 /0 /II	SCHOOL GIRL (First Trip to School, Girl)	4¼ 5 7½	29.50 38.00 D?	51		1950-	?	Also called "Little Scholar" Rare - See Sec. II for inform. and prices
82	/2/0 /0 /II	SCHOOL BOY (School Truant, Boy)	4 5 7½	29.50 38.00 D/R	52		1950- 1950- ?		Rare w. TMK-2. Reissue expected in 1977 or later. See Sec. III
83		ANGEL SERENADE (Pious Melodies)	5½	D/R	98		1950-	?	D/R Standing Angel with banjo - see 214/D/11 (sitting)
84	— /0	WORSHIP (At the Wayside, . . . "shrine")	? 5	? 45.50	57		1950 -		

TABLE IV.

No.	Size Mk.	a. English Name / b. German	Size Inches	$ Price/Status	Illus. on Page No.	Date of Copyr't.	Date of Issue	Date Discont'd.	Remarks
84	/II		?	D					Insufficient data to date
	/III		?	D					Insufficient data to date
	/IV		?	D?					Insufficient data to date
	/V		12¾	450.50					Added in 1977 Catalog
85		SERENADE	?	?	52				
	/0	(Serenade, Boy w/Flute)	4¾	31.50			1950-		
	/I		?	D?				?	Insufficient data to date
	/II	7½					1950		Oversize example reported.
86		HAPPINESS	4¾	30.50	45		1950-		
		(Hiking Song, Girl)							
87	—	FOR FATHER	5½	43.50	43		1950-		"Father's Joy" in 1950
		(For the Little Father, Radish Boy)							catalog
88	—	HEAVENLY PROTECTION	9	D	45		1950-		This size listed in 1950 as
	/0	(Guardian Angel)	?	D				?	"GUARDIAN ANGEL"
	/I		6¾	92.00		1962		?	in 1950 catalog, listed as
	/II		9	149.00	100			?	88 (only) 9" high.
89	—	LITTLE CELLIST	?		47				
	/0	(Homeward Bound, Bass Violinist)							
	/I		6	45.00			1950-		
	/II		7½	126.50					See Sec. III for variation
90	/A&B	B.E. Wayside Devotion and Adoration	?	D				?	No record of examples
91	/A&B	HWF: Angel at Prayer (Angel Looking Left (B)) (Angel Looking Right (A))	2x4¾	18 pr.	61		1950-		
92		Plaque: Merry Wanderer Wanderer (Boy)	4¾x5	40.00	65	1938 R1968			Reissued in 1977 catalog. Original size listed as 5x5½
93		Plaque: Little Fiddler (Little Fiddler,)	5x5½	D	65	1938 R1968		?	Rare. See Sec. III for price
94	/3/0	SURPRISE	4	34.50	54		1950-		Listed in 1950 catalog
	/2/0	(Hansel and Gretel)	?	D	102			?	See Sec. III for comment
	/0		?	D	102			?	and price
	—		?	D					Insufficient data to date
	/I		5½	52.50			1950-		Listed in 1950 catalog
95		BROTHER	4¾	34.50	39				Called "Our Hero" in 1950
		(Village Hero)							
96		LITTLE SHOPPER	5½	29.50	48		1950-		"Errand Girl" in 1950
		(Gretel)							
97		TRUMPET BOY	4¾	29.50	55		1950-		Oversize example reported
		(The Little Musician)							
98	/2/0	SISTER	4¾	29.50	53	1963			
	/0	(The First Purchase)	5½	34.50					
	—		?	D?			1950-	?	Insufficient data to date
99		EVENTIDE	4¾x4¼	67.50	42		1950-		
		(Evening Song)							
100		Lamp Base, Shrine (Lamp Base w/Figure)	7½	D				?	Examples are rare see Sec. III
101		Lamp Base: To Market (LB: Little Brother & Sister)	?	D				?	See Sec. III for comment
102		Lamp Base: Volunteers LB: (no name)	?	D/R				?	Rare. Reissue expected in 1978 or later
103		Lamp Base: Farewell L.B. (no name)	?	D				?	Very rare - see Sec. III for information
104		Lamp Base: Wayside Devotion LB: Evening Song, Shrine		D				?	Rare. Prices similar to 101-3
105		ADORATION WITH BIRD		P	98				Previously listed as a cancelled number. Example found in 1977. See Sec. III
106		Plaque, Merry Wanderer	UNK	D					See Section III for comment
107		Plaque, Little Fiddler	UNK	D					See Section III for comment
108		(UNKNOWN)		C					No example reported to date
109	—	HAPPY TRAVELLER	?	D					Date discontinued unknown
	/0	(Out into Far Places)	5	31.50			1950-		
	/I		?	D?				?	Insufficient data to date
	/II		7½	126.50			1950-		

123

1	2	3	4	5	6	7	8	9	10
No.	Size Mk.	a. English Name b. German	Size Inches	$ Price/ Status	Illus. on Page No.	Date of Copyr't.	Date of Issue	Date Discont'd.	Remarks
110	—	LET'S SING			47	1939			
	/0	(Heini, Accordion Player)	3¼	D		R1967	1950-		Listed in 1950 catalog
	/I		4	41.50			1950-		
III/110		CBX. - Let's Sing	6	57.00	61				New style has straight sides and cap top. Old style was bowl shape with inset lid.
111	3/0	WAYSIDE HARMONY	4	30.50	56		1950		See Sec. III for inform.
	/2/0	(Father's Cleverest)	?	D?				?	Insufficient data to date
	—		?	D?		1939		?	Insufficient data to date
	/I		5	49.00		R1967	1950		Oversize examples reported
112	/3/0	JUST RESTING	4	30.50	46				Original called "Fence Duet"
	/2/0	(Mother's Most Beloved)	?	D?			1950	?	Insufficient data to date
	—		?	D?		1939	?	?	
	/I		5	49.00		R1967	1950		
113		HEAVENLY SONG (Silent Night, Advent Group)	3½x4¾	D/R				D/R	Similar to #54 Silent Night. #413 Child has halo. Left figure no flower
114		Ashtray: Let's Sing (Ashtray: Heini)	3½x6¼	43.00	57		1950-		
115		Cand'h'r - Christmas Angel (Girl with Bouquet)	3½	48.00	59				w. Nosegay - one set of three sold as set
116		Cand'h'r - Christmas Angel (Girl with Pine Tree)	3½	48.00	59				w. Fir Tree - one of set of three sold as set
117		Cand'h'r - Christmas Angel (Boy with Wooden Horse)	3½	48.00	59				w/Horse - one of set of three sold as set
118		LITTLE THRIFTY (Savings - Little Hummel)	5	41.50	49				This a bank w. metal door on bottom w. lock and key
119		POSTMAN (Special Messenger)	5	43.50	51		1950-		
120		JOYFUL - LET'S SING	?	D				?	Two figures on wooden base. No examples reported to date
121		WAYSIDE HARM. - JUST RESTING	?	D				?	Two figures on wooden base. No examples reported to date
122		PUPPY LOVE - SERENADE HAPPINESS	?	D				?	Three figures on wooden base. No examples reported to date
123		MAX AND MORITZ (Max and Moritz)	5	42.50	49	1950			
124	—	HELLO	6¾	D	46		1950-		Listed in 1950 catalog as 17cm. HUMMEL book lists as "Chef, Hello"
	/0	(The Boss)	6¼	38.00					
	/I		7	D				?	Date discontinued unknown
125		Plaque: Vacation—Time (Vacation Friends)	4x4¾	61.00	66				See Sec. III for inform.
126		Plaque: Retreat to Safety (Coward)	4¾x4¾	D?	66			?	Insufficient data to date
127		DOCTOR (Doll Doctor)	4¾	39.00	41		1950-		
128		BAKER (The Little Confectioner)	4¾	38.00	37		1950-		Oversize example reported
129		BAND LEADER (The Bandleader)	5	45.00	37		1950-		
130		DUET (Singing Pair)	5	60.50	42		1950-		
131		STREET SINGER (Chamber Singer)	5	34.50	54		1950-		Called "Soloist" in 1950
132		STAR GAZER (Star Gazer)	4¾	45.00	54		1950-		For old mark and blue shirt See Sec. III
133		MOTHER'S HELPER (Mother's Helper)	5	46.50	50		1950-		
134		Plaque: Quartet (The Quartet)	6x6	85.00	66				
135		SOLOIST (Heroic Tenor)	4¾	30.50	53		1950		Called "High Tenor" in 1950
136		FRIENDS			43	1954			Not in 1950 catalog
	/I	(Good Friends)	5	43.50					

TABLE IV.

No.	Size Mk.	a. English Name b. German	Size Inches	$ Price/ Status	Illus. on Page No.	Date of Copyr't.	Date of Issue	Date Discont'd.	Remarks
	/II		?	D					Insufficient data to date
	/III		?	D					Insufficient data to date
	/IV		?	D					Insufficient data to date
	/V		10¾	333.50	99				See Section III for Arabic 5 mark
137		Plaque: Child in Bed (Child in Small Bed)	2¾x2¾	24.00	65				Reported marked 137A & 137B. If found add 30% see Sec. II
138		(UNKNOWN)		C					No examples reported to date
139		Wall Ring: Flitting Butterfly (Sitting Child w/Butterfly)	2½x2½	D		197-?			Reported in 1977 to be reissued
140		Plaque: Mail Coach (Plaque: Ta-dum, The Mail Is In)	6¼x4¼	73.00	65				Similar to figurine 226. HUMMEL book lists as "Mail Is Here"
141	/3/0	APPLE TREE GIRL (Girl in Tree (Spring))	4	29.50	98			1950-	Called "Spring" in 1950
	/2/0		?	D?					Insufficient data to date
	/0		?	0?	37				Insufficient data to date
	/I		6	60.50	98			1950-	
	/II		?	?					These intermediate sizes may have been passed over to date. No example
	/III		?	?					
	/IV		?	?					
	/V		10	333.50	98			1968	
	/X		29	P				1976	Produced in 1976. Examples reported sold from $6,500-$9,000
142	/3/0	APPLE TREE BOY	4	29.50	37			1950	Called "Fall" in 1950 catalog
	/2/0	(Boy in Tree, Autumn)	?	D?					Insufficient data to date
	/0		?	D?					Insufficient data to date
	/I		6	60.50				1950	
	/II		?	?					Insufficient data to date
	/III		?	?					Insufficient data to date
	/IV		?	?					Insufficient data to date
	/V		10	333.50				1968	These intermediate sizes may have been passed over to date. No example reported
	/X		29	P				1976	Produced in 1976. Examples reported sold from $6,500-$9,000
143	/0	BOOTS	5½	38.00	39			1950-	
	—	(Master Important)	?	D?					Insufficient data to date
	/I		6½	D	98			1950-	Listed in 1950 catalog. See Section III
144		ANGELIC SONG (Singing Child w/Small Angel)	4	42.00	37			1950-	
145		"LITTLE GUARDIAN" (Praying Child w/Small Angel)	4	42.00	48			1950-	
146		Font: Angel Duet (Small Group of Angels)	3¼x4¾	14.50	61			1950-	
147		Font: Devotion (Angel)	3x5	14.50	62			1950-	HUMMEL book lists as ANGEL SHRINE
148		(UNKNOWN)		C					No examples reported to date
149		(UNKNOWN)		C					No examples reported to date
150	/2/0	HAPPY DAYS	4¼	49.00	45				
	/0	(House Music, Pr. of Children)	5¼	D	100			?	Not currently available
	—		6	D			1950-	?	Listed in 1950 catalog. This size only.
	/I		6¼	D/R				?	Reissue expected in 1977 or later. See Sec. III
151	/W	MADONNA, SEATED & CHILD	12	D					White. Not in 1950 catalog
	/II	(Sitting Madonna w/Sitting Child)	12	D					Very rare "Blue Cloak" Madonna (Sec. III) also with "Brown Cloak"
152A	—	UMBRELLA BOY	?	?	55				Insufficient data to date

1	2	3	4	5	6	7	8	9	10
No.	Size Mk.	Name a. English b. German	Size Inches	$ Price/ Status	Illus. on Page No.	Date of Copyr't.	Date of Issue	Date Discont'd.	Remarks
	/0	(Sheltered Safe, Boy)	4¾	161.00		1957			
	/I		?	D		R1972	?	?	Insufficient data to date
	/II		8	500.00			1951		
152B	—	UMBRELLA GIRL	?	D?	55				Insufficient data to date
	/0	(Sheltered Safe, Girl)	4¾	161.00		1951			
	/I		?	D?		R1972		?	Insufficient data to date
	/II		8	500.00			1951		
153		AUF WIEDERSEHEN	6¾	D	37		1950-		Called "Goodbye"
	/0	(Good-bye, See You Again)	5	52.50					Rare Model - Boy w/Hat (Sec. III)
	/I		7	D				?	Not currently available
154		WAITER	6½	D/R	56	1951	1950+		Reissue expected in 1978 or later
	/0	(Head Waiter)	6	45.00	103	R1972			
	/I		7	D	103			?	Not currently available - See Sec. III
155		(UNKNOWN)		C					No examples reported to date
156		(UNKNOWN)		C					No examples reported to date
157		(UNKNOWN)		C					No examples reported to date
158		(UNKNOWN)		C					No examples reported to date
159		(UNKNOWN)		C					No examples reported to date
160		(UNKNOWN)		C					No examples reported to date
161		(UNKNOWN)		C					No examples reported to date
162		(UNKNOWN)		C					No examples reported to date
163		WHITSUNTIDE (Bell Tower with Angels)	7	D	56		1950-	1959+	Also known as "Christmas." Known size variations. Reissue expected. Very rare (Sec. III)
164		Font, Worship (At the Wayside)	2¾x4¾	17.00	62		1950-		Unnamed in HUMMEL book.
165		PLQ: Swaying Lullaby (Child w/Hammock & Birds)	5¼x5¼	D				?	Rare, see Sec. III. Not cataloged at present. TMK-2 or 3
166		Ashtray: Boy with Bird	3¼x6¼	51.00	57		1950-		
167		Font: HW-Angel w/Yellow Bird (Sitting Angel)	3x4¾	D	61		1950-	?	Official name unknown. This name assigned for convenience
168		Plaque: Standing Boy Standing Boy w/Heart & Bottle	5¾x5¾	D/R					Discontinued. May be reissued in 1978 or later
169		BIRD DUET (Song of Spring)	4	39.00	38		1950-		
170	—	SCHOOLBOYS	?	D?	52			?	Insufficient data to date
	/0	(Difficult Problem)	?	D?		1961		?	Insufficient data to date
	/I		7½	333.50					
	/II		?	D?				?	Insufficient data to date
	/III		10¼	851.00		R1973			Limited production since early 1970s
171		LITTLE SWEEPER (Sweeping Liesl)	4¼	29.50	48		1950-		Called "Mother's Helper" in 1950
172	—	FESTIVAL HARMONY with MANDOLIN	?	D?	43				Insufficient data to date
	/0	(Advent Angel w/Mandolin)	8	76.50	99				TMK-1 had flowers in front See Sec. III
	/I		?	D?					Insufficient data to date
	/II		10¼	149.00					See Section III for comment
173	–	FESTIVAL HARMONY with FLUTE	?	D?	43			?	Insufficient data to date
	/0	(Advent Angel with Flute)	8	76.50					TMK-1 had flowers & bird in front. See Sec. III
	/I		?	D?				?	Insufficient data to date
	/II		10¼	149.00					See Section III for comment

No.	Size Mk.	a. English Name b. German	Size Inches	$ Price/ Status	Illus. on Page No.	Date of Copyr't.	Date of Issue	Date Discont'd.	Remarks
174		SHE LOVES ME, SHE LOVES ME NOT (Loves Me Loves Me Not)	4¼	43.50	53		1950-		Reported in "eyes open" add 30%. See Sec. III
175		MOTHER'S DARLING (Market-Christel)	5½	45	50				See Sec. III & illus. for color variation in two bags
176		HAPPY BIRTHDAY (Well-Wishers)	5½		45		1950-		In 1950 catalog, replaced by 176/0
	/0		5½	52.50					
	/I		6	D/R				?	See Sections II & III for comment. Reissue expected in 1978 or later
177		SCHOOLGIRLS (The Masterpiece)	?	D?				?	Insufficient data to date
	/0		?	D?				?	Insufficient data to date
	/I		7½	333.50		1961			
	/II		?	D?				?	Insufficient data to date
	/III		9½	851		R1973			Limited production since early 1970s
178		THE PHOTOGRAPHER (The Photographer)	5¼	57.50	51	1950			In 1950 catalog. Same w/ 1948 date See Sec. II
179		COQUETTES (The Deadheads)	5	60.50	41		1950-		See Sec. III for variations & price
180		TUNEFUL GOOD NIGHT (Sitting Child w/Trumpet)	5x4¾	D/R				?	Rare—reissue expected in 1978 or later. See Sec. III for comment
181		(UNKNOWN)		C					No examples reported to date
182		GOOD FRIENDS (Girl With Kid)	4	41.50	44		1950-		Called just "Friends" in 1950
183		FOREST SHRINE (Forest Shrine)	9	D/R	99			?	Very rare, see Sec. III. Discontinued. May be reissued in '78 or later
184		LATEST NEWS (The Latest News)	5	60.50	47		1950-		
185		ACCORDION BOY (On the Mountain Pasture)	5	39.00	36		1950-		"On Alpine Pasture" in 1950
186		SWEET MUSIC (To the Dance. Bass Violinist)	5	43.50	54		1950-		
187		Plaque, "Hummel" Display	4x5½	D	104	1948	1950-	1971-	Old style "ENGLISH" Display Plaque. See Sec. III
187C			5½x3⅝	33.50	65		1972		New style "ENGLISH" Display Plaque
188		CELESTIAL MUSICIAN (Heavenly Sounds)	7	80	39	1950	1950+		Not in 1950 catalog. In early 50s price list
189		(UNKNOWN)		C					No examples reported to date
190		(UNKNOWN)		C					No examples reported to date
191		(UNKNOWN)		C					No examples reported to date
192		CAN, Candlelight (Angel With Candle)	6¾	D/R	59	1950	1950+	?	Reissue expected. See Sec. III Illustrated with short candle. Also long candle style
193		CAN, Angel Duet (Silent Night, Sml. Grp./ Angels)	5	49	59	1950			Angel holds candle cup. "ANGEL DUET" #261 Angel has no holder. ("Not ANGELIC SONG")
194		ANGELIC CARE (Guardian Angel)	6½	60	37	1950	1950+		Small angel w/candle looking at child in crib w/four legs. Called Watchful Angel in HUMMEL book
195	/2/0	BARNYARD HERO (Coward)	4	38	38		1959–		
	/0		?	D?				?	Insufficient data to date
	—		?	D?		1950	1950+	?	Insufficient data to date
	/I		5½	65					Add 30% for oversize
196	/2/0	TELLING HER SECRET (The Secret)	?	D?	55			?	
	/0		5½	65	102		1950+		
196			5¼±	D?		1950	?	?	See Sec. II for price
	/I		6½	D/R			1950+		Reissue expected in 1978 or later. See Sec. III for prices with TMK-2 or 3.

TABLE IV.

127

1	2	3 a. English Name b. German	4 Size Inches	5 $ Price/ Status	6 Illus. on Page No.	7 Date of Copyr't.	8 Date of Issue	9 Date Discont'd.	10 Remarks
No.	Size Mk.								
197	/2/0	BE PATIENT (Little Duckling Mother)	4¼	38	38		1959 –		
	/0			D?				?	Insufficient data to date
	—		?	D?		1950	1950+	?	Insufficient data to date
	/I		6¼	57.50		1948?	1959 –		See Sec. III for variation and price
198	/2/0	HOME FROM MARKET	4¾	34.50	46		1959 –	1966 ±	See Illus. Sec. III for "Old" & "New" look
	/0	(Happy Purchase)		D?	100			?	Insufficient data to date
	—		?	D?	100	1950	1948	?	Insufficient data to date. In early 50s price list
	/I		5½	43.50			1948+	1966 ±	
199	—	FEEDING TIME (In the Chicken Run)	?	D?	42		1950+	?	Insufficient data to date
	/0		4¼	43.50					See Sec. III for variation
	/I		5½	53.50					and price
200	—	LITTLE GOAT HERDER (Goatboy)	?	D	48	1950	1950+	?	Found w/1948 date
	/0		4¾	41.50	100				See Sec. III illustration
	/I		5½	53.50	100				
201	/2/0	RETREAT TO SAFETY (With a Thousand Fears)	4	38	51		1948?	?	Not in 1950 catalog. In early 50s price list
	/0		?	D?					Insufficient data to date
	—		?	D?		1950		?	May have decimal mark
	/I		5½	63					
202	—	(UNKNOWN)		C					No record of examples to date
203	/2/0	SIGNS OF SPRING	4	39	53				See Sec. III for variation and price
	/0	(Spring Idyll)	?	D?				?	Insufficient data to date
	—		?	D		1950	1950+	?	Date discontinued unknown In early 50s price list
	/I		5½	52.50					
204		WEARY WANDERER (In Clearstream I . . .)	6	41.50	56	1950	1949+		
205		Plaque 'HUMMEL DISPLAY	4x5½	D	104				In German, old style w. Bee on top. See Sec. III
206		Font w/Angel Cloud (Child With Flower)	2¼x4¾	D		1950	1949?		Not in 1950 catalog but in early 50s price list
207		Font H.W. Heavenly Angel (The Little Christ Child Comes)	2x4¾	15	62	1950	1950+		
208		Plaque HUMMEL DISPLAY	4x5½	D	104	1947?	1947	?	In French, old style w. Bee on top. See Sec. III
209		Plaque HUMMEL DISPLAY	4x5½	D				?	In Swedish, old style w. Bee on top. See Sec. III
210		Plaque HUMMEL DISPLAY	4x5½	D				?	In English, old style w. Bee on top. See Sec. III
211		Plaque HUMMEL DISPLAY	4x5½	D				?	In English, (a variation) old style w. Bee on top. See Sec. III
212		Plaque HUMMEL DISPLAY	4x5½	D				?	"Schmid Bros" on bag. Old style w. Bee on top. See Sec. III
213		Plaque HUMMEL DISPLAY	4x5½	D				?	In Spanish, old style w. Bee on top. See Sec. III
214/A&B/II		NATIVITY SET	Var	111			1959-		3 pcs. Madonna, St. Joseph and Child in color
214/A&B/W		Holy Family - 3 pieces		75.50					
214 /A/B/F/ G/J/K/L/ M/N/O/II & 366		NATIVITY SET - 12 pieces	Var	400.50			1959-		12 pc. set - includes #366 Flying Angel in color
214 /A/B/C/ D/E/F/G/ H/J/K/L/ M/N/O/II & 366		NATIVITY SET - 16 pieces	Var	509.50	64	1952			16 pc. set - includes #366 Flying Angel in color
214	S/I		*	36					
214	S/II		*	19.50					
		NATIVITY COMPONENTS (small) Madonna and Child,							
214 AM&K/W		2 pcs., White	M-6¼"	40.50					
214 AM&K		2 pcs., Color	C-3½"x 1½"	66.50					
214/A/M/11		Madonna	M-6¼"	50.50					

1	2	3	4	5	6	7	8	9	10
No.	Size Mk.	a. English Name b. German	Size Inches	$ Price/ Status	Illus. on Page No.	Date of Copyr't.	Date of Issue	Date Discont'd.	Remarks
214	/A/K	Infant Jesus Only	3½ x1½	16.00	46				
214	B/W	St. Joseph White	7½	35.00	52				
214	B/11	Color	7½	44.50					
214	/C/11	Goodnight	3½	22.50	44				
214	/D/11	Angel Serenade	3	19.50					
214	/E/11	We Congratulate	3½	37.00					
214	/F/11	Shepherd w/Sheep - 1 pc.	7	51.50					
214	/G/11	Shepherd Boy	4¾	32.00					
214	/H/11	Little Tooter	4	30.00	49				
214	/J/11	Donkey	5	18.00					
214	/K/11	Cow	6¼"x3½	21.50					
214	/L/11	King (Standing)	8¼	50.00					
214	/M/11	King, Kneeling on one Knee	5½	45.00					
214	/N/11	King, Kneeling on two Knees	5½	37.00					
214	/O/11	Lamb	2"x1½	4.50					
HX 306/O/6		Camel	8¼	73.00					
	366	Flying Angel/Color	3½	30.00					
	366/W	Flying Angel/White	3½	11.50					
215		(UNKNOWN)		C		1964			Cancelled. No record of examples
216		(UNKNOWN)		C					Cancelled. No record of examples
217		BOY WITH TOOTHACHE (Diminish, Pain)	5½	41.50	39		1950 +		
218	/2/0	BIRTHDAY SERENADE (Birthday Serenade)	4¼	43.50	38	1966			
	0		5¼	D			1952	?	Date discontinued unknown
	—		?	D?		1953			Insufficient data to date
219		GIRL WITH FROG	?	D	99	1953(?)		?	Recently discovered. Number had been classified as C-UNKNOWN. See Sec. III
220		WE CONGRATULATE (Pair of Children)	4	39	56	1959R	1952		Similar to 214/E/II but 220 has base added in 1977 catalog
221		(UNKNOWN)		C					No record of examples to date
222 PLQ		Plaque: Madonna (Picture of the Madonna)	4x5	D				1959 +	Known example. Rare, see Sec. II & III Madonna in Red w/Metal Frame
M223		Lamp Base: To Market (Little Brother & Sister)	9½	141	63				
M224	/I	Lamp Base: Wayside Harmony	7½	103.50	63				
	/II	(Father's Cleverest)	9½	D/R				?	See Section II & III for more information. Reissue expected in 1978 or later
M225	I	Lamp Base: Just Resting (Girl)	7½	103.50	63		1966±		
	II	(Mother's Most Beloved)	9½	D/R				?	See Sec. II for more information. Reissue expected in 1978 or later
226		MAIL IS HERE (Ta-dum, The Mail Is In)	6x4¼	172.50	49	1954	1952		
M227		Lamp Base: She Loves Me - She Loves Me Not (Loves Me, Loves Me Not)	7½	103.50	104				
M228		Lamp Base: Good Friends (Friends, Girl with Kid)	7½	103.50	63				
M229		Lamp Base: Apple Tree Girl (Spring, Girl in Tree)	7½	103.50	63				
M230		Lamp Base: Apple Tree Boy (Autumn, Boy in Tree)	7½	103.50	63	1955	1959		
M231		Lamp Base: Birthday Serenade	9½	D				?	See #218 same name for picture. Also refer to Sec. II & III
M232		Lamp Base: Happy Days	9½	D				?	See #150, same name, for picture. Also refer to Sec. II & III
233		(UNKNOWN)		C					No examples known to date
M234		Lamp Base: Birthday Serenade	7½	D		1955	1954	?	See #218, same name, for picture. Also refer to Sec. II & III

TABLE IV.

No.	Size Mk.	a. English Name b. German	Size Inches	$ Price/ Status	Illus. on Page No.	Date of Copyr't.	Date of Issue	Date Discont'd.	Remarks
1	2	3	4	5	6	7	8	9	10
M235		Lamp Base: Happy Days	7½	D				?	See #150, same name, for picture. Also refer to Sec. II & III
236		(UNKNOWN)		C					No record of examples to date
237		(UNKNOWN)		C					No record of examples to date
238	/A	ANGEL TRIO (B) - with Banjo	2½		59	1967			Set of 3 separate sitting figures. Angel w/Banjo, Angel w/Accordion, Angel w/Horn, See #III 38, 39 & 40 Candle-holders, set of 3 also called "Angel Trio" (A)
	/B	ANGEL TRIO (B) - with Accordion	2	42	59	1967			
	/C	ANGEL TRIO (B) - with Horn	2½		59	1967			
239	/A	CHILDREN TRIO (A) - Girl w/Flower	3½		40	1967			Set of 3 standing figures each on a separate base. A - Girl w/nosegay; B - Girl w/doll; C - Boy w/horse. See #115, 116, & 117 for same figures called Christmas Angels as candleholders
	/B	CHILDREN TRIO (A) - Girl w/Doll	3½	48.00	40	1967			
	/C	CHILDREN TRIO (A) - Boy w/Horse	3½		40	1967			
240		DRUMMER (Drummer)	4¼	34.50	41		1955		*HUMMEL* book calls this "Little Drummer"
241		(UNKNOWN)		C					Cancelled. No record of examples
242		(UNKNOWN)		C					Cancelled. No record of examples
243		Font: Madonna and Child (no translation)	3x4	D	62	1956	1955-		Date discontinued unknown Not available in U.S.? See Sec. II
244		(UNKNOWN)		C					No record of example to date
245		(UNKNOWN)		C					No record of example to date
246		Font: Holy Family (Holy Family)	3¼x4	18	62	1956	1955		
247		(UNKNOWN)		C					No record of example to date
248		Font: Kneeling Angel (no translation)	2¼x5½	14.50	62	1959			*HUMMEL* book calls this Guardian Angel
249		(UNKNOWN)		C					
250	A	BE: LITTLE GOATHERDER	5½	93.50	58		1966-		Price for pair
	B	BE: FEEDING TIME (Goatboy & In the Chicken Run)	5½		58				
251	A	BE: FRIENDS	5	93.50					Price for pair
	B	BE: SHE LOVES ME, SHE LOVES ME NOT	5						
252	A	BE: Apple Tree Girl (Spring)	5	69	58		1966-		Price for pair
	B	BE: Apple Tree Boy (Autumn)	5		58				
253		(UNKNOWN)		C					No record of examples to date
254		(UNKNOWN)		C		1963			No record of examples to date
255		STITCH IN TIME (Two to the right-Two to the Left)	6¾	51.00	54	1963	1964		
256		KNITTING LESSON (Will It Work?)	7½	126.50	46	1963	1964		
257		FOR MOTHER (For the Little Mother)	5	34.50	43		1964		
258		WHICH HAND? (Guess!)	5½	34.50	56	1963	1964		
259		(UNKNOWN)		C					No record of examples to date

No.	Size Mk.	a. English Name b. German	Size Inches	$ Price/ Status	Illus. on Page No.	Date of Copyr't.	Date of Issue	Date Discont'd.	Remarks
260	(A-R)	NATIVITY SET, LARGE	(16 pcs)	1679.00	64	1968	1968		
260	/S	Stable only, to fit 16 pc. 260 set		191.50					
	260A	Madonna	9¾"	158.50					
	260B	St. Joseph	11¾"	164.00					
	260C	Infant Jesus	5¾"	35.50					
	260D	Good Night	5¼"	40.00					
	260E	Angel Serenade	4¼"	35.50					
	260F	We Congratulate	6¼"	109.00					
	260G	Shepherd, Standing Sheep (Standing)	11¾"	180.00					
	260H	w/Lamb	3¾"	27.00					
	260J	Shepherd Boy, Kneeling	7"	87.00					
	260K	Little Tooter	5⅛"	41.50					
	260L	Donkey	7½"	37.00					
	260M	Cow	6"x11"	47.50					
	260N	Moorish King	12¾"	187.00					
	260O	King, Standing	12"	175.50					
	260P	King, Kneeling	9"	149.50					
	260R	Sheep (Lying)	3¼"x4"	13.00					
261		ANGEL DUET (Silent Night, w/o Cndlhldr.)	5	55.50		1968	1968		Similar to Candleholder #193 Angel Duet HUMMEL book. (Angelic Song)
262		LULLABY	3¼x5	36	49	1968	1968		Similar to Candleholder #24 Lullaby.
263		PLQ: MERRY WANDERER	4¾x5	D			?		See Section III for more inform.
264		ANNUAL PLATE 1971 (Heavenly Angel)	7½	D	66	1970	1971	1971	See Section II for original issue prices and current guide prices
265		ANNUAL PLATE 1972 (Hear Ye, Hear Ye)	7½	D	66		1972	1972	See Sec. II
266		ANNUAL PLATE 1973 (Globetrotter)	7½	D	66		1973	1973	See Sec. II
267		ANNUAL PLATE 1974 (Goose Girl)	7½	D	66		1974	1974	See Sec. II
268		ANNUAL PLATE 1975 (Ride into Christmas)	7½	D	66		1975	1975	See Sec. II
269		ANNUAL PLATE 1976 (Apple Tree Girl)	7½	D	66		1976	1976	See Sec. II
270		ANNUAL PLATE 1977 (Apple Tree Boy)	7½	D	67		1977	1977	See Sec. II
271		ANNUAL PLATE 1978 (Happy Pastime)	7½	65	67				Listed in 1978 catalog
272		(ASSIGNED)		A					For future announcement
273		(ASSIGNED)		A					For future announcement
274		(ASSIGNED)		A					For future announcement
275		(ASSIGNED)		A					For future announcement
276		(ASSIGNED)		A					For future announcement
277		(ASSIGNED)		A					For future announcement
278		(ASSIGNED)		A					For future announcement
279		(ASSIGNED)		A					For future announcement
280		Anniversary Plate 1975 (Stormy Weather)		D		1975			Issued in 1975 @ $100. See Sec. II
281		OPEN		0					Open for assignment to subject
282		OPEN		0					Open for assignment to subject
283		OPEN		0					Open for assignment to subject
284		OPEN		0					Open for assignment to subject
285		OPEN		0					Open for assignment to subject
286		OPEN		0					Open for assignment to subject
287		OPEN		0					Open for assignment to subject
288		OPEN		0					Open for assignment to subject

TABLE IV.

1	2	3	4	5	6	7	8	9	10
No.	Size Mk.	a. English Name b. German	Size Inches	$ Price/ Status	Illus. on Page No.	Date of Copyr't.	Date of Issue	Date Discont'd.	Remarks
289		OPEN		0					Open for assignment to subject
290		OPEN		0					Open for assignment to subject
291		OPEN		0					Open for assignment to subject
292		OPEN		0					Open for assignment to subject
293		OPEN		0					Open for assignment to subject
294		OPEN		0					Open for assignment to subject
295		OPEN		0					Open for assignment to subject
296		OPEN		0					Open for assignment to subject
297		OPEN		0					Open for assignment to subject
298		OPEN		0					Open for assignment to subject
299		OPEN		0					Open for assignment to subject
300		BIRD WATCHER		A		1956	1978 +		New issue - expected in '78 or later
301		DELIVERY ANGEL WITH BASKETS		A		1958	1978 +		New issue - expected in '78 or later
302		KNIT ONE PURL ONE		A		1955	1978 +		New issue - expected in '78 or later
303		SCHOOL LESSON		A		1955	1978 +		New issue - expected in '78 or later
304		ARTIST (The Artist Painter)	5½	49.00	37	1955	1971		
305		BUILDER (The Heavy Worker)	5½	53.50	39	1955	1971 1964 +		
306		LITTLE BOOKKEEPER (Substitution)	4¾	70.50	47	1955	1971 1962		
307		GOOD HUNTING (Good Sport)	5	53.50	44	1955	1962 +		
308		LITTLE TAILOR (Little Tailor)	5½	60.50	48	1955 R1972	1971		
309		GREETINGS		A		1955	1978 +		New issue - expected in 1978 or later
310		SEARCHING ANGEL		A		1955			New issue - expected in 1978 or later
311		KISS ME! (Love Me!)	6	52.50	46	1955	1961		Restyled in 1972
312		JAM POT		A		1955	1977 +		New issue - expected in 1978 or later
313		ASSIGNED		A		(1955?)			For future announcement
314		CONFIDENTIALLY (Dialogue)	5½	53.50	41	1955 R1972	1972		Redesigned. Older models have no bow tie. See Sec. III
315		MOUNTAINEER (I Have Achieved It!)	5	53.50	50	1955	1966 ±		
316		ASSIGNED		A		(1955?)			
317		NOT FOR YOU! (Nothing For You!)	6	52.50	50	1955	1961		Oversize add 30%
318		ASSIGNED		A		(1955?)			
319		DOLL BATH (Doll Bath)	5	51	41	1957	1962		
320		PROFESSOR	6	43?		1955	1978 ±		New issue - expected in 1978 or later
321		WASH DAY (Big Wash)	6	52.50	56	1956	1963 ±		
322		LITTLE PHARMACIST (The Pharmacist)		53.50	48	1955	1960		See comment in Sec. II & III

1	2	3	4	5	6	7	8	9	10
No.	Size Mk.	a. English b. German Name	Size Inches	$ Price/ Status	Illus. on Page No.	Date of Copyr't.	Date of Issue	Date Discont'd.	Remarks
323		MERRY CHRISTMAS		A		1955	1978+		New issue - expected in 1978 or later
324		OTHER SIDE OF FENCE		A		1956	1978+		New issue - expected in 1978 or later
325		MOTHERS AID		A		1956	1978+		New issue - expected in 1978 or later
326		NAUGHTY BOY		A		1956	1978+		
327		RUNAWAY (The Happy Wanderer)	5½	55?	51	1956 1972	1972		Mark #4 or #5 - see Sec. III
328		CARNIVAL (Carnival [Mardi-Gras])	6	39	39	1956	1963+		
329		KINDERGARTEN ROMANCE		A		1956	1978+		New issue - expected in 1978 or later
330		KNEADING DOUGH		A		1956	1978+		New issue - expected in 1978 or later
331		CROSSROADS (At the Crossroad)	6¾	107.50	41	1956	1972		Mark #4 or #5
332		SOLDIER BOY (At Attention)	6	34.50	53	1956	1963+		
333		BLESSED EVENT (The Big Event)	5½	100.50	38	1956	1964		
334		HOMEWARD BOUND (Return Home from the Fields)	5¼	100.50	46	1956	1971		
335		ASSIGNED		A		1956	?		For future announcement
336		CLOSE HARMONY (Birthday Serenade)	5½	68.50	40	1956	1966		
337		CINDERELLA (Cinderella)	4½	64.50	40	1961 R1972	1971		Mark #4 or 5
338		BIRTHDAY WISH		A		1956	1978+		New issue - expected in 1978 or later
339		WALKING HER DOG		A		1956	1978+		New issue - expected in 1978 or later
340		LETTER TO SANTA CLAUS (Letter to the Christ Child)	7¼	80.50	47	1957	1971		
341		BIRTHDAY PRESENT		A		1956	1978+		New issue - expected in 1978 or later
342		MISCHIEF MAKER (The Mischief Maker)	5	64.50	50	1961	1972		
343		SINGING ANGEL		A		1957	1978+		New issue - expected in 1978 or later
344		FEATHERED FRIENDS (The Swan Pond)	4¾	63	42	1957	1972		
345		A FAIR MEASURE (The Merchant)	5½	52	36	1957	1972		Mark #4 or #5
346		SMART LITTLE SISTER (The Clever Little Sister)	4¾	53.50	53	1957	1962		
347		ADVENTURE BOUND (The Seven Swabians)	8¼x7½	1092.50	36	1957	1971		
348		RING AROUND THE ROSIE	6¾	793.50	51	1957	1967 1972		Scarce. Extra premium when found w/TMK-3 or 4
349		FLOWER LOVER		A		1961	1977+		New issue - expected 1978 or later
350		HOLIDAY SHOPPER		A		1965	1977+		New issue - expected 1978 or later
351		REMEMBERING		A		1972			New issue - expected 1978 or later
352		MUSICAL GOOD MORNING		A		9/65	1977+		New issue - expected 1978 or later
353 — 0 I		SPRING DANCE (Summer Dance)	6¾	? D/R 161	54	? R1963	1964	?	Insufficient data to date Discontinued date unknown. May be reissued in 1978 or later
354		ASSIGNED		A		(1961?)			For future announcement

TABLE IV.

1	2	3		4	5	6	7	8	9	10
No.	Size Mk.	Name	a. English b. German	Size Inches	$ Price/ Status	Illus. on Page No.	Date of Copyr't.	Date of Issue	Date Discont'd.	Remarks
355		AUTUMN HARVEST	(Fall Blessing)	4¾	53.50	37	1964	1972		Mark #4 or # only unknown
356		GAY ADVENTURE	(Happy Wandering)	5	53.50	43	1971	1972		Was also called Joyful Adventure
357		GUIDING ANGEL	(Kneeling Angel w/Lantern)	2¾	26	45	1961	1972		Mark #4 or #5 known
358		SHINING LIGHT	(Kneeling Angel w/Candle)	2¾	26	53	1961	1972		
359		TUNEFUL ANGEL	(Kneeling Angel w/Horn)	2¾	26	55	1961	1972		
360A		WV: Boy & Girl		6¼	D/R		1958		?	Discontinued date unknown May be reissued in 1978 or later
360B		WV: Boy		6¼	D/R		1958		?	Discontinued date unknown May be reissued in 1978 or later
360C		WV: Girl		6¼	D/R		1958		?	Discontinued date unknown May be reissued in 1978 or later
361		FAVORITE PET	(Easter Greeting)	4¼	53.50	42	1961	1966		
362		THOUGHTFUL		?	A		4/61	1978+		New issue - expected in 1978 or later
363		BIG HOUSECLEANING	(Big Cleaning)	4	67.50	38	1961	1972		
364		MADONNA and CHILD		?	A		4/64	1978+		New issue - expected in 1978 or later
365		WEE ANGEL		?	A		4/64	1978+		New issue - expected in 1978 or later
366		FLYING ANGEL (color)	(Hanging Angel)	3½	25	42	1964	?		Part of #214 Nativity set cataloged in color 366 & 366W
366W		FLYING ANGEL (white)		3½	10					
367		BUSY STUDENT	(Model Pupil)	4¼	38.50	39	1967?	1964		
368		ASSIGNED		?	A		1967?			For future announcement
369		FOLLOW THE LEADER	(Follow the Leader)	7	281.50	42	1967	1972		Mark #4 or #5 known
370		Assigned			A		1965?			For future announcement
371		Assigned			A		1965?			For future announcement
372		ASSIGNED			A		1965?			For future announcement
373		ASSIGNED			A		1965?			For future announcement
374		LOST STOCKING	Lost My Stocking	4¼	43	49	1965	1972		
375		ASSIGNED			A		1965?			For future announcement
376		ASSIGNED			A		1972?			For future announcement
377		BASHFUL	(Forget Me Not)	4¾	43	38	1971	1972		
378		EASTER GREETING	(Easter Greeting)	5¼	53.50	42	1971	1972		
379		ASSIGNED			A		1972?			For future announcement
380		ASSIGNED			A		1972?			For future announcement
381		FLOWER VENDOR	(To the Flower Market)	5¼	53.50	43	1971	1972		
382		VISITING AN INVALID	(Visit to a Patient)	5	64.50	55	1971	1972		
383		ASSIGNED			A		1972?			For future announcement
384		EASTER TIME	(Easter Playmates)	4	63	42	1971	1972		
385		CHICKEN-LICKEN!	(Chicken Liesl)	4¾	67.50	40	1971	1972		
386		ON SECRET PATH	(On Secret Paths)	5¼	64.50	50	1971	1972		
387		VALENTINE GIFT		4½±	43	55	1972	1977		Limited Edition - Members of Goebel Collectors entitled to buy one

No.	Size Mk.	Name	a. English b. German	Size Inches	$ Price/ Status	Illus. on Page No.	Date of Copyr't.	Date of Issue	Date Discont'd.	Remarks
388		CAN: LITTLE BAND (Group of Children)		4¾x3	P	60		1970		Same as #392 but with candleholder. (389, 390, 391) on base w/candle-holder
388	/M	MBX: LITTLE BAND		4¾x5	120.50	64	1968	1970		Music box w/candle and 3 seated children
389		CHILDREN TRIO (B)- Girl with Sheet Music				40	1968	1970		Sold as a set under name of Children (Trio) B
390		CHILDREN TRIO (B)- Boy with Accordion		2¼	60	40	1968	1970		Same seated figures as Little Band but not mounted on
391		CHILDREN TRIO (B)- Girl with Horn				40	1968	1970		a common base
392		LITTLE BAND (Group of Children)		4¾x3	77	64	1968	1970		Same as three seated children on base as #388 but without candleholder
392	/M	LITTLE BAND		4¾x5	99?	47		1970		Music box without candle, same three children.
393		OPEN			0					Open for assignment of subject
394		ASSIGNED			A		1972?			For future announcement
395		ASSIGNED			A		1972			For future announcement
396		RIDE INTO CHRISTMAS (Ride (Drive) Into Christmas)		5¾	115.50	51	1971	1972		Scarce. Premium price for TMK-4 See Sec. II
397		OPEN			0					Open for assignment of subject
398		OPEN			0					Open for assignment of subject
399		OPEN			0					Open for assignment of subject
	HU-2	"HUMMEL" BUST		5¾	15.50			1977		Small version in 1977. Larger version discontinued, date unknown See Sec. II
700		FIRST ANNUAL HUMMEL BELL		4"x3½"x6¼"	50	57	1978	1978		

FROM THE DESK OF

John F. Hotchkiss

NEW RELEASES

As this book went to press two unofficial announcements indicated there would be fifty-two discontinued items reissued and twenty-seven new designs released. The seventy-nine items have been included for the reader's information only. There is no assurance of when or if these additions will be made. Names shown for items still to be issued are unofficial and coined for use in this book only.

DIE ECHTEN HUMMEL-KUNSTPOSTKARTEN
ORIGINAL HUMMEL FINE ART POSTCARDS

208 Gl, Geb, Na   820   207 Gl, Geb, Na

825   221 A   824

202 Gl, Geb, NJ   816 Geb   203 Gl, Geb, WN

Bei Bestellung genügt die Angabe der Nummer. Bei Glückwunschkarten bitte Nummer und Zeichen angeben.
When ordering, please only mention the numbers.

3

4.

Hummel Prints, Pictures, and Other Paper Items

Two Dimensions in Hummel Art

By 1934 the Western World was at the bottom of the worst depression of the twentieth century. It was hardly an auspicious time for an artist to expect to find ready acceptance for sketches and paintings. Seemingly least likely to find success would be a graduate from a teachers' academy who had just decided to become a novice in a secluded convent. But almost overnight success did happen to such an artist because of ability and courage.

Berta Hummel had an abundance of ability. She had a magic touch with pencil or brush coupled with a creative insight in portraying children in a way pleasing to both adults and children, themselves. Fun, frolic, awe, fear, and play were all portrayed in scenes common to the daily life of little ones. Her drawings are almost irresistible to all who see them.

How Berta Hummel's talent found sponsors with the courage to invest in her work at such an inauspicious time in history is a complex and involved story. It appears that there were two pioneers in the effort of translating the originals of Berta Hummel into faithful lithographic reproductions, items that could be inexpensively enjoyed by millions. The German publishers, Verlag Ars Sacra, Josef Müller of Munich,[1] and Verlag Emil Fink of Stuttgart were these two innovators. Between them, they obtained the licenses to reproduce an abundance of Sister Hummel's work.

Opposite page: Original Hummel postcards from Verlag Emil Fink catalog. Courtesy of Verlag Emil Fink.

---

[1]There is no association between the "Ars Sacra" (Sacred Art) used in conjunction with the name Josef Müller and the Ars Sacra used for a few years during the 1940s by Herbert Dubler, Inc. of New York for a line of inferior Hummel figurines they copyrighted, produced, and distributed during World War II. Whether the name and rights were expropriated due to the war has not been determined.

Their catalogs have grown to a collective total of some five hundred different prints of originals. Perhaps two-thirds of these are controlled by the Muller firm, who have confirmed that they own outright most of Sister Hummel's original works for which they have reproduction rights. This fact is interesting since most collectors have been under the impression that these originals were owned by the convent.

As early as 1934 publisher Emil Fink had the foresight to copyright selected sketches and drawings of Sister Hummel and to couple these with Margarete Seemann's poems in book form. *The Hummel Book* shows not only the whimsical representations of children at play, prayer, and other tasks but also incorporates some of Sister Hummel's deeply religious work. Her Madonna in Red shown on page 139 is one especially fine print reproduced in this book. The book was not actually printed until 1950, several years after Sister Hummel had died in the convent. The popularity of this book is evidenced by the fact that there had been seventeen printings of it up to 1973. It is, of course, available in English.

Other books and publications have been issued using the work of Sister Hummel. One such book is *Sketch Me*, a biography written by an American Franciscan nun. It has been published in English, but at the present time is out of print and as rare as some of the discontinued M. I. Hummel figurines produced by W. Goebel Company. Copies, when found, have been known to sell for one hundred dollars. Another widely distributed book that is still in print is *The Hummel* copyrighted in 1939 by Verlag Ars Sacra, Josef Müller. It is similar in format to the Fink book and does full justice to the Hummel touch and color. The verses accompanying each illustration also do their part in highlighting the theme. An example is the verse with a picture of two children peering over a wooden gate:

Here's a gate,
Strong and stout;
It shuts you in
When you want to be out.
A gate to hate.

Madonna in Red by Sister M. I. Hummel.
Courtesy Verlag Emil Fink

Unfortunately, the distribution of prints, pictures, cards, and calendars has not been as wide in the United States as that of the figurines. They have been issued for many occasions such as New Year's, Christmas, birthdays, or general greetings, as well as notepaper for one's own thoughts. There are many colorful reproductions from which to choose.

The original plan for this book called for publishing a wide assortment of the reprints available from Müller and Fink. It was hoped that the publishing of these reprints would serve two purposes. For the first time more people would be able to see and enjoy the great variety of Sister Hummel's work and realize the possibilities in collecting her art in two-dimensional form. Figurine collectors would be interested in seeing the extensive reservoir of her work that remains as a potential for future three-dimensional adaptations.

The second purpose was to give figurine collectors their first opportunity to see a replica of the original art in the way it was created by Sister Hummel. They would then be able to compare it side-by-side with their three-dimensional figurine interpretations. In some cases the similarity is striking and in others the two-dimensional art contains something that had to be sacrificed to the practical production of the three-dimensional version. An album of cards or selected, large framed prints would complement nicely any collection of figurines, just as the annual plates do already.

656

697

800

215 a

Original Hummel postcards from Verlag Emil Fink catalog. Courtesy of Verlag Emil Fink

There are also some collectors who specialize in collecting only the two-dimensional examples.

It was necessary to modify the original plan, however, and to limit the number of examples to be printed because of time and problems in obtaining the necessary clearances. However, a sampling of the broader objectives was shown in the preceding pages, which have been reproduced from the Verlag Emil Fink catalog. Of particular interest to Hummel collectors are the reproductions of original drawings of older people. Sister Hummel has infused these drawings with a vitality and joy of living not unlike her drawings of children. Of special interest to collectors, also, are Moonlight Return, the original upon which the Schmid 1977 Berta Hummel Mother's Day Collection is based, and Heavenly Angel, the original upon which the famous 1971 Goebel "M. I. Hummel" Annual Plate is based. An unusual original drawing is the portraitlike rendering of the boy. The tone of this drawing is quite different from most of those of her other "children." It seems to be more formal and posed, as if done of a specific child for a specific purpose.

Not all of the illustrations are available in all the formats such as fine arts postcards, small Hummel pictures in the 2¾" x 4¼" size, and the larger Hummel wall pictures with sheet sizes of 7¾" x 11¾" and 9¾" x 14¼". The postcards cost around twenty-five cents and the small prints are sold by the hundred for about five dollars. The wall pictures' prices depend on the size of the work, with the largest costing about fifteen dollars, unmounted and unframed. When found in this country they may be priced higher. *The Hummel* by Sister Hummel and Margarete Seemann sells for about ten dollars here and about half that in Germany.

About twice as many of Sister Hummel's originals have been published by Verlag Ars Sacra,[1] Josef Müller as those by Verlag Emil Fink. These items are in the form of note cards, greeting cards, posters, postcards, folders, wall pictures, and miniatures. As transfers they appear on candles. The exact sizes and prices of these were not available at the time this was written. Müller's book, *Hummel*, and calendar are also part of the line, although apparently neither is distributed as widely in this country as the book by Fink. In Germany the price of *Hummel* is about five dollars. Listed in Sources in the back of this book are the two places found where postcards are carried in this country in a limited assortment. The Verlag Ars Sacra, Josef Müller address is listed in Sources as is that of Verlag Emil Fink. Some readers may wish to write for more information on availability and prices to one of these publishers or to one of the German retailers also listed in Sources.

[1] There is no association between the "Ars Sacra" (Sacred Art) used in conjunction with the name Josef Muller and the Ars Sacra used for a few years during the 1940s by Herbert Dubler, Inc. of New York for a line of inferior Hummel figurines they copyrighted, produced, and distributed during World War II. Whether the name and rights were expropriated due to the war has not been determined.

Hummel Calendars

A final category of two-dimensional Hummel art is calendars. Located inconspicuously under the catchall category of "Miscellaneous" at the very end of the M. I. Hummel Figurine Price List is the entry "Hummel Calendar — $3.50." With such a back seat and so little promotion, it is surprising how rapidly these calendars are becoming of interest to collectors. They have been published for about twenty-five years in English and in German — possibly longer in German. The earliest date suggested so far has been 1952 for both issues. The oldest one located in the research for this book was an incomplete 1954 edition illustrated here. The available examples from that time through the 1977 edition are illustrated on pages 142 through 145.

An M. I. Hummel figurine is represented in a photograph on the cover of each calendar (8¼" x 11½", or 21 x 30 cm) followed by a 7" x 9" color picture of a different figurine for each of the twelve months. Careful study of these calendars reveals many interesting details. Illustrations in the German editions precede those in the English ones by one year. The only exception found so far is between the 1975 German and 1976 English issues. While both show an Annual Plate on the cover, the subject of the plates is different. The dates of the plates correspond with the dates on the calendars. However, the monthly pages of these two different years are identical with respect to illustrations. Also, in addition to the language difference, there is also a difference in the form used for the German days and weeks of the month as compared to the English method.

The fine creative photography used in arranging the individual figurines for each cover and month is evident in the pleasing results. In recent years many scenes have been designed around the figurines to give a natural, real-life background which suppresses the presence of the base of the figure. An example is the August, 1976, figure #386 On a Secret Path which seems to be actually trudging through a forest on a narrow trail. Alert collectors will note that in this example, as in many others, special modeling, detail, and coloring seem different from normal production examples. Another dissimilarity between these figurines used for calendar photographs and those in normal production is that the "M. I. Hummel" is incised on the front rather than the rear of the base. In these cases the signature has been highlighted with black to show the incised name in contrast to the base. Certainly these unique pieces would be prized possessions in any collection.

Both Verlag Ars Sacra, Josef Müller and Verlag Emil Fink also publish calendars. For 1977 Verlag Ars Sacra, Josef Müller has two, a larger one than Goebel's in English and French and a smaller one than Goebel's in German. At press time permission had not been received to illustrate them. Emil Fink also has a small one shown in the illustrations, that is similar to Ars Sacra.

At the present time there is no known secondary market for the two-dimensional lithographic reproductions of Hummel art. The calendars, however, are a notable exception. The price for the current year calendar is $3.50. The prices on back issues vary according to how old they are and the particular year. Seemingly, the most difficult year to find is the 1970 issue, except for any of the 1950 decade. Anything dated in the 1950s will probably soon be priced around twenty-five dollars. As interest in collecting calendars grows, prices of 1960 issues could range from ten to twenty dollars. It seems reasonable that the prices of these calendars will advance faster than the rate of inflation, reaching the point where they are taken apart and the individual pictures framed and sold for five or ten dollars apiece.

Hummel Calendars

English, 1954, Heavenly Protection. (Called Guardian Angel in 1950.)

English, 1956, Candlelight.

English, 1957, School Girls.

English, 1959, Meditation.

English, 1960, Stormy Weather.

English, 1961, Bookworm.

English, 1962, Flower Madonna.

English, 1963, Telling Her Secret.

English, 1964, Serenade.

English, 1965, Goose Girl.

English, 1966, Spring Dance.

English, 1967, School Girls.

English, 1968, Duet.

English, 1969, Mail Is Here (Mail Coach)

English, 1970, Ring Around the Rosie.

143

English, 1971, To Market.

English, 1972, Stormy Weather (close-up).

English, 1973, Adventure Bound.

English, 1974, Umbrella Boy.

English, 1975, Happy Days.

English, 1976, Apple Tree Girl.

Emil Fink, 1976; print from original art.

German, 1977, Follow the Leader.

English, 1978, Follow the Leader.

M. I. Hummel calendars. Left, 1976
German version. Right, 1977 English
version.

German issue M. I. Hummel 1975
calendar featuring 1975 Annual Plate,
Ride into Christmas.

Left, 1976 German issue. Right, 1977
English issue with identical format.

August, 1976, from English version
showing figurine in naturalistic setting.

Non-Hummel 1977 calendar by Alfred
Mainzer. Artist unknown.

Non-Hummel 1977 calendar by Alfred
Mainzer. Artist unknown.

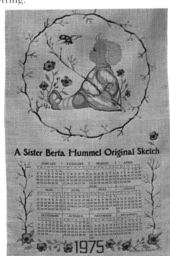

Sister Berta Hummel 1975 calendar towel
by Schmid Brothers.

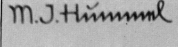

Dolls

Brought to you from W. Goebel the manufacturer of the world famous "Hummel" Figurines. The costumes are all hand sewn and are of authentic German dress. Attractively packaged in round clear acetate self-display box. Each doll is tagged with the World Famous Hummel Trademark.

Hansl und Gretl
10"

00 002   00 001

10 inch high

12 052

12 048

Der Artikel 12 052 auch in hellblau (12 036) lieferbar

Vroni, Rudi, Seppl,

8 inch high

Mariandl, Jackl, Rosl

00 058   00 057   00 059   00 060   00 061   00 056

Strickliesl, Radi-Bub, Wanderbub,

10"

Gänseliesl

146

5.

Goebel and Hummel Dolls

Hummel dolls first appeared in America in 1951. At that time, Mrs. Elsie Clark Grug wrote in her newsletter for collectors: "They are perfect to give to American small fry without raising an objection from a father who 'doesn't want his son to play with dolls.' Nobody could object to one of these Hummel boys being in his son's play room."

Today the emphasis has switched from whether a doll is suitable for a boy to questions on authenticity and price and value as a Hummel collectible. Because the names Goebel and Hummel have been used so interchangeably, the question "What is a Hummel doll?" is a most pertinent one. A short quick answer is: "All 'M. I. Hummels' are made by Goebel but all Goebel items are not Hummels." For a more complete answer, the easiest method may be to trace Goebel's role as a doll manufacturer.

Goebel and Bisque Dolls

An early example of Goebel's work is a head made with his 1871 mark, a triangle over a quarter moon. This bisque head was made for Max Hanwerk's "Bebe Elite" dolls. The Goebel trademark on the back of the head of these dolls is shown in Illustration

1. 1871 Goebel trademark. Courtesy Mrs. Coleman's *Collectors' Encyclopedia of Dolls.*

Opposite page: Illustration from 1976 Goebel catalog of genuine "M. I. Hummel" dolls.

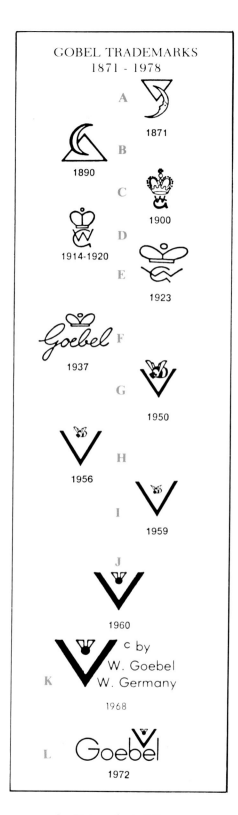

GOBEL TRADEMARKS
1871 - 1978

A
1871

B
1890

C
1900

D
1914-1920

E
1923

F
Goebel
1937

G
1950

H
1956

I
1959

J
1960

K
c by
W. Goebel
W. Germany
1968

L
Goebel
1972

2. Picture of a half-figure woman shown on page 45 of *China Half Figures Called Pincushion Dolls* by Frieda Marion, figure 44 from collection of Eleanor Lar Rieu. Courtesy of Frieda Marion.

#1. Under the trademark was printed, "Max Handwerk's, Bebe Elite, Germany." This doll is illustrated in Coleman's, *Collectors' Encyclopedia of Dolls*, page 56, #126. Later, Goebel adopted a crown above the entwined letters "W.G." as his trademark on bisque half-figure and full-sized dolls. Because Goebel may have used variations on his trademark before or after they were registered, it is difficult to conclusively date his half figures. However, recent correspondence with W. Goebel Porzellanfabrik states that the half figures were produced only until 1920, according to Frieda Marion in *China Half Figures Called Pincushion Dolls*. An example of a Goebel half figure or pincushion doll can be found in Illustration #2.

3. Pincushion head, same as Figure 43
on page 44 of *China Half Figures Called
Pincushion Dolls* by Frieda Marion.
Same mark as figure 40 first on left.
Courtesy of Margaret Woodbury Strong
Museum.

4. Pincushion head. Lightly tinted bisque
with blonde mohair wig and velvet
ribbon band through her hair. Lower
eyelashes only. Painted features. Carries a glazed porcelain tray, teapot, and
cup and saucer. Trademark #Od.

Marked as #648 on page
255 of Coleman *Encyclopedia* but only
a number 5 on the right side and no
Germany mark. Courtesy of Margaret
Woodbury Strong Museum.

Marion describes these half figures as "of such fine quality
that it is no wonder that they are sought by discriminating collectors." Among the characteristics she points out are blossoms in
the figures' hands, unusual design and fidelity of period, and the
painting of lower eyelashes but not uppers. The Goebel trademark is often found on the base of the half-figure dolls, but was
sometimes a paper label which could be removed. Two more fine
examples of these pincushion, half-figure dolls are shown and
described in Illustrations #3 and #4.

5. All bisque, swivel neck, jointed at hips and shoulders, molded Dutch cap. The white front band is incised with small seven-petal flowers, and the back part of the cap is brown flocked finish. Marked with Goebel mark shown in Angione book, page 153. Courtesy of the Margaret Woodbury Strong Museum.

6. Bisque head with painted, molded features. Molded hair with blue ribbon and pink flowers. Composition body, jointed at shoulders and hips, painted blue shoes. Head marked GB 13/0. Pictured in Coleman *Encyclopedia*, page 255. Courtesy of Margaret Woodbury Strong Museum.

More uncommon are the all-bisque dolls, especially when marked. Genevieve Angione in *All Bisque and Half Bisque Dolls* compares several dolls. The one pictured in Illustration #5 carries a Goebel trademark indicating a date of 1914-20. Illustration #6 shows another doll with bisque head, but in this example the body is composition with original gauze dress. The picture also appears in Coleman's, *THE COLLECTOR'S ENCYCLOPEDIA OF DOLLS*. She theorizes that these irregularities can be explained by the possibility that the all-bisque doll aspect of the Goebel Company was a training ground for artists. Probably it was used to keep the factory operating at full speed and as also a source of income.

Goebel and Hummel

When did the name Goebel become confused with Hummel? In 1934 the Hummel figurines were introduced. Patterned from the drawings of Sister M. I. Hummel, they helped contribute to Goebel's growth so much that by 1958 the company had expanded to four plants. Dolls and toy animals were made in an affiliated rubber plant in 1952. About this time, Goebel adopted the letter "V" with a bumble bee superimposed on top. The word "hummele" in German means bee so it was natural for the public to conclude that anything with this mark was a Hummel when actually it is the Goebel mark for all of their products.

The original Hummel doll was introduced to the United States in 1951. Made of rubber and overpainted a tannish flesh color, many of these early dolls have suffered a breakdown in the rubber compound causing them to collapse. By 1963, the dolls were made of rubber and vinyl. *The Doll Collectors Manual* in 1964 reprinted a page from a pamphlet by Goebel that describes the dolls as "made of rubber and vinyl—work done by hand—hygienic —washable—free from poison—unbreakable." The dolls are now made of all polyvinylchloride (PVC) plastic in a realistic flesh color.

W. Goebel obtained the right to make Hummel dolls and figurines from the Franciscan convent where Berta Hummel became Sister Marie Innocentia Hummel in 1933. A genuine Hummel must bear the signature M.J.Hummel. Unless a doll is signed in a facsimile of Sister Hummel's signature, the doll is not a Hummel. It may be another Goebel product by another artist if it bears one of Goebel's trademarks. Hummel dolls will always have this signature on the back of the neck and usually the name M. I. Hummel sewn in the garments. In addition, a pendant with the artist's signature, the name of the doll, and Goebel's trademark is also attached to currently produced Hummel dolls.

Johana Gast Anderton in *More Twentieth Century Dolls* describes Hummel dolls as among the best marked lines of collectibles available today. However, even with these detailed

7. Gretl, an original "M. I. Hummel" doll. 1976, 10 inches high, vinyl, made by W. Goebel Company, W. Germany. Trademark #5.

8. Rose, an original "M. I. Hummel" c. 1970, 10 inches high, made by W. Goebel Company, W. Germany. Trademark #3.

9. Catalog sheet by W. Goebel Company for 1976 showing "M. I. Hummel" dolls for sale. Trademark #5.

```
      HUMMEL DOLL PRICES 1976
      ==========================


   order No.        name              size      US-$ each

   12o52         Hummel baby pink     lo "        8.9o
   12o36         Hummel baby blue     lo "        8.9o


   ooo58         Vroni                8 "        11.9o
   ooo57         Rudi                 8"         11.9o
   ooo59         Seppl                8 "        11.9o
   ooo60         Mariandl             8 "        11.9o
   ooo61         Jackl                8 "        11.9o
   ooo56         Rosl                 8 "        11.9o


   oooo2         Hansl                lo "       15.9o
   oooo1         Gretl                lo "       15.9o
   oooo5         Strickliesl          lo "       15.9o
   ooo17         Radi-Bub             lo "       15.9o
   oooo6         Wanderbub            lo "       15.9o
   ooo14         Gaenseliesl          lo "       15.9o



   ALL DOLLS ARE NOW IN STOCK AGAIN!

   ==================================
```

10. Pumuckl, a 12-inch vinyl doll made by W. Goebel Company c. 1960. Trademark #3, Illustration 11.

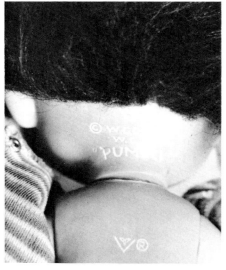

11. Trademarks on back of "Pumuckl" doll showing marking of doll name, the maker (Goebel), and trademark #3 used about 1960. This is a Goebel doll.

markings, there is still confusion unless the collector remembers that the only positive identification is the facsimile M.J.Hummel on the back of the neck.

Another problem for the collector is that while all Hummel dolls have a special look about them, there are sometimes only slight differences between the individual dolls. For example, 1976 Gretl, pictured in Illustration #7 is quite similar to Rose shown in Illustration #8. Both dolls are hatless, carry baskets and have braids. The differences lie in the colors of the costumes and styles of shoes. In addition, the company may also use the same name for different appearing dolls.

Buying and Selling Hummel Dolls

A doll price guide lists a twelve-inch rubber Hummel doll for $125. A recent response to an ad in *Hobbies* asked $125 for Rose in Illustration #8.

For contemporary dolls, retail prices in Germany for the 1976 Hummel line shown in Illustration #9 range from $8.90 for the ten-inch babies to $11.90 for the eight-inch Vroni, Rudi, Seppl, Mariandl, Jackl, and Rosl to $15.90 for ten-inch Hansl, Gretl, Strickliesl, Radi-Bub, Wanderbub, and Gaenseliesl. The dolls have fixed brown glass eyes, molded hair, and are dressed in a variety of hand-sewn costumes. The Goebel distributor, Hummelwerk, does not sell them in the United States to dealers. However, there is an importer in New York City who does sell Hummel dolls. Many dealers in this country buy them from overseas at approximately the same prices. By the time they get here, the retail prices of Hummel dolls range between thirty to forty dollars, or more than double their retail price in Germany.

"Where can I buy or sell Hummel dolls?" you may be asking yourself. Some of the large gift shops that carry Hummel figurines also sell the current line of dolls. Their names are listed in the Sources section of this book. If you are interested in buying one of the older dolls, your best source is one of the specialized doll dealers in your area or one of those who advertise in abundance in national collectors' magazines like *Hobbies*, The *Antique Trader Weekly*, and many others. When buying by mail, it is customary to make the purchase subject to a three- to five-day inspection of the doll and to have the privilege of returning it for a full refund if not satisfied. For more details on buying by mail, consult the chapter on buying and selling. This is especially applicable to Hummel dolls because of the widespread confusion between the terms Goebel and Hummel. In placing an order, it is well to state in your letter that the doll must be marked M.J.Hummel®. Even then, your order should be subject to personal inspection and acceptance since you still might be sent one of the wild *henna*-haired, devil-may-care "Pumuckl" dolls, also made by Goebel, as

14. Fiber tags and paper label used in addition to backmarking on "M. I. Hummel" dolls.

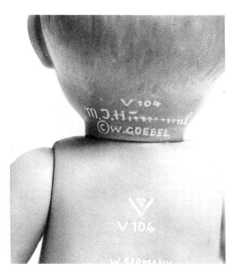

12. Trademark #3 on the back of the head of a genuine "M. I. Hummel" doll, #V104. This is a 10½-inch vinyl baby doll made about 1960. Incised on the back of the body is the trademark in use at that time, the doll make number, and the country of origin. This is a Goebel doll.

13. "M. I. Hummel baby vinyl doll V104.

was the author in researching material for this book. (See Illustrations #10 and #11.)

When it comes to selling one or more Hummel dolls, the large doll dealers are again the most likely buyers. In such cases, the price will be less than that indicated in this section, as the dealer may have to do some reconditioning and is also entitled to a margin of profit. Other ways to sell your doll(s) are outlined in the section on buying and selling.

All genuine "M. I. Hummel" dolls made since the early 1950s should have some numbers incised (hot stamped) along with the Goebel trademark and in some cases, the name of the doll. These numbers have been assigned by the W. Goebel Company and help in the positive identification of a specific model (Illustration #12). The authors of some of the doll books have also used a numbering system for all of the dolls described and illustrated in their books. Advertisers and collectors frequently use these numbers in writing about any doll. These numbers do not mean much unless you have the particular book in which the doll was illustrated. It is suggested that in addition to or in place of any such numbers that the number on the back of the doll under discussion be used to further pinpoint the doll. In a later edition of this book when a more active secondary market has developed, it may be possible to publish the numbering codes that the W. Goebel Company uses to further assist collectors in locating hard-to-find specimens.

As Hummel figurines continue to gain more and more status as collectibles, Hummel dolls also grow in popularity. These high-quality dolls serve as a good addition to the collections of Hummel figurine lovers and doll collectors.

6.

Berta Hummel Art by Schmid

As a young girl, Berta Hummel would sketch on odd scraps of paper, on the blackboard, and in the margins of letters. From that time until she entered the convent in 1933, she produced numerous drawings. This wealth of art went primarily unnoticed until the late 1960s when Schmid Brothers, Inc., an importing firm, gained the exclusive rights to reproduce all art done by Sister Hummel prior to her entering the convent.

The association between Hummel art and the Schmid Brothers began nearly thirty years before this agreement. In a story by Marge Rosenberg in The *Plate Collector*, Paul Schmid III relates how his family became associated with Hummel art. Paul Schmid II, son of the company's founder, stepped into a little shop in Germany in 1935. Attracted by a Hummel figurine, Schmid placed an order with W. Goebel Company. From that time until 1968 when Schmid and Goebel terminated their relationship, the Boston-based firm served as an important importer of Hummel figurines.

Schmid Brothers 1977 limited edition items based on an early Berta Hummel drawing of her brother entitled "Midnight Return."

In an undated special notice to Schmid customers, as reprinted above, Paul A. Schmid clarifies the relationship between the Hummel family and the Schmid Brothers since the separation of W. Goebel and the importers. Schmid confirms that: "Mrs. Viktoria Hummel, the late artist's mother and legal heir, has granted exclusive and undisputed rights to Schmid to utilize all those works of art which Sister Hummel created before she became a nun, and which she left behind in her parents' home."

Schmid notes that the new line of products based on Berta Hummel's art will include ceramic and other figurines. "The Schmid figurines should not be confused by our customers with the products of the German firm of W. Goebel Porzellanfabrik, none of which are catalogued or sold by Schmid. Our exclusive collector's items can be readily identified by the back or bottom stamp which will show a copyright by Schmid Brothers, by V. Hummel, or by J. Hummel."

This warning, unfortunately, may have been too late to help all collectors. During Christmas, 1971, W. Goebel and Schmid

Brothers each issued a limited first edition plate based on the same well known drawing of Sister Hummel's, the Heavenly Angel. The Schmid plate is called a Christmas Plate and is a two dimensional transfer printed design in matt finish muted colors. The Gobel plate is an Annual Plate molded in bas relief with brighter and shinier colors. Both of these plates are illustrated at the bottom of the page."

Another interesting item in Schmid's special notice is his reference to Sister Berta Hummel's mother. For the first time since her daughter's death in 1946, Mrs. Hummel is earning royalties on her daughter's works. The convent, under agreement with W. Goebel, is reported to have earned upwards to four million dollars on Sister Hummel's work.

Schmid Brothers until 1977 had produced a large diversified line of well over one hundred Hummel art items. These have been produced in unlimited quantities. Music boxes and Hummel pictures were the items most prominently displayed in the twelve-page catalog. The wooden music boxes were shaped in rectangles, hearts, and ovals and play a variety of popular American songs. A decoupage technique using Hummel prints decorates the boxes. Many of the larger boxes also contain a lined jewel compartment. Schmid offered gilded metal rectangular and heart-shaped musical jewelry boxes with Hummel prints on a satin covering.

An assortment of pictures was offered. Large single pictures or groups of smaller prints were available to the collector. Pictures ranged from close-ups of the children's faces to prints with lines of verse under the Hummel drawings. Several rather unique Hummel items were also offered, such as a Hummel key rack and a wide assortment of candles with many different Hummel scenes that could be coupled with an equally wide assortment of either wrought iron or wooden candleholders. And even a musical Hummel key chain was listed for the dedicated collector of Hummel-ania who had everything.

All of that changed. These items that were available in unlimited quantities have been discontinued and, as a result of that, the quantities available for future collectors are those that

Heavenly Angel 1971 ANNUAL PLATE, Hum. 264. Goebel's plate is done is bas-relief with bright, hand-painted colors.

Heavenly Angel 1971 Christmas Plate by Schmid Brothers. Note design was transfer-printed in soft, muted colors.

have been produced to date—some of which were made in very large quantities and others in very limited numbers. At the present time there is no active secondary market in these items because they can still be found on dealers' shelves in varying degrees. Some time hence when these first begin to appear at flea markets, later at collectors' shows, and still later at antiques auctions and shows, a secondary market at prices equal to or greater than the previous retail prices should emerge if these run true to the pattern of all other discontinued items of decorative art, and there seems to be no reason to expect otherwise.

In addition to the variety of unlimited articles, Schmid Brothers, as already mentioned, have produced a limited edition Christmas plate since 1971. This series has been continued each year and is shown through 1976 on page 159. By 1977 a number of other limited edition companion articles carrying the same motif as that year's plate have been added. Paul Schmid, III, the recently elected president, has indicated that in the future the Berta Hummel series will be limited to a family of limited edition items similar to the 1977 Christmas group shown on page 160. Each year another of the paintings or sketches that Berta Hummel did before entering the convent will be selected as the motif for that year for both Christmas and Mother's Day.

In 1972 Schmid Brothers introduced their first Mother's Day limited edition plate. This series has been continued each year since and is shown on page 159. For 1977 the very interesting sketch that Berta Hummel made of her brother called Midnight Return is the theme for the entire group of Mother's Day articles. All of these appear on page 154, including the stained glass plaque. One version of the story is reported as follows:

> *Sister Berta's family was typically solid, middle-class Bavarian, proud of its position in commerce. But the Great Depression was exceedingly cruel in Germany and the three children took jobs before and after school.*
>
> *Late one afternoon Berta's brother, Adolf, fell asleep in the haystack of a neighboring farm, bone-tired. He awoke at half past midnight, and the picture shows him hurrying home with the moon high over his shoulder and hay falling from beneath his arms. Probably, Berta added the two crickets for luck, suspecting he would be strongly spanked when he got home.*

An "M. I. Hummel" figurine produced by the W. Goebel Company, #386, On Secret Path, is based on the same original art.

Starting in 1976 a limited edition plaque of stained glass was introduced with the same motif as the Christmas and Mother's Day plates for that year. This innovative use of the revived stained glass technique which is now so popular, has added a new

Schmid Brothers Limited Edition plates of Berta Hummel's art for Christmas and Mother's Day

Schmid Bros. Limited Edition items of Berta Hummel's art for Christmas 1977

dimension to the ever-expanding group of limited edition collectibles which are pictured with the rest of the "family" on the previous pages for Mother's Day and Christmas of 1977.

PREVALENT PRICES

The secondary market for limited edition plates is well established for all makes. The history of Schmid plates has not followed the established pattern set by many others. Usually the first year of issue turns out to be the one with the highest premium in years to come. Schmid's 1971 plate was issued at $15 and is now being offered for around $90, or almost three times as much as the present 1971 price offering. The other years vary, but fall in between these two limits. In the case of the Mother's Day plate first issued in 1972 at $15 it is the 1973 issue (also $15) that carries the biggest premium today of $40. The retail prices for the current year on both series is $27.50, and the new stained glass plaques having the same design sell for $37.50. In the other articles having the same design, the 1971 Bell sells now for around $40. The current price on the Bell for 1977 is $22.50, the Child's Cup, $15, the Music Box, $22.50. The Christmas Ornament is $4.50 and the Christmas Candle is $6.50 for 1977. Those interested in either buying or selling these items in the secondary market can obtain current prices at any time from the advertisements in the *Antique Trader Weekly* or The *Plate Collector* that is published each month. The latter magazine also publishes The *Bradford Exchange* (something like stock quotations), but these appear to always be above the advertised prices.

7.

Reproductions of Hummel Art

Real, Fake, or Reproduction

Strangely enough, there are only a few hundred pieces of Hummel art that are not reproductions. Some reports place the number of original sketches by Sister Hummel between five and six hundred. All others are copies or reproductions of these original creations of hers. These reproductions take many forms, such as the best known, genuine "M. I. Hummel" figurines made by the W. Goebel Co., the prints, posters, and cards made by Verlag Ars Sacra, Joseph Müller and Emil Fink publishing companies, the dolls also made by Goebel in the likeness of some piece of original Hummel art, the transfers used on plates, candles, and eggs by Schmid, and the copies of copies made by various firms in Japan, Korea, Taiwan, and elsewhere.

Many collectors have come to regard a reproduction as something bad, cheap, illegal, dishonest, or inferior. The American Heritage Dictionary defines "reproduce" as follows: "To produce a counterpart, image, or copy of." There seems to be no implication of undesirability.

Opposite page, School Girl, 5½″ high. Produced c. 1947 by unknown maker.

Certainly the first reproductions of great consequence were very desirable. The invention of movable type made possible the first replicas in the form of the limited number of Guttenberg Bibles made in the mid-fifteenth century. The making of reproductions in the form of etchings and engravings by great artists, such as Rembrandt and Durer, was another great stride in the wider distribution of original art in either limited or unlimited editions so that the masses rather than the classes could own and enjoy it.

Figurine reproductions of Hummel art accomplish the same end. By adapting Sister Hummel's works of art to a three-dimensional form by a carefully controlled molding process, creators of these "reproductions" have given millions of collectors a chance to enjoy and cherish what she created. The modeling and molding carefully preserve all the warmth, sentiment, and the action of her original creations. In fact these reproductions are done so well many people regard them as they would an original piece of art. To support this position, even the United States Customs classifies them as "original works of art" as shown earlier in this book. Since "M. I. Hummel" figurines have taken on the status of pieces of original art themselves, they, in turn, are now being copied. Unfortunately, most of these copies are not made to the same high standards as the "M. I. Hummels" and are unlikely to ever be classed as "works of art."

The story of the figurines made by Herbert Dubler, Inc., during World War II in New York is a good example of such reproductions. They were made, according to published information, under a license from the Siessen Convent and for which royalties were set aside. Almost everyone who has seen them agrees that they do not compare favorably in execution, workmanship, or materials to those made by Goebel. This fact, perhaps, could somewhat be accounted for by wartime shortages. Examples of these figurines are illustrated on pages 169 and 170.

They are not good reproductions of original Hummel art, but neither are they fakes. A "fake" implies fraud. These reproductions by Herbert Dubler, Inc., and those from Japan, Taiwan, or elsewhere are not so much "fakes" as they are inferior representations of Sister Hummel's work. Like eggs, there are good reproductions, mediocre reproductions, and "bad" reproductions. Sister Hummel's originals have been rendered in all of these degrees of quality.

Since the words "Hummel reproduction" have come to mean something made to look like the "M. I. Hummel" figurines, this seemingly widely accepted meaning has been used in this book. Many examples of such reproductions have been made in the past and are currently being made. Illustrations of as many as possible are pictured on pages 165 through 175. The reproductions are shown with two ideas in mind. First, to illustrate how widely these reproductions vary in quality and appearance from the accepted standard "M. I. Hummel" ones. Some, like Dubler, are authentic but inferior interpretations. Others may be unauthorized copies that may or may not violate copyright laws, with only the courts being able to make that determination. There are also others designed to appear Hummel-like without being an actual copy.

1. *At the Well*, 4¼″, unnumbered, maker unknown, Korea, c. 1975.

2. *Go Get It*, 4″, no marks, c. 1940.

3. *Backpacker*, 4½″, unnumbered, maker unknown, Occupied Japan, c. 1946.

4. *To the Mailbox*, 4½″ unnumbered, maker unknown, Japan (?), c. 1976.

Secondly, these various styles and ages of reproductions are shown to identify them with a source, if possible, and to record them for easy reference by collectors. These illustrations should go a long way to reassure collectors that most copies differ in so many respects from their Goebel counterparts that they have no real worry about being confused. if there is ever any doubt, a collector can check for the M.J.Hummel incised mark which, so far as could be ascertained, has never been used by anyone other

165

5. *Banjo Stroller*, 4″, unnumbered, maker unknown, Japan, c. 1976.

6. *Dry Shelter*, music box, 7″, unnumbered, maker unknown, Japan, c. 1976.

7. Unnamed, similar to FOREST SHRINE, Hum. 183, 4¼″, unnumbered, c. 1965.

8. *Goose Girl*, ARNART, 22/620, 4¾″, Japan, c. 1976.

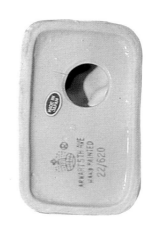

9. Base of *Goose Girl*, ARNART.

10. *Shoe Shine*, Picci La Ca, 90014, 3¾″, Taiwan, c. 1976.

12. Wax candle, 7″, no marks, c. 1976.

13. *To School*, wax candle, 6¾″ unnumbered, maker unknown, Japan, c. 1976.

14. *April Showers*, NAPCO, C8747, 7″, Japan, c. 1976.

than Goebel. Furthermore, to the best of our knowledge, all Goebel examples have been incised with this designation. The prices on even the best of the copies illustrated are about 10 percent to 20 percent of a genuine "M. I. Hummel" of similar design and size.

Figurines are not the only Hummel art that has attracted similar but not identical copies. Similar enough to attract the eye of the buyer but dissimilar enough to deter any legal action are greeting cards, calendars, and other paper likenesses drawn in the Hummel "style and manner." For example, Henry Mainzer, Inc. produces a line of Christmas and greeting cards that on first glance appear to be photomechanical copies of original Hummel drawings. However, they contain the name of no artist and no copyright date. Pictures of these items are shown on these pages to illustrate their Hummel-like style.

As with other reproductions, some are good values while others may vary widely in quality. For example, a Mainzer 1977 calendar was seen and purchased because of its similarity to Goebel's annual Hummel calendar. Close inspection showed items to have visual defects that would not be tolerated by any first-rate publisher. However, this example may have been an extreme exception. The prudent approach is to bypass such bargains unless you have real expertise in appraising reproductions.

However, avid knowledgeable collectors seek out reproductions for two reasons. First, because they supplement a collection of authentic articles and may even enhance it since imitation is the sincerest form of flattery. Second, these reproductions add meaningful contrast and, in some cases, may even make a separate, interesting collection. Dubler figurines are acquiring status as collectibles, although they will never be works of art in years to come.

Many of the categories of reproductions have attracted their own independent following. In some collectible classifications, individual items have attained or even exceeded the price of the original articles. "Poor Man's Tiffany" (Carnival Glass) is one example. Some pattern glass goblets made to imitate expensive, hand-cut crystal sell for as much or more than their original counterparts. Genuine ancient glass from the first or second century A. D. will usually bring only a fraction of what a reproduction made by Tiffany and Carder will bring at auction.

Many collectors wonder if the same thing will happen in various forms of Hummel art. There appears to be a better-than-even chance that it could in isolated cases, but probably not "across the board." Even if most "M. I. Hummel" collectors wanted only one Herbert Dubler figurine to supplement their collections for contrast, there are so few "Dublers" available that they could become worth more than comparable "M. I. Hummels" in the secondary market. The demand versus the supply will provide the answer in the future.

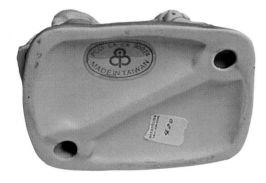

11. Base of *Shoe Shine*, Picci La Ca.

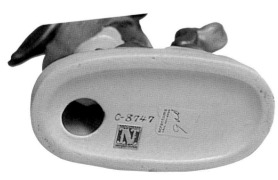

15. Base of ARNART *April Showers*.

167

Herbert Dubler Figurines

Herbert Dubler, Inc. copyrighted, produced, and sold Hummel figurines for a short time, although they are relatively unknown. Prior to World War II an individual named Herbert Dubler was an importer of greeting cards and other paper products. Some if not all of these imports, were products published by Verlag Ars Sacra, Josef Müller of Munich[1], Germany. Müller was one of the first two publishers to obtain reproduction rights to Sister Maria Innocentia Hummel's drawings and paintings about 1933. Perhaps due to embargoes and the war in Europe, Dubler sold his business in about 1939 to three men living in or near New York. The capitalization was set at $2,000 or $100 a share. The incorporation was under the laws of the State of New York with the original owners and their holdings being: John P. McArdle, ten shares; Herman Van Mell, five shares; and Lawrence B. Wardrop, five shares. The purpose of the corporation was to continue the business of Herbert Dubler at 15 Barclay Street, New York, New York, and to manufacture, print, publish, and circulate innumerable forms of paper products and related properties. The date of this certificate of incorporation was April 29, 1939.

From April 1939 until mid-1942 no records of their products or activities were found. About 1942 this corporation decided to produce Hummel figurines, no doubt because at this time no imports from Germany were allowed. From June 1942 until May 1943 a total of seventeen copyrights were registered in the name Herbert Dubler, Inc. According to the copyright the models were executed by Joseph Josephu after the original work of artist Berta Hummel. About that time the company issued a brochure about Berta Hummel and the story behind these figurines. So far as is known this brochure quoted below is being published for the first time.

> These figures are authentic Hummel figures created after the original designs by Berta Hummel. They are not copies of any previously made. All our figures by Hummel or other artists as well as our greeting card designs and prints, published by us in this country, are fully protected by copyright. Any attempt to copy them will be prosecuted.
>
> A royalty from the sale of the figures will go to the artist who designed them. In the case of Sister Hummel, the royalty will be paid to a trust fund in her name, to be distributed among the Franciscan Convents in this country at her discretion. Sister Hummel is a Catholic Nun and as such had to take a vow of poverty which does not allow her to personally own any money. No amount of money, large or small, will leave this country.

From this statement it is deduced that Herbert Dubler, Inc. was publishing the greeting cards and prints, as well as the figurines, in

---

[1]There is no association between the "Ars Sacra" (Sacred Art) used in conjunction with the name Josef Müller and the Ars Sacra used for a few years during the 1940s by Herbert Dubler, Inc. of New York for a line of inferior Hummel figurines they copyrighted, produced, and distributed during World War II. Whether the name and rights were expropriated due to the war has not been determined.

16. *Leap Frog*, NAPCO, C8837, Japan, c. 1976.

17. *Horn Blower*, C7655, 4½″, Japan, c. 1976.

18. *A High Note*, NAPCO(?), C8502, 4½″, Japan(?), c. 1976.

19. *Baker w/Dog*, 5″, no name or numbers, Japan, c. 1976.

20. *Young Gardener*, Royal Crown, 4½″ 11/541, Japan, c. 1976.

21. Back stamps and label from *Young Gardener* by Royal Crown.

22. *Little Mailman*, Dubler 35, 5″ New York,© 1942.

23. *Sleepy Baby*, Dubler 39, 4″, New York,© 1942.

24. *Bawling Benny*, Dubler 44, 5″, New York,© 1942.

25. *Dentist Dodger*, Dubler 48, 3¼″, New York,© 1942.

26. Unnamed, unnumbered Dubler, similar to MEDITATION, Hum. 61, 4¾″, New York, 1942-5(?).

27. Unnamed, unnumbered Dubler, similar to RETREAT TO SAFETY, Hum. 201, 5″, New York, 142-5(?).

28. Unnamed, unnumbered Dubler, similar to DOLL MOTHER, Hum. 67, 4″, New York, 1942-5(?).

29. Unnamed, unnumbered Dubler, similar to PLAYMATES, Hum. 58, 3½″, New York, 1942-45(?).

30. Unnamed Dubler plaque similar to Hummel plaque, Vacation Time, 4″ x 5″, New York, 1942-5(?).

31. Unnamed Dubler plaque similar to APPLE TREE GIRL, Hum. 141.

32. *Heavenly Angel*, 4½″, possibly Dubler, c. 1947.

33. *Let's Move*, 5¼″, no maker or numbers, c. 1947.

170

this country because of the war. The list of figurines which were copyrighted and listed in this brochure is quoted verbatim below. One copyright, G42188 on May 5, 1943, described as "Boy with Flute," is not included in the list.

These are the titles of the new figures created by Herbert Dubler, Inc.[1]

No. 31 —	THE LITTLE SKIPPER	by E. O. Jones
No. 32 —	THE LITTLE BOOKWORM	by B. Hummel
No. 33 —	THE TINY CHERUB	by E. O. Jones
No. 34 —	THE LITTLE MOTHER	by B. Hummel
No. 35 —	THE LITTLE MAILMAN	by B. Hummel
No. 36 —	THE LITTLE COBBLER	by B. Hummel
No. 37 —	THE DOLL'S DOCTOR	by B. Hummel
No. 38 —	THE LITTLE CHEMIST	by B. Hummel
No. 39 —	THE SLEEPY BABY	by B. Hummel
No. 40 —	MOTHER'S HELPER	by B. Hummel
No. 41 —	HELLO! BIRDIE	by B. Hummel
No. 42 —	THE FLOWER LASS	by B. Hummel
No. 43 —	CACTUS PUSS	by B. Hummel
No. 44 —	BAWLING BENNIE	by B. Hummel
No. 45 —	MADONNA AND CHILD	by B. Hummel
No. 46 —	ANGEL'S SONG	by B. Hummel
No. 47 —	THE BAD MASTER	by B. Hummel
No. 48 —	THE DENTIST DODGER	by B. Hummel

Pictures of these figurines are shown on pages 169 and 170 together with their Dubler names and numbers (35, 39, 44, 48). They produced more than were listed in the above brochure. Six of these are shown with the corresponding "M. I. Hummel" name and number but no record of a Dubler name or number. The quality of these figures does not compare with that of the Goebel Company in either material or decoration and varies between examples. Apparently the Dubler figurines were made of plaster of paris or similar soft material. Some carried an aluminum foil label on the bottom saying "Authentic Hummel Figure, Produced by Ars Sacra[1], Made in the USA." They were also incised around the base with the name "Herbert Dubler, Inc." It is not known how long these figures were made and sold, but considering their quality and wartime conditions, they must have had a short life.

Shortly after World War II the name of the business was changed to Crestwick. According to reports, the new owner was a Mr. Wick. From December 8, 1947, until March, 1962, this firm distributed greeting cards under its own brand name. Where these cards were made has not been determined. The only existing example found to date is an advertising bookmark from Robert's Book Shop, Inc., 5556 Broadway, New York 63, New York. It shows a color picture of a small girl knitting by the light of a lamp. It is obviously not an adaptation from a Hummel original. The

[1]There is no association between the "Ars Sacra" (Sacred Art) used in conjunction with the name Josef Müller and the Ars Sacra used for a few years during the 1940s by Herbert Dubler, Inc. of New York for a line of inferior Hummel figurines they copyrighted, produced, and distributed during World War II. Whether the name and rights were expropriated due to the war has not been determined.

name of the picture is Little Knitter. One report says that Wick retired in 1962 when the corporation was purchased by a subsidiary of the W. Goebel Company known as Hummelwerk Sales. This subsidiary was only an American distribution and sales operation and had nothing to do with the manufacture of Hummel figurines, as its name would seem to imply. The new name became Crestwick-Hummelwerk Sales, Inc.

Sometime during the next ten years this corporation took over part of the distribution of M. I. Hummel figurines after the Goebel agreement with Schmid Brothers was terminated. From then until the present, this distribution has been shared in the United States apparently on a nonexclusive basis with a Philadelphia firm. The distribution of greeting cards and related material was carried on along with the Hummel figurines for some time, possibly until 1971, when the name changed to Hummelwerk Sales, Inc. On April 30, 1971 Mr. Morris Kule, who had been with Crestwick, became president of Hummelwerk Sales, a position he still holds. These changes are only a few of about nine that were made in the original corporation since 1939. Today the only other firm known to have copyrighted and produced figurines from the original work of Sister Hummel has become a subsidiary of the original producer of them, the W. Goebel Company of West Germany.

Based on the above information, it appears that the Dubler Hummel figurines are authentic though much inferior to the ones produced by Goebel. Since they were discontinued many years ago, they are a collectible in their own right and of interest to some M. I. Hummel figurine collectors as examples to use for comparison. Even though they are not plentiful, they are still found at conservative prices from time to time. Depending on the model and its condition, the price can range from as low as five dollars to as high as about twenty-five. As more collectors become interested in related collectibles of Hummel art it is not unlikely to assume that these will escalate in price.

Hummel-like Figurines

In addition to Goebel and Dubler copyrighted Hummel figurines, on which royalties have been paid for the privilege of reproducing original Hummel art, there are untold examples of other unauthorized Hummel reproductions. These not only cover a broad range of quality but as wide a range of intent. Some of these reproductions may have been issued to deceive customers into thinking they were genuine "M. I. Hummel" figurines made by the Goebel Company. If so they probably should be classed as "fakes" conceived with the intent of fraud. Since there seemed to be no proof of this fact, they are probably more correctly called unauthorized reproductions which may or may not infringe on existing copyrights.

While the initial intent is not always evident with respect to some of the reproductions that closely resemble "M. I. Hummel" figurines, there are many others that only remotely resemble any genuine Hummel. There are some examples that seem to have been created by using component parts from well-known original art in such a manner as to create the illusion of its being a genuine Hummel figurine. These examples could be referred to as "Hummel-like" or perhaps "Hummel-inspired." They are likely to have been taken from original modeling of another artist who was commissioned to sculpt a model approaching original Hummel figurines in appeal and public acceptance. Frequently another objective may have been a lower sales price. These "cheaper" items are just another proof that imitation is the sincerest form of flattery and at the same time annoying and confusing for collectors.

In the accompanying illustrations in this chapter there are also some examples that would never be mistaken for authentic "M. I. Hummel" figurines. A few of these radically different appearing figures are included to illustrate the extent and variety of childlike figures and to emphasize that there are many small children in various attitudes and actions that are not at all related to Hummel art and are beamed at a different group of buyers and collectors.

Some of the oldest reproductions illustrated were made about thirty years ago. Numbers 32, 33, 34, 35 all came from the same source and were part of an extensive collection of at least fifty different models found in an antique shop in Arkansas. The dealer said that she had purchased them from a lady who was certain they had originally been made in Germany. There seems to be little doubt that they are reproductions of original Hummel art, authorized or unauthorized. Illustration 36 shows the close resemblance between the "M. I. Hummel" figurine, Merry Wanderer on the right of the picture and the unidentified one of Strolling Along on the left. The similarities are striking, but so are the differences. The closer the inspection the more the dissimilarities are apparent. Side by side the quality difference is as apparent

34. *School Girl*, 5½", no maker or numbers, c. 1947.

35. *Shepherd's Boy*, 5¼", no maker or numbers, c. 1947.

173

as the difference between the dog and the valise in the picture. Modeling, mold quality, painting, and features of the unidentified example are all drastically inferior.

The Strolling Along example had no marking of any kind, but two in the same group do have the international copyright insignia and the year 1947 incised on the rear of the base. One in illustration 35 is in the likeness of Shepherd Boy and the other, 34, is in the likeness of School Girl. These two examples are especially interesting because of the religious association highlighted by quotations from scripture incised on specially designed backgrounds. One is "The Lord Is My Shepherd" and the other "Trust in the Lord." Not only are the quotations incised but they have been highlighted with a contrasting color to accentuate them. The quality of the material, which is plaster of parislike, and all other aspects are as inferior to "M. I. Hummel" counterparts as was Strolling Along. Two experts in Hummels who reviewed the color slides of these pieces thought there was such a similarity that they probably were Dubler figures in spite of the 1947 copyright date. Whatever the origin, they represent an interesting unknown that needs to be researched to complete Hummel art history. The prices on these items ranged from about ten dollars for single figures to forty dollars for some of the multiple figure groups.

Illustration 3 is an example that is also about thirty years old and is identified as being made in Japan. This seemed to be "Hummel-inspired" as there seems to be no Hummel art counterpart. It is typical of the imitative products and inferior quality that characterized Japanese exports of that time. Whether this item is of interest to Hummel collectors is immaterial, as it is desirable as a collectible for quite another reason. It is marked "Made in Occupied Japan" and anything so marked has a rapidly expanding following of collectors who specialize in examples so marked. Because of the limited period of time in which this mark was used, examples are not common. However, at present they are still very inexpensive. This figure would probably be valued at five to ten dollars because it is "Made in Occupied Japan" and not because it is a work of art.

Other identified figurines that are currently distributed in the United States are those of the National Potteries Company of Cleveland, Ohio. Examples of which are found in illustrations 16 and 14. They are part of a numbered series imported from Japan. The boy leapfrogging is C8337 marked underglaze on the bottom. The girl figure that seems to have possibly been inspired by "M. I. Hummel" #5 Strolling Along is marked C8747. The only other identification is the foil label of Napcoware with a large letter "N". Once the label is removed identification as to the origin of the model numbers would be difficult or impossible to trace. The drastic improvement in quality from the earlier example of "Made in Occupied Japan" should be obvious even in the small picture. Hand-held, the contrast is dramatic. With retail prices of four and nine dollars respectively they are excellent values and probably will turn up as valuable collectors' items in the years to come.

The second extensive line of figurines widely distributed in this country at this time is imported from Japan by Arnart of New York City. Two examples are shown, one of a boy with watering can (20) and the other of a girl with geese (8). Neither of these pieces is a replica of any original Hummel art, either, but do show "Hummel influence." Both are marked with underglaze "Royal Crown—Hand Painted, 11/541." In addition there is a small oval paper label with "Made in Japan" attached temporarily. The girl is marked "Arnart 5th Ave-Handpainted, 22/620" and with a similar dishwater-susceptible paper label. With the paper label removed, no country of origin would show and the "5th Ave" would imply the United States. The prices on these are somewhat less than the previous two, as well they should be.

Taiwan is represented by illustration 10 of a boy and girl, which are currently distributed in this country at a retail price of about four dollars. This is finished in colored bisque finish as is 1 , which is a small girl figure with a pitcher. This was made in Korea and is currently found for sale in discount stores for one dollar. Perhaps the furthest removed from original Hummel art concept are the figures of the girl and boy shown in illustrations 12 and 13. They are also the most perishable, being wax candles.

Thus reproductions from Sister Hummel's drawings and paintings range from authorized, finely done works of art made by the W. Goebel Company through the authorized figures of Herbert Dubler, Inc., to the somewhat inferior, unauthorized "Hummel-like" items of all types. The collector of "M. I. Hummels," with interest and practice, and using certain clues detailed above, can soon learn to distinguish among all types of Hummel reproductions.

36. *Strolling Along*, no maker or numbers, c. 1947. Right, MERRY WANDERER, Hum. 11/0, TMK-3, c. 1960.

37. Bases of *Strolling Along* (left), and MERRY WANDERER (right).

38. Hummel-like reproductions of greeting cards.

8.

Where to Buy and Sell Hummel Art

Buying Hummel Figurines

There is a scarcity of "M. I. Hummel" figurines, especially if you are trying to buy certain new models. New figurines are defined as those listed in the current distributor's catalog and not previously owned. Very few dealers have an extensive inventory; that is, more than one hundred on hand at any one time. There are some who may not have any to sell for weeks until their next allocation arrives. However, a customer interested in purchasing an "M. I. Hummel" figurine with no particular model or size requirements should have no trouble finding one he likes. It is different if you are a collector or if you are selecting a certain model and size as a gift to a collector and you do not want to duplicate something he already has.

Interviews and answers to some three hundred questionnaires indicated that you may be lucky and find what you want, but the chances are if you deal exclusively with one dealer you may have to wait three months or more. A longer wait may be necessary if

Opposite page: Large group of collectors and dealers examining figurines offered in secondary market.

the figurine you want is not part of the line used to fill allocations. In other words, a special order. Many dealers maintain want lists to minimize this problem. Some have special cards that customers fill out giving the name, number, and size of the figurine(s) they want for their collection, together with their name, address, and telephone number. When the dealer receives his allocation and finds models that are wanted, he calls those customers to let them know that he now has what they are looking for. A typical "want card" is shown in the illustration on this page. Most dealers report that they never know what models they will get in their allocation. The model mix is determined by the distributor unless the dealer places an order and uses part of his quota to order "specials" that are not shipped with regular allotments.

From the survey, it appears that many of the large "M. I. Hummel" dealers having several hundred to over one thousand pieces obtain some of their requirements from several sources in order to have larger selections for their customers. Some of these large dealers buy from overseas sources paying the retail price from authorized Goebel dealers in those countries. In many cases, because of the short markup on overseas purchases, the dealer adds a small percentage over list price on these items. One gift shop that was contacted bought all their requirements from overseas and added a straight 10 percent to the standard list prices. It was the owner's opinion that the customers did not mind the extra 10 percent when they were able to find what they wanted.

Because of supply problems, many an active collector is not content to take his chances on getting what he is looking for from dealers, especially if his dealer's allocation is small — perhaps, twenty-five pieces. Such a collector uses several methods to obtain what he wants more quickly. By filing want cards with more than one dealer he can improve his chances. There are a number of large "Hummel" dealers who sell by mail and advertise what they have for sale in one of several national magazines for collectors, one of which is The *Antique Trader*. The active collector usually subscribes to one or more of these and as a result buys some of his requirements in this way. Some of these advertisers, including ones from Germany and Denmark, are listed under Sources in the Appendices. Normally, they do not list their inventory but welcome inquiries and will "Want List" a collector's needs.

As a convenience to collectors and other buyers of "M. I. Hummel" figurines, we have included a list of dealers who maintain a larger than average supply of figurines on hand at all times and in many cases have some with old trademarks or unusual variations, all of which carry a premium price. This list is not all-inclusive but was compiled as a result of personal inspection or replies to a questionnaire. The intention is to expand this list with future additions as more information becomes available. There are some dealers who try to maintain a wide variety of models and sizes ranging from six hundred to twelve hundred pieces. Usually

CUSTOMER'S WANT CARD

Name _____ Date _____
Street _____ Tele. _____
City _____ State ____ Zip _____
Model No. _____ Name _____
Size _____ Wanted Until _____ Price _____
Comments: _____
_____
Rec'd _____ Notified _____ Hold Until _____
Delivered _____ How _____

they have many of the special order items on hand. In the list are some dealers who handle mail orders and some who do not. Those who advertise at frequent intervals in collectors' magazines are also noted, both in the United States and overseas. Many of these dealers also sell "M. I. Hummel" figurines with older marks. Of course, these items carry a premium price depending on the marks. More details are included in the second part of this chapter.

Selling Hummel Figurines

Now it is time to discuss how to sell some figurines that are no longer wanted. Most of the discussion of buying figurines that preceded applies here. It is just a question of looking at the transaction from the opposite side of the table. It's time to locate the person who wants to acquire this particular example more than anyone else. It is usually impractical for an individual to spend the time, money, and effort to locate the ideal buyer. What are the alternatives?

The quickest and surest way to sell one figurine or a whole collection is by auction. There is almost invariably a buyer at an auction if it is an unrestricted one. (One in which the seller did not agree with the auctioneer on a minimum price below which the auctioneer was not to sell.) While it is quick, you have to pay for the speed. The auctioneer usually charges 20 to 25 percent commission and sometimes the conditions for selling are less than ideal. Perhaps the weather is bad and the attendance low. Maybe the item is offered at the end of a long sale. Many buyers had to leave to get home for dinner and the ones that are left have already exceeded the amount of cash they intended to spend.

There is the other side of the coin though, when prices on most items exceed average expectations and also when some individual ones made new highs. Sometimes it is a new collector or a collector that does not have many of the pieces. These buyers boost the average selling price. And with two or more such people wanting the same figures at the auction the lid can blow off.

Not long ago a "Hummel" figurine was for sale in an antique shop for $250—a fair price which a local collector thought was $50 too high—and the dealer did not want to sell badly enough to come halfway or all the way down to $200. A few months later the dealer was forced to liquidate the business. Did she sell the figurine for $200? She did not. The whole figurine inventory was sent to a well-known auction gallery along with her other antiques and collectibles.

Our collector went to the auction confident he could buy at his price. If he did, the dealer would only realize about $160 after paying the commission. When the one he wanted was offered, the first bid was $50, second $100, third $150, fourth $200, and from there to $1,000 in $50 leaps. After a pause and some encouragement from the auctioneer, another round of raises in $25 steps came rapidly until it was finally knocked down, to the amazement of our collector, for $1,125.

Why did this item that had been for sale for months, all of a sudden bring more than four times the shop price? The answer, in this case, was because two collectors from different parts of the country needed this particular mark and size to fill a hole in their collections and each was determined enough not to let the other have it.

What was the right price? There was no "right price." Probably $250 was a fair estimate of its normal value, but certainly not over $400. It is unlikely that if another one shows up within a year, it will bring $1,000. It may bring more than $250 because of the publicity on this first sale. This demonstrates rather dramatically that the selling price of any collectible, figurines included, can and does vary greatly from any published guide price due to different conditions.

Private sale, sometimes called "house sale," or "tag sale" is another way to sell a collection locally, usually as part of a whole household of furnishings. This is also quick. The disadvantage is the lack of a broad market and reaching out-of-town buyers. The buyers at these sales usually expect to buy at less than normal retail prices.

A more time-consuming method requiring considerable effort is to advertise the item or items for sale in a collectors' magazine with national distribution. This reaches a broad market of other collectors and dealers all over the country. The fairly priced items and "sleepers" (ones worth more than the owner realizes) will usually sell quickly by telephone the same day the magazine is received. If there are quite a few items, some will be sold in the next week by telephone and mail. Some items may not attract any offers.

Then the work begins. Once the checks arrive by mail, the seller usually deposits them and waits ten days for them to clear. No doubt some duplicate checks received too late have to be returned. More information has to be given on some items, and many times pictures are requested in advance.

After a waiting period, unless drafts or money orders were received for immediate shipment, the figurines have to be carefully double packed, addressed, and taken to UPS or other carrier. Most purchasers make their offers subject to personal inspection, with the privilege of returning for refund within three to five days of receipt any item they find unsatisfactory. Anything returned not sold has to be re-advertised or perhaps given to some local dealer to sell on consignment in his shop or shows where he exhibits. The usual commission is 10 percent. Many collectors use consignment selling when they have only one or two items to sell.

Another problem connected with advertising in a national magazine is what prices to use for your figurines. Several avenues are open, such as asking what you paid for them. If your collection was purchased over many years, you will probably jam the telephone lines, since the prices will be below the market. You can also see what other advertisers have asked for the same or similar items in past issues. Whether those offerings were disposed of there is no way of telling.

Having an appraisal made by an experienced appraiser who knows "Hummel" figurines may be well worth the cost if you have only a limited knowledge of market prices. This is especially a wise move if these figurines were a gift and you never had·occasion to know what the retail prices were. Charges for an appraisal are often on an hourly basis and will vary between individuals. Many times the cost of this professional assistance may run from ½ to 1½ percent of the market value, or $50 to $150 on a collection worth $10,000.

One selling suggestion that applies to all kinds of Hummel art (figurines, dolls, plates, or anything related with Hummel collecting) is to give it away. This may sound somewhat strange when you have paid good money for them. Nevertheless, there are good reasons for considering this method of disposing of your individual items or extensive collections. Before selling anything, consider the possibilites of an outright gift, if financial circumstances permit, to various beneficiaries in the following order or priority:

1. An immediate member of the family such as a son or daughter, who will not only enjoy the gift but will also cherish the sentiment attached to it more and more as the years pass. It will have an increased attachment if this practice is followed in succeeding generations. Recently, a descendant of General Lafayette purchased his relative's sword at auction for about $150,000. There must be at least $100,000 of sentiment in that purchase price.

2. A friend or neighbor that has expressed interest in the item. Some have collections of their own that it would enhance. Others will appreciate one as a memento of your friendship or thoughtfulness.

3. A museum or historical society that will be able to use it from time to time in the special exhibits it arranges either locally or as loans to similar organizations. This practice has great merit in sharing your acquisitions with people of all ages for their education and enjoyment in perpetuity. Not every museum will accept all types of gifts. This is especially true if there are a lot of strings attached, such as wanting it

permanently displayed in a prominent place with the donor's name in large bold type.

4. Any other charitable organization. The list is long, ranging from the Salvation Army or Goodwill Industries to your college or church. There is a difference in gifts given to such organizations. Invariably, any charitable organization will, in return, try to find a buyer and liquidate your gift to meet its operating budget or endowment fund. In such cases, there is considerable satisfaction in helping to finance some charitable or educational institution. Most of these organizations get two to ten times the mileage of each gift dollar as Uncle Sam does through welfare rolls and public education.

Uncle Sam is a smart old fellow who has learned a lesson or two in the two hundred years he's been around. He is also wise to how charitable and educational institutions stretch every dollar and pinch every penny. As a result, he has ruled that such gifts are deductible from your income taxes to the same extent as the coin in the Sunday offerings. There are many other ramifications of this charitable deduction. If your gift is large enough, you might talk to your tax lawyer. In some of those cases it may be practical to set up a residual trust where both you and the recipient also can share in a gift deduction and additional income as long as you live.

The older Uncle Sam gets, the smarter he gets. For awhile the "fast buck" boys took him to the cleaners on his offer. They found that by inflating the real value of gifts like some kind of bubble gum, they could get a bigger tax credit. Uncle Sam retaliated by siccing his hounds (they wear a dog tag, I.R. for Internal Revenue) on them. It was not long before their fangs took all the air out of blown-up gift values and, in some cases, the seat of the pants of some of these phony donors.

All of this is just to say if you plan to go this route, it is all perfectly legal if you follow government rules and don't value a few pieces of "Hummel" art at slightly more than the Mona Lisa. How can you be sure that you're playing the game straight? The easiest way is to get a recognized third party who is considered an expert on the fair price of the articles you are donating to set the amount you deduct. For example, museum experts will not do this for gifts to them (or anyone else) as they are not a third party. An appraiser is the best bet and he will give you a signed authentification of the fair market value that you can keep on file in case your phone rings and the voice on the other end says, "Uncle."

Buying and Selling Other Hummel Art

Dolls, prints, pictures, cards, candles, music boxes, and calendars — these are some of the other adaptations of Hummel art besides figurines and plates. There should be no difficulty in buying any of the items new. However, there may be some information accumulated in the survey that could save some time and even some money.

For example, "M. I. Hummel" dolls (refer to the chapter on dolls for more information) are not distributed in the United States by the two distributors of "M. I. Hummel" figurines. Some of the large dealers in figurines also carry dolls but buy them from another distributor in New York City. Others buy them from dealers overseas. The retail prices of the dolls vary considerably. One shop had them for around $30. The highest price encountered was $40. One of the reasons they are not found in more gift shops and doll dealer shops is the price. Generally, doll collectors consider them overpriced compared to other American and imported dolls. Many Hummel collectors have reported that they can buy them overseas for $16 and are therefore reluctant to pay the markup in local gift shops.

All other Hummel art articles are made by other licensed manufacturers or publishers or by those that make reproductions which are Hummel-like and are not licensed. As already mentioned, the Hummel prints are made by two firms in West Germany and have been for as long or longer than Goebel has been making figurines. Each one of them, Emil Fink and Ars Sacra, Josef Müller, also have a book of Hummel pictures and appropriate verses accompanying each illustration. These are listed in the Bibliography at the end of the book. The books, postcards, and greeting cards are carried in those gift shops that handle Hummel figurines. The books are about ten dollars. Individually, the greeting cards and postcards run from twenty-five to fifty cents. A number of the designs are sold in boxes as Christmas cards, with appropriate sentiments printed on the inside, and also as boxed notepaper. In the Sources section, we have listed several large dealers who carry them. There are probably many others.

The prints do not seem to be distributed as widely. Some of the smaller ones, 3" x 4", 4" x 5", are purchased by manufacturers of music boxes, plaques, and boxes to apply to these items by the decoupage method. A good percentage of the larger prints are religious ones and are probably more available in Europe than the States.

While these paper items can be bought new, as indicated in many locations, it is not easy to sell them individually, or as a collection, at the present time. They have not acquired sufficient following as yet to justify the interest necessary for an active secondary market (with the exception of annual "M. I. Hummel" calendars).

If the occasion arises to sell any appreciable quantity of such art, the owners might find it worthwhile to offer items in an advertisement in a national magazine like those listed in the Sources section. There are more and more Hummel figurine collectors becoming aware of other Hummel art and adding it to their collections to add interest and comprehensiveness. At present, a fair offering price might be about half of their original cost or half the present retail price, whichever is higher. An exception is "M. I. Hummel" dolls because they are really bought and sold in the secondary doll market rather than a Hummel secondary market which has thousands of dealers, full and part-time, and certainly tens of thousands of collectors of "pre-owned" dolls. Collectors interested in buying or selling dolls will find many dealers buying and selling through the pages of national collectors' magazines and particularly *Hobbies Magazine.* All of the discussion on buying and selling in the after market or secondary market applies to dolls as well as figurines. There are enough selected prices for the various Hummel dolls included in this book to guide the buyers and sellers in obtaining equitable prices. At this time, there is not the demand, variation, or rarities in the older dolls to necessitate as extensive table as that for figurines.

When buying or selling "M. I. Hummel" dolls, it is essential to remember the confusion and interchangeability that exists between the names Hummel and Goebel. If it is not imprinted M.J.Hummel it is a Goebel.

Schmid Brothers of Boston is another major distributor of Hummel art in various forms. Most of their items are termed "Berta Hummel" rather than "Sister Hummel." You'll find illustrations of these in this book. They are probably best known for their limited edition annual plates. They not only started the same year (1971) as Goebel did with theirs, but they both used the same subject, The Heavenly Angel.

In the ensuing five years the fireworks have died down. The resulting court decision is too voluminous for this book. As a mini-abstract, the Goebel name is associated with "M. I. Hummel" and the works that Sister Hummel produced in the convent. The Schmid name uses the earlier Hummel art done while she was still Berta Hummel.

Buying of any of the broad range of Berta Hummel items distributed by Schmid is no problem. In any medium-sized city or larger, there should be one or more gift shops that handles their current line of limited edition articles. Buying of older Schmid limited editions, articles such as plates, candles, eggs, and bells is the same for all other similar limited edition products. There is an established secondary or after market of specialized dealers listed in the Source section. The *Antique Trader* and *Collector's News* has many more in this category.

Selling any Schmid items that are other than limited editions is fully covered earlier in this section on other products where there is no secondary market. As mentioned before, be prepared to sell them at about half price for the present, or give them where they will be appreciated.

To summarize this section on buying and selling Hummel art other than figurines, it can be concluded that except for the ones that are limited editions, there is not a very good market where collectors can sell individual items or collections. The reason being that there is no secondary market to speak of, which is due to rather passive interest by collectors. If history repeats, it may not be too many years before there is a drastic change. After all, it has not been many years since older "M. I. Hummel" figurines came to be considered highly collectible. Prior to that they were a gift item with a universal appeal and extensive following. The antique and collecting fields abound in similar case histories. One expert said, "Any item of decorative or fine arts has to have a hibernation period of from two to three generations." When granddaughter discovers it is quaint and in short supply, the hobby is off and running. It is pretty obvious that it is already true of "M. I. Hummel" figurines and the chances seem better than ever that the other associated Hummel art will follow suit as has happened in so many other categories.

9.

Caring for Hummel Art

Displaying

Trips totaling eight thousand miles looking and talking about Hummel art proved that professionals and collectors are effectively using many ideas to show Hummel art to full advantage. Some of these ideas are passed along here.

Starting with figurines, many small collections are displayed on open shelves intermingled with books or other art objects. Most of them are out of reach - and, of course, out of bounds for subteen-agers. One collector's home had a 1971 Annual Plate standing on a small stand and resting against the wall. When the value of this plate ($1,000+) was discussed, the plate was removed from the path used by lively six-year-old-twins and placed in a breakfront behind glass doors.

Opposite page. WAYSIDE HARMONY, Hummel 111.

Many plates are mounted on the wall, utilizing the two mounting holes drilled in the raised edge on the underside in almost all Annual Plates. It has been reported that the plates sent to one European country do not have the mounting holes because there was a lower import duty if they were omitted. All of which makes an interesting variation for the alert collector to add to his collection.

Whether hanging plates or Hummel prints, which come in various sizes, the type of hanger which is secured by a nail driven on a slant seems more secure than some of the new pressure-sensitive adhesive mounts. Many collectors are adding a touch of interest to one or a group of Annual Plates by purchasing round wooden frames that act as a frame for the plates and thereby also add insurance against breakage.

A more recent trend is the rectangular shadow box. This is a glass-fronted box trimmed in wide molding. The most popular now are the ones that are large enough to enclose both the plate and the corresponding figurine. There are mounts for both of these included in the shadow box. Against the dark background, the figurine and matching plate are in an effective contrast. The glass front keeps both objects clean and secure. These combinations have become so popular that the figurine Ride into Christmas which matches the 1975 plate is in very great demand. In fact, the price during 1976 reached $150 instead of $86 shown in the official price list published by Goebel. In the Sources section of this book, the names of two manufacturers of many varieties of these frames are listed.

As personal collections grow, most owners group them together in some sort of display cabinet. Half-round French and antique china cabinets are two of many types used. Those with glass shelves and mirrored backs are most effective. The cabinets not only provide more security and cleanliness but offer the option of installing lighting for further attractiveness. Standing or custom designed built-in cabinets with lighting included are used to provide uniform housing as the collection grows. The supports for the shelving should be checked for adequacy. Glass shelves should be heavy plate glass. A personal experience of finding a heap of shattered Steuben glass due to a presumably defective glass shelf is a vivid reminder of the damage potential. In this instance, a fine arts floater insurance policy covered the $3,400 loss, but not the bereavement suffered for some of the very rare pieces.

If the lighting has to be added to existing freestanding or built-in cabinets, it should be as uniform and as diffused as possible. If fluorescent lights are used, the cool white or daylight types do not distort the true colors as much as other types. Very effective displays have been noted where spotlighting was also used to highlight important items. In any event, care must be exercised to keep the light sources screened from normal viewing angles, which is difficult to do with mirrored-backed cabinets.

If open shelves are used, consideration should be given to using bell jars to emphasize important pieces and at the same time keep them dustproof and touchproof. In either type installation a neutral, dark-colored background seems to be used more frequently and makes the lighter colored figurines stand out.

Where the collection is not too numerous, very effective displays can be made with one or two figurines in settings that are appropriate to the subject. For example, the Little Fiddler could be on a simulated stand or small stage giving a concert to an audience of a few small seated figurines. Introducing woodland or street scenes, snowy hills for the skier, barnyard animals to scale for the Goose Girl, and many more can be very effective.

The more recent Hummel calendars published by Goebel have twelve such arrangements in each year, one for every month. These offer unlimited ideas which can be adapted to the figure and space available. Dealers in miniature replicas now provide a wide variety of scale model items for collectors which can be utilized just as doll collectors do when they want to make small doctors' offices for a doctor and nurse dolls. Farmyard, bedroom, patio, garden—name your wants and you can design your own background to complement your favorite figurine. Chances are you can find a source that has ready-made articles to fit the scene. If not, model train hobby stores have many items that fit in. Do-it-yourself is another whole and satisfying approach.

A discussion of scenes which fit one or more figurines would be incomplete without mention of the Hummel Nativity sets (illustrated and itemized in this book), because Goebel has designed the appropriate background to complement the figures and has added some non-Hummel figures such as the camel to further enhance the scene. Fortunately, these smaller sets can be purchased by individual pieces so they can be added to year by year until the whole assembly is complete. Even with only the essential three figures of Virgin, Child, and Joseph an appropriate background can be improvised at a small cost.

Some of the large collections suffer from overcrowding. What was adequate space several years ago, is now so jam-packed that the collection looks like a TV shot of Times Square in New York on New Year's Eve. The most effective displays are those in which the individual figurines have elbowroom to be enjoyed individually. "How many make a mob scene?" you might ask. It depends entirely on the taste of the collector — a fact sometimes lost sight of from the standpoint of others. And after all, one of the pleasures of collecting is to share your effort with others. Shoulder to shoulder arrangements won't show the collection to the best advantage.

As department store owners have their display windows changed at frequent intervals, so do collectors change the arrangement of theirs. If the collection is exceptionally large, it can still be more fully appreciated by arranging new figures "front and center" two or three times a year. A few collections may be like museums' where only the tip of the iceberg shows. In many museums, there is less than 10 percent of their fabulous collections on public display. The other 90 percent, thank Providence, gets viewed on a rotating basis. If you have a "museum size" collection of figurines or other Hummel art, try their workable formula of giving each portion its day in the sun rather than trying to get them all sunburned at once. Your friends and fellow collectors will be the beneficiaries of your efforts.

One other museum procedure worth considering is "sharing the wealth." Lending portions of a collection to others on a temporary basis deserves consideration. Perhaps there is an Oktoberfest in your area that would appreciate an added attraction — so might your public library, one of the branches, a bank, hobby show, antiques fair, or a dozen other worthwhile extracurricular activities. So much for display of figurines and other Hummel art, as the principles apply to dolls, prints, plates, postcards or what have you. Now, a few paragraphs on what some of your fellow collectors and those interested in other types of antiques or collectibles are doing to protect their acquisitions.

Insuring and Protecting

In seeking to protect valuables, two paths sometimes are straddled in hopes of attaining a satisfactory solution. One choice is to insure the collection to its full value and then relax and enjoy it. The second is to build high fences, install floodlights, automatic detection, direct-dial police devices, and then sit back and relax. The third approach is, obviously, to have the best of both worlds—go for both—with double the relaxation—and invoices. In fact some types of insurance are only written after specified protection is installed.

For the first path—insurance—the man to listen to is your agent. All this book can do is to provide some generalities and examples because protection of most good collections is customized to fit the circumstances. Since the introduction of comprehensive insurance policies on your home, its contents, and quite a list of hazards, most homeowners have obtained much broader coverage at much more reasonable rates. It may be that some policyholders have considered this a cycloneproof umbrella. That may not be the case. One hazard that figurines are subject to is breakage. This is not covered in many policies. The limits of the comprehensive or "homeowners" may not be sufficient to cover a large collection. There may be other exclusions and low limits depending on the insurance company.

The so-called fine arts policy or floater policy is designed to fill in some omissions and limitations of conventional policies and, of course, is an additional charge. For a Hummel figurine collector, it should cover breakage. The art glass example is a good illustration of what can happen. Vandalism or robbery are other important coverages. The comforting part of this insurance contract is the inventory and values of the articles covered by it. With a valid appraisal made by an experienced professional there is not much question about the existence or value of the component parts of the collection. The adjustment should be fast and equitable based on the written contract. Some such policies have a 20 percent clause that can be very valuable to an active collector. This provides for full coverage of items not inventoried at the time the contract was signed. In other words additions to the collections up to 20 percent of the value of the collection at time of issuance are covered until the next inventory or renewal of the contract. Some policies cover items that are not in the home such as items purchased while traveling.

"What's a package like this cost?" is usually the first question asked. Again that can best be determined for your particular requirements by talking to a local insurance agent. Some policies in the fine arts category cost around ½ percent of value per year. On a $20,000 collection the premium might range around $100 per year for each of the three years of the contract. Some insurers require submitting a revised inventory each year or notification of no change in status. One specialist in writing fine arts policies is listed in the Sources section.

Many of the collectors that carry this type of extra policy say, "In case of a breakin there is no incentive to risk a confrontation resulting in a loss of life or physical impairment. Let the intruders have what they want — it's fully covered." This plus coverage of breakage and mysterious disappearance are features that could prove to be very advantageous.

The other path of preventing loss or damage to a collection is by protective devices that will circumvent a breakin or give an automatic signal of any attempt. The sophistication of these systems varies widely, and rapid advances are frequently making the headlines. Some utilize a combination of electronic and ultrasonic detection. The alarm may be given inside the house or inside and outside of the house. Others, in addition, are connected to some protective agency or directly to the local police. Many are custom-designed to the requirements of the clients and the features of the house.

Obviously, the costs of such systems vary widely. There are a number of agencies in most cities listed in the Yellow Pages which provide such services. Estimates from their representatives are necessary to have any reliable figure on which to base a decision. Information from various collectors indicates that an installed

system with complete coverage may cost upwards to $5,000. Others may run under a thousand and seem entirely adequate for the specific application.

Once again manufacturers have recognized the do-it-yourself market by designing self-contained plug-in ultrasonic units beamed to cover specific zones such as doorways. Any change in the reflected sound pattern will trigger the alarm and in some cases a reporting mechanism. There are several makes, one of which is by 3M, that have a unit which looks like a book. These self-contained units cost somewhat over one hundred dollars each.

The simplest and least expensive system encountered consists of three small labels that were purchased for one dollar. Applied to the doors of a house, they advise callers that the house is protected by something like the "National Alarm Service." Whether the effectiveness of these is relative to their cost probably depends a great deal on the interest and determination of the "uninvited guest."

A final suggestion to protect valuables is to mark the items themselves. The marks can be a social security number, initials, a special accession number assigned the piece by the owner, or any other recognizable code. These numbers can be engraved with a special engraving tool produced by Dreml and available at hardware stores. Diamond point pencils will also permanently mark possessions. There is also an invisible marking pen kit available for $2.50 (see Sources). It makes marks that can be read under ultraviolet light. An illustration from a recent Brookstone Company catalog is reproduced here to give more information and prices.

Many collectors follow a routine procedure of regularly updating the inventory of their collections, including a complete file of photographs showing each item. A recent inventory accompanied by recent photographs is an invaluable aid to a claims adjuster in the event of a loss. If this inventory and list of photographs are kept in a safety deposit box, and if they are regularly updated and reviewed, items can also be more easily identified if recovered by the police.

Whether elaborate or simple, there are suitable methods of protection for any size or type of collection. It is important that the collector choose one that suits him. Then he can relax and enjoy his collection.

Cleaning

The M. I. Hummel figurines provoke more questions about cleaning than any other form of collectible in this book. Many questioners express concern about what washing might do to the finish and colors. A good answer to these questions can be found in a recent newsletter of the Hummel Collectors Club. Dorothy Dous, the editor, says, "When I come home (from an auction) I wash each Hummel with a heavy detergent—believe me 'Top Job,' 'Grease Relief,' 'Janitor in a Drum,' and I would imagine any other heavy detergent will not harm your old Hummel. It will only make them super clean and beautiful again. It will also remove most of the paint from areas that have been 'touched-up'."

While Hummel figurines are detergent proof, they are too fragile to be dishwasher proof. The reason they will tolerate rugged detergents is that they are a quality product. The colors are sealed in under a glass-hard surface produced from the final high temperature firing of the coating covering all decoration. One possible caution in a complete deep wash might be with respect to trapping some of the solution of detergent inside. Large openings found in figurines made years ago show an unglazed surface which might absorb the standing solution over a long period of time. Chances of damage seem slim if the figurines are rinsed and drained thoroughly. The newer figurines with solid bottoms must have small ventholes added in inconspicuous places for the hot gaseous moisture to escape in the firing. These holes are probably too small to allow much water to enter. If there is any doubt or concern, the collector can temporarily or permanently plug these holes.

The extra dividend mentioned by Dorothy Dous gained from washing the figurines bears repeating. This treatment is likely to remove any touch-up paint added to cover small blemishes. This added cover-up is over the glaze and probably would not readily adhere. If such a "super-wash" does not reveal any "added decorations," a black light will.

The advantages of keeping figurines in a glassed-in display cabinet were mentioned in the section on displaying. Yet another advantage is that once cleaned, no strong detergent cleaning should be necessary for a long, long time. When it is time for cleaning, the job can be done "on location," which will minimize the risk of breakage possible from transporting the figurines to and from the kitchen as well as damage in the sink. Many makes of treated cleaning cloths, including professional tack rags are effective. Some of the foam and spray cleaners can also be used successfully near the display case. This same method, possibly with increased frequency, also can be used on figurines on open shelves.

In the remote chance that a reader has an original work of Hummel art in the form of a charcoal or pastel drawing, or even one of Sister Hummel's paintings, the best suggestion for cleaning such a work of art is **DON'T**. The cleaning or restoring of fine art should be turned over to a capable professional. There should be little need for such service, however, if the original has been properly framed and not subjected to unusual light or humidity. The prints and pictures made from these originals are probably not valuable enough to warrant a professional restoration, especially since new ones are still available at a nominal cost. For a well-framed print, the only part that might need cleaning is the glass in front of the frame, which is usually done as part of the general cleaning schedule anyway.

Repairing

"M. I. Hummel" figurines are probably the only example of Hummel art that are valuable enough to consider having professionally repaired. Even then it would probably have to be an item worth over a hundred dollars to justify a repair that may cost twenty to forty or more dollars. Often sentiment may be a more important factor in the decision than the value. A fine old example handed down through the family, one purchased on a special trip, an important anniversary gift, a remembrance sent home by a son or daughter on duty in Germany are examples that may be treasured for more than the dollar value. Here economics and eventual resale price are of little consequence.

Does professional repair that is undistinguishable by the average collector restore the item to a price equal to an unrestored or mint example? Collectors have already answered this question in numerous cases recorded at auctions and private sales. The broad rule of thumb seems to be that the value of an average figurine with minor imperfections (i.e., a flake in an inconspicuous place or a fine repair of more serious damage) will center around 50 percent of the value of the same item in mint condition.

This rule falls apart for the scarce, rare, unusual, or unique examples. Just as the market price of perfect ones in this category will have no stable price, so will the value of repaired examples vary widely from 50 percent to perhaps 90 percent of the perfect ones. It is important to know that advanced collectors and museums are perfectionists. They will tolerate only the finest specimens to be had, with one exception. When a unique (one-of-a-kind) example appears with some damage most collectors and museums accept it. They have no choice. Museums, especially, seem willing to make exceptions for extremely rare pieces. They feel a real obligation to preserve and display the whole or entire scope of an art, craft, or whatever their specialty. Did the Vatican scrap Michelangelo's, *LaPieta* because some unbalanced individual used a sledge hammer on it? Of course not. Did the Corning Museum of Glass display just the fragments of the world-famous Venetian Dragon-stem Goblet after the flood had subsided? Not at all. Were the hundreds of books and paintings by the great Italian artists left waterlogged in Florence after their disastrous flood? Again a resounding "No." All of these cases looked hopeless. Today after scientists and expert artisans teamed up to develop new products and techniques for repair and restoration these priceless items are again available for public education and enjoyment. In many cases the damage is invisible to an unaided eye. The same principles apply to Hummel art. The greater the rarity of an item the greater the time and money that will be spent restoring any imperfections. The value of such items will approach the value of a similar perfect piece.

To sum up—while normally a damaged piece may only be worth about half that of a perfect example — sentiment, historical value, and rarity may make major restorations not only acceptable but mandatory. The restored piece will be almost equal in value to a perfect one.

In replying to our questionnaire, Hummel collectors indicated a need for more information on where to get Hummel figurines repaired. Since their porcelain is so hard and brittle, the figurines can and do suffer occasional accidental damage. To assist collectors or dealers who have had this happen to their pieces, a list of restorers has been added to other sources listed in the back of the book. It is certain there are many more qualified professionals who should be listed. Information on additional sources is welcome and will be incorporated in later editions. The experts listed are there as a result of recommendations by satisfied customers. The only exceptions to complete satisfaction have been an almost unanimous comment on how long it takes to get the job done, but followed with an expression of gratitude that the results were worth waiting for.

While the cost of repair is high because of the skill and time involved, customers seem to understand and appreciate the results, feeling them to be worth the charge. Most people want to know the cost involved before giving approval for repair. It seems to be quite common practice to take or send the damaged object to a qualified restorer with a request for an estimate of the cost to be incurred and the time involved for the repair. Restorers are usually willing to hold the article until they hear from the customer and then proceed with the repair or return the item.

For those readers having no experience in shipping fragile articles, extreme care should be taken not to provoke more damage by the way items are packed or shipped. Briefly, select a corrugated container about 50 to 100 percent bigger than the object. Wrap the figure in tissue, then twice more in soft wrapping paper or newspaper. Fill the voids in the box with crumpled newspaper to form a cushion on all sides. Only one article to a box is a must. Place the sealed box(es) in another larger carton and fill in the voids on all sides with newspaper or professional packing material like the new polyurethane foam "popcorn." After sealing and labeling it "fragile" send it by United Parcel Service, insured for its full value. The United States Postal Service is a poor second choice but may have to be used in some areas. Air Express or Freight and Greyhound buses are other alternatives.

With the giant strides made during the last twenty-five years in the repair and restoration of porcelain, how do Hummel buyers protect themselves from buying skillfully repaired pieces at mint condition prices? In two ways; both of which are used extensively. The first and by far the easiest and best way is to know the seller. If he is a longtime dealer with an impeccable record for honesty and fair dealing you're home free. He is probably more solicitous in checking what he buys than you are. He has his reputation to protect. He has his years of experience to guide him and has probably developed a sixth sense in detecting any deviations from standard. Furthermore, if at a later date it turns out he was in error, he not only will want the return of the figurine for a full refund—he will insist on it.

Should there be any skepticism concerning the authenticity or condition of a high-priced figurine, it is good business to request a written statement on the bill of sale when buying from an unknown source. It should contain words to the effect that the article is perfect and as described; and if found not to be, it may be returned for a full refund within a reasonable time (five to twenty days). Where it is necessary to buy figurines by mail this statement is practically mandatory and will not be resented by reliable dealers.

The second method of assurance has come into extensive use with the much higher priced figurines such as Royal Worchester's Dorothy Doughty birds which are priced in the thousands and the similarly high priced Edward Marshall Boehm bird sculpture limited editions. It is the employment of ultraviolet light to disclose imperfections. This is commonly referred to as "black light." Many dealers have units for their own protection when they buy, and make them available for the use of their customers. Advertisements for a scarce example frequently specify that any piece offered for sale must pass the "black light" test. Insistence on black light examinations should not be resented. It is a protection for both parties. Some almost invisible repairs can only be distinguished by such means.

Certainly, someone is saying, "That's all very fine for the few collectors who have figurines that are worth hundreds or even thousands of dollars, but what about the majority of us who may have only a few inexpensive ones that have been damaged?" The tried-and-true formula for repairs that has been successfully used by thousands of collectors of every conceivable kind of object is "do-it-yourself." Just as many advances have been made for amateur repairing and restoring as there have been for professional. In some cases, it is the same material. In the Bibliography there are several books listed on repairing which include detailed illustrations, steps, and lists of materials. Complete kits can be purchased for mending ceramics. With such guides and materials and with patience and care your chances of success are good. The dividends in satisfaction are enormous whether it is only the repair of a wing tip or the assembling of several pieces in perfect alignment. The savings in cost are added inducements. Who knows—you may be on your way to another absorbing hobby.

Next to figurines, perhaps dolls are the most subject to damage, especially since they are made to be played with and not just for display. As doll collectors know, there are many fine doll hospitals. If there is not one near you, there are some as near as your mailbox. The owners of these "hospitals" have a deep attachment for dolls and usually do a superb job of repair, including providing new eyes, wigs, and new outfits.

The one bit of bad news on Hummel dolls concerns the ones made of rubber some years before the introduction of the improved vinyl. The early ones were painted to give more natural flesh colors. For some reason, a percentage of them collapsed. Sometimes the knees buckle; sometimes the face creases across the eyes. In any event, according to information from several doll authorities, these older dolls do not lend themselves to repair.

As for remaining Hummel art, prints, pictures, and cards are the most numerous. The repair of prints, paintings, and pictures is a highly specialized craft. Tears, rips, and yellowing of the paper can be restored by experts if the original piece is valuable — as it would certainly be if you were fortunate enough to have an original signed M.J.Hummel . Damaged frames, mats, or glass can be repaired by any good picture framing company in the larger cities or by the owner. Some suggested sources for both the artwork and frame are listed.

Other articles using Hummel art such as boxes, bells, plates, eggs, candles, and others can be restored if worthwhile by specialists in the materials used. At present, most of these items would not be worth repairing, except for sentiment, since replacements can be bought for less than the cost of any major repair.

10.

The Future of Collecting

Hummel Art as an Investment

These comments were purposely put in the back of the book. Just as this section may be one of the last things to be read, so should the idea of buying figurines or any other adaptation of Sister Hummel's work as an investment be the last thing to enter a collector's mind. Buy art for art's sake. Buy because you like what you see. Buy because it will give you more satisfaction as the years pass. Hummel art was meant to be enjoyed. Buy it for that reason, not because next year the price may go up 10 percent, or in hopes that in ten years it may pay off the mortgage on the house, or because someone said this was a better way of making money fast. Horse races, numbers games, and state lotteries were designed for people who want to make money fast. Hummel art should be bought for one purpose—enjoyment.

Opposite page. VISITING AN INVALID, Hummel 382.

If it is bought to enhance the surroundings, then there is better than a thousand-to-one chance the purchaser will not only get what he paid for, but even more in most cases. First, the longer a piece is owned, the more satisfaction and enjoyment will be derived from it. Thousands, yes millions, of purchasers of Hummel art will surely subscribe to this. Since the attachment and intangible value will increase with time, the buyer invariably has made an excellent investment in personal well-being.

There are many instances in which Hummel art that was purchased for its artistic merit and intangible value turned out to be more valuable than the buyer had anticipated. This news frequently comes as a pleasant surprise. A surprise because enhanced monetary value was not the primary motivation, as it should not have been. For example, a collector might have made an initial purchase of a Merry Wanderer, #7/0 about 6″ high in Germany in 1950. At that time the price was 18.70 deutsche marks or about $4.70. This popular "M. I. Hummel" figurine is still available in the latest price list. The price in the United States is now $60.50. Imagine, about thirteen times more than the 1950 price. What a terrific investment! Maybe, during that time interval, at least half the increase, or five times the original price, is due to inflation. Some of the price spread is also due to devaluation of the U.S. dollar. Collectors now pay about 40 percent more for figurines from Germany due to "floating rates of exchange." Except for one factor, the owner of this 1950 Merry Wanderer probably would be able to sell his figurine today to a dealer for about one-hundred eighty dollars. Everything considered, he got his money back and then some, but his real gain was the twenty-seven years of enjoyment he got from owning the piece.

In selling the figurine above, the exception noted was the law of supply and demand. This law has been operating during the twenty-seven year interval and has changed numbers rather drastically. The supply of 1950 "M. I. Hummel" Merry Wanderer figurines has remained about constant, excluding loss or breakage, but the number of people wanting the old examples has increased dramatically. So many collectors want the few examples made in 1950 that today the going price for them is as much as four times the present retail price for the identical figure in current production. That is forty times the original 1950 price. Now that is appreciation! Five dollars to two-hundred in twenty-seven years is an increase comparable to receiving almost 15 percent compounded on five dollars invested in 1950. Even if the original owner sells it to a dealer for about one hundred dollars, he will still be receiving the equivalent of about 12 percent on his money.

Two more examples will further illustrate the possibilities. In 1971 the first "M. I. Hummel" Annual Plate was issued to commemorate the founding of the W. Goebel Company in 1871. The retail price of the plate was $25. These plates, with a bas-relief likeness of the Heavenly Angel, were only available during that year. Therefore the quantity, unlike the Merry Wanderer, was limited to the number produced during that year. The issue was a smash hit. As Jimmy Durante said, "Everyone wanted to get into the act." With the demand greater than the supply, the price started moving upward at an accelerated pace until six years later the asking price for this plate is one thousand dollars or more. A twenty times increase in six years is almost unbelievable. The rate of return is incredible and amounts to something like 70 percent a year on the original investment. Certainly those who purchased 1971 plates for decoration and enjoyment have received quite an added and unanticipated bonus in appreciation. The obvious conclusion from these two examples is that "M. I. Hummels" are one of the best investments in the world. They must be a surefire way of making money, so why bother with any other motive for buying them? Just put your savings into buying all the figurines possible, store them for twenty years or less, and reap a big fat profit. For readers attracted to this reasoning, let's look at a final example.

Since 1971, a new Annual Plate has been issued each year. After the smashing success of the 1971 plate, thousands who missed that bargain wanted to catch up with the front-runners, so the next year many bought more than one plate as an *investment*. (It is doubtful that two plates are likely to give twice as much visual enjoyment.) The retail price of the 1972 plate was $38. Although the number sold has never been made public, with the demand sky-high, it seems likely it was much greater than the number sold in 1971. Today, five years later, these plates are listed for about $76 each.

What kind of investment did this 1972 plate turn out to be? Since 1972 there has been at least one year of "double-digit" inflation with an average of perhaps 7 percent a year. If the $38 had been invested at 7 percent, five years later it would be worth about $53. A profit of $76 − $53, or $23 more than a savings account? No, because a dealer will only pay a collector about $40 for one, or $2 over the original price. The "investor" has lost $53 − $40, or $13 when compared to putting this money in a savings account.

It appears that with Hummels, like any other investments, there are some that turn out well and some that don't. A great deal seems to depend on the law of supply and demand. Will history repeat itself? Will some present Hummel items be great investments in years to come and others a losing proposition? What do the chances look like? The chances look exceptionally good for the future buyers of Hummel art to receive huge dividends in enjoying their acquisitions for what they are—a work of art. There is also always the possibility, but an uncertain one, of realizing an additional cash dividend when and if they have to be disposed of.

For the investors and/or speculators the picture is unclear or muddy to say the least. One dealer published a list of fifty-some discontinued figurines that may be reissued in the next few years.

The number and form of these reissues will have a major effect on the value of similar ones now in collections. New fads, new artists, depressions, wars, and many other imponderables, including the dwindling supply of energy, will influence the answer. So, for those who want to make money investing in Hummel art there is always the crystal ball and tea leaves to provide answers. A million or more buyers have probably discovered the best approach. They buy it if they like it—and reap the rewards in personal pleasure.

The Hummel Collectors' Club

Many of you reading this already know about the club. Many more are learning about it from present members. For those of you who don't, you should get to know Dorothy Dous, one of the country's more advanced collector-dealers. In addition, this dedicated lady had been publishing a quarterly newsletter. The *Hummel Collectors Newsletter* is loaded with unpublished information about this young hobby. And, she has been doing this singlehandedly since 1976. There is a rumor that her husband gets drafted as an assistant now and then. Prior to this, she published it as the *International Goebel Collectors Club Newsletter*. The name was changed in 1976 at the request of W. Goebel Company, which then formed a club called Goebel Collectors Club. Details on this club are given in the following section.

Renaming the club "Hummel" was a "giant step" forward for the hobby, thanks to Goebel. Goebel is only one company producing decorative arts and crafts which have been inspired by an original work of art by Sister M. I. Hummel nee Berta Hummel (1909-1946). Collectors are already confused by the true relationship between these two names, Goebel and Hummel. This relationship is discussed in detail in an earlier section of this book in an effort to eliminate this unfortunate confusion. Renaming the club also serves the same end.

For Hummel figurine collectors, the *Club Newsletter* has another valuable feature. It contains short, concise ads from members who want to sell all or part of their collection or from those who are trying to buy certain figurines to fill a spot in theirs. In arranging this, Dorothy has assigned a number to each ad so that the advertiser's privacy is maintained. Members interested in an ad send a letter addressed to the number shown, care of the club. Dorothy then forwards the unopened letter to the advertisers for any further action. Ready for the good news? The ads are free to club members.

On learning about the club, the most frequent comment is, "Where is the catch?" If there's any catch, it's Dorothy who is caught in the middle of trying to write, edit, duplicate, and mail this *Newsletter* every quarter without going broke on the membership dues of ten dollars a year. Those wanting more details should address their inquiries to Mrs. Dorothy Dous, 1261 University Dr., P. O. Box 257, Yardley, Pennsylvania 19067.

The Goebel Collectors' Club

The W. Goebel Company of Rodenthal, West Germany initiated the Goebel Collectors' Club in 1977 through its subsidiary Goebel Art, Inc., of 105 White Plains Rd., Tarrytown, New York 10591. For an annual fee of ten dollars members receive a membership card, four issues of *Goebel Collectors News*, a gold binder for the newsletters, brochures, and catalogs detailing new products, a chance to purchase special figurines available to members only, discounts on charter flights to Germany, charter trips to Coburg with a special tour of the factory at Rodenthal (including a Bavarian lunch), and a commemorative plaque proclaiming their membership.

The Goebel Collectors' Club is just what the name says. It is a club for collectors of Goebel products of all types — figurines by Charlot Byj, "M.I. Hummel," Janet Robson, Hanns Welling, and Lore, as well as their other plates. Emphasis is on the company, its history, and its products of all kinds.

Hummel Look-Alike Contest

In addition to sponsoring The Goebel Collectors' Club, the W. Goebel Porzellanfabrik of West Germany has sponsored for many years a Hummel figurine Look-Alike Contest. The contestants are children from two to eight years old posed and costumed as much like Hummel figurines as possible. The winners are chosen from photographs submitted to the company. Entry blanks may be obtained from Hummel dealers, and there is no fee for entering. Prizes can be as much as $1,000 in cash and a portrait.

Your Two Cents' Worth

"Your two cents' worth" is sincerely solicited. It will be welcomed warmly. To many readers, the term "two cents' worth" may be a derogatory slang expression. Please think of it like this—it takes fifty people, each contributing two cents, to make a whole dollar. Five hundred such contributions makes ten dollars and a bowl full of pennies — 1,000.

It is advice that is wanted, not coin of the realm. Perhaps you may consider it as only two cents' worth. Be assured there are hundreds, more likely thousands, that will value your contributions much more generously. A two-cent effort on your part, may be well worth hundreds or even thousands of dollars worth of satisfaction to many collectors. Many are anxiously waiting for your comments, for you to share your discoveries and opinions with them. As might be expected, the sharing of "two cents' worth" is not a one-way street. Your offerings may be returned many times by what you learn from someone else's "two cents' worth."

Readers are urged to write to the author if they have questions, or wish to point out errors in this or other books, are able to fill in missing information, or just want to sound off. When you're reading the book and feel a comment coming on, jot it down right then. Jot what down? Here are a few for instances:

1. You find a mistake in the book.
2. This book and something else you read, don't agree.
3. Something was omitted that you wanted to know more about.
4. You know something the book did not mention.
5. Anything you read which you do not fully understand.
6. An idea(s) of how this book could be more help to dealers and collectors.
7. Comments about your unusual Hummel art.
8. Anything else that comes to your mind.
9. Or, just to say "Hello."

"That's great," you say, "but, after I go to all that trouble what good will it do?" Here's the plan. Address your letter to John F. Hotchkiss, 306 Bay Village Dr., Rochester, N.Y. 14609. Put a stamp on it and drop it in the nearest mailbox. Then what happens? It could be one of several things. When a question is asked, it is hoped that many of them will be answered by Dorothy Dous in the Hummel Collectors Club Newsletters, issued four times a year. (See preceding pages for more details on this club.) In case you're not a member it may be possible to send you a complimentary copy of the bulletin that includes your answer if you have included a self-addressed stamped (#10) envelope. If your letter relates to the contents of the book, the author should be able to reply within a reasonable time. Perhaps some of your replies will be bundled together for forwarding to the Goebel Company or to any other producer of Hummel art from whom action or comment has been requested. Some of the new information on Hummel art collecting and price changes will be accumulated and incorporated in later editions of this book. In fact, who knows, you may get nominated for the best contribution or even for the Hummel Board of Consultants, as it is always in need of members who want to help Hummel art collecting be more enjoyable for everyone.

Appendix I

History of Goebel Company —
How Figurines Are Made

All "M. I. Hummel" figurines are made by the Goebel factory, located in the southern part of West Germany. The factory, currently headed by the fifth generation of the Goebel family, began in 1871 by making slate, blackboards, and marbles. In 1879, a porcelain kiln was built, and dinner services, beer steins, egg cups, and other such practical items were produced, as well as bisque doll heads. Ceramic figurines were added to the line in 1926, but Hummel figurines, based on drawings by Sister Maria Innocentia Hummel were not produced until 1935 after the company made contractual arrangements with her convent. With World War II limiting the export business, the firm concentrated on the domestic dinnerware market. After the war production boomed. Some sources attribute it to the GI's stationed in West Germany. So much so, in fact, that Goebel set up a U.S. subsidiary called Hummelwerk to do some of the distribution in the States. During the 1960s, W. Goebel Company, employing over 1,400 people, had established itself dramatically—especially with its world-famous "M. I. Hummel" figurines.

The Hummel figurines that were added to the Goebel line in 1935 were the result of a special agreement, including royalties, between the Siessen Convent of the Franciscan Order, to which Sister Hummel belonged, and the Goebel firm. The convent and Sister Hummel agreed to allow Goebel to use the sister's original sketches of art in order to adapt her two-dimensional works into three-dimensional figurines. All such work was strictly subject to convent approval and changes of each item before it could be produced and sold. While still alive, Sister Hummel took an active part in reviewing all models. One report indicates that she even participated in the sculpting of them.

Once a new design is approved for production, the original model of the figurine is cut into many parts, separating arms, legs, heads, and bodies, each to be made into an individual mold. These little molds are used to create plaster of paris forms which, in turn, are used to create the acrylic working models. From these acrylic working models, plaster of paris working molds are created in which the parts are actually cast (see illustration #1). These production molds are filled with a thin, creamy mixture of porcelain slip. The porous plaster of paris mold rapidly absorbs the excess water leaving a soft, damp, solid replica of the part to be removed when the two halves of the mold are opened.

1. Goose Girl, 200. A new working mold for body of the girl showing special, black, production-standard body piece in place from which the mold was formed.

2. Finished "green" (unfired) body of Goose Girl at left, small parts in foreground and the completely assembled figure.

One report states that prior to 1954 the Goebel firm made their working models out of plaster of paris as well. As a result, the model expanded about 1 percent at each pouring. Therefore, the figurines sometimes "grew" as much as 10 to 20 percent. This condition may explain many of the size variations in the older figurines. With the introduction of acrylic working models, firgurine sizes are now much more standard.

After the figurine sections are removed from their respective molds, the assembler puts them together using a thin slip to bond them and following a master model identified by a special metal seal (see illustration #2). The assembler also puts the venthole in the bottom of the figurine or some inconspicuous place to prevent its exploding upon being fired. For this first, "bisque," firing, because the figurines are still rather moist clay, support pieces are used to maintain the correct shapes. After being slowly cooled they are then coated with a sizing and sent to the decorating department (see illustration #3).

The figurines are then painted by expert craftsmen who have served a five-year apprenticeship in their craft. Since the 1950s, with the development of metallic oxide paints, the colors of these more recent figurines do not fade, dull, or mellow as did the older figurines. After most of the figurine is painted, special craftsmen paint the face to insure uniformity of expression (see illustration #4). It is at this point that the artist's mark may be put on the bottom. This tiny brush mark is reported by one source to be that of the artist who painted the face.

After final firings, the figurines are inspected and packed into custom-formed styrene inner packs for distribution to millions of Hummel fanciers the world over.

3. The assembled figure at the left. A similar figure after dipping in a blue glaze before firing in the center. On the right the glazed porcelain figure after emerging from the kiln. (The blue color disappears in the firing.)

4. Steps in painting the figurine requiring different levels of skill. From left to right: (a) lips, eyebrows, and hair finished; (b) dress added; (c) bonnet and geese bodies colored; (d) completed piece with face, costume, and base ready for final firing.

Appendix II

Sources: Auctioneers, Buying and Selling, Display, Insurance, Other

The names in this section have been put here for you to help yourself. They are here to assist you when there is a problem. Perhaps you need an "M. I. Hummel" figurine for your daughter's birthday next week. A concern over how to protect your collection may have been unduly prolonged for lack of information. An uninsured figurine that was damaged in a house move has been teasing to be made whole again. New developments like black lights or marking instruments may not have been known. The answers to these and other problems should be found in the groups of names listed.

This list includes only a small percentage of the number of people willing and interested in solving your problems. Some names have been obtained through favorable personal contacts by the author and others. Some sources have expressed a desire to be listed and are believed to be competent in their specialty. In either case it is up to the reader to assure himself that any of the persons meets his standards and requirements. Further names of other sources of satisfactory service will be welcomed and passed along to others in later editions. Perhaps this list should be expanded to include other categories. Any suggestions or ideas will be appreciated and used, if possible.

Think of this section as a Help-Yourself Exchange—of ideas.

Auctioneers

Lufkins

26916 La Sierra

Mission Viejo, California 92675

Twice a year mail bid auction in addition to "on-the-spot" buying. Accepts small quantities of figurines to sell by mail.

L. Sones, Auctioneer

1009 Chestnut Street

Newton, Mass. 02164

617-964-0923 or

617-627-0286

Specializes in selling unwanted Hummel figurines at periodic auctions.

Buying and Selling

Antiques Journal

Box 1046

Dubuque, Ia. 52001

Ads for buying and selling Hummel items.

Antique Trader Weekly

Box 1050

Dubuque, Ia. 52001

Ads for buying and selling figurines, dolls plates, anything collectible.

Campbell Graphics, Inc.

Suite 110

Mt. Carmel-Tobasco Rd.

Cincinnati, Ohio 45230

513-752-8820

Illustrated advertising brochures and catalogs.

Collector News

606-8th St.

Grundy Center, Ia. 50638

Ads for buying and selling any Hummel items.

Ernest Gilbert Bentley

1308 Juanita

Mesquite, Tex. 75149

214-285-1249

Photographs items for ads or catalogs. Color or black and white. Call for rates, information, reference, sample photos, or prints.

Hobbies-Magazine for Collectors

1006 S. Michigan Ave.

Chicago, Ill., 60605

Ads for buying and selling dolls, plates and other collectibles.

How to Deal in Antiques

Donald Cowie and John Mebane

Babka Publishing Company

P.O. Box 1050

Dubuque, Ia. 52001

$4.95. Order from publisher.

Plate Collector
 100 E. San Antonio
 Box 1041
 Kermit, Tex.
 Ads for buying and selling plates, figurines, and Hummel art.

Dealers-U.S.A.

ABC Gift Shop
 8849 McGaughey Road
 Indianapolis, Ind. 46239
 Mail order, calendars, old and new figurines. Buys from collectors.

Albatross Antiques
 Box 900
 Manchester, NH 03105
 Call Toll Free 800-258-3595 (Mail order only).

Pat Arbenz
 1968 Golf Links Rd.
 Sierra Vista, Arizona 85635
 Extensive inventory of old and new figurines. Buys from collectors.

Beru's, Inc.
 10051 East Washington St.
 Indianapolis, Ind. 46229
 Mail order. Does not buy from collectors.

Brumelda
 P.O. Box 5007
 Mission Hills, Calif. 91345
 Mail order.

Cameo Gift Shop
 22 N. Main Street
 Chagrin Falls, Ohio 44022

Carol's Gift Shop
 17601 South Pioneer Blvd.
 Artesia, Calif. 90701
 Mail order.

Chaikalena
 1206 West 38th Street at "26 Doors"
 Austin, Tex. 78705
 512-459-3187
 Large retail display.

Clark China and Gallery
 73 Westfield Avenue
 Clark, N.J. 07066
 Mail order.

Dorothy's Treasures
 1512 East 54 Place
 Tulson, Okla. 74105
 Mail order.

Crestwood Flowers
331 East 55th Street
Kansas City, Mo. 64112
Mail order.

Danish Imports, Inc.
34 Edison Mall
Fort Myers, Fla. 33901
Mail order.

Denbos
Box 578
Claremore, Okla. 74017

Dorothy Dous
1261 University Drive — P.O. Box 257
Yardley, Pa. 19067
Mail order. Extensive inventory of old and new figurines. Buys from collectors.

The Gallery
Gifts and Graphic Arts
3954 West 69th Terrace
Prairie Village, Kans. 66208

Sam F. Jackson
417 University Blvd.
Tuscaloosa, Ala. 35401
205-758-2711 or 205-758-2712
Mail order.

Jeral's Gift shop
Morris Hills Shopping Center
Parsippany, N.J. 07054
No mail order.

JuDee Kay's
P.O. Box 292
Bremen, Ind. 46506
Extensive inventory of old and new figurines. Buys from collectors.
Mail order.

Ruth Laudien
4940 Hayes Street
Gary, Ind. 46408

Leo's Jewelry and Gifts
34900 Michigan Avenue
Wayne, Mich. 48184
Extensive inventory of old and new figurines. Buys from collectors.

The Lion's Den
Fontana Shopping Center
Box 35663, Tulsa OK 74135
Buys & Sells - Mail Order

Mader's Restaurant and Gifts
1041 N. 3rd
Milwaukee, Wisconsin
Mail order: Old and scarce items.

Miller's Supermarket
Eaton, Ohio 45320
Extensive inventory of rare/old figurines.

Misty's Gift Gallery
205 Fry Blvd.
Sierra Vista, Arizona 85635
Large inventory of new, old and rare figurines and other related material.

Old Towne Colonial Corner
6692 Crenshan Dr.
Parma Heights, Ohio 44130

The Old World
The Quadrangle
2800 Routh
Houston, Tex. 75201

Rankins
512 Scott Drive
Green Bay, Wis. 54303

Scottsdale East
8011 East Roosevelt
Scottsdale, Arizona 85257
Mail order.

Serendipity Shop
1203 Old Town in the Village
5500 Grenville Ave.
Dallas Tex. 75206
Extensive inventory of new figurines, dolls, cards and other Hummelania

Shirley Ann-Tiques
3905 South Delaware
Independence, Mo. 64055

Shirley Niz
8725 Elm
Hinsdale, Ill. 60521

Margie Simpson
P.O. Box 520113
Miami, Fla. 33152
Sells both old and new figurines.

Spencer
3001 Fondren
Houston, Tex. 77063

Tiffany's Treasure, Ltd.
14019 Midland Road
Poway, Calif. 92064

Pat Upton
Woodhollow Court
Syosset, N.Y. 11791

Sam Yeagley
44 East Main Street
Annville, Pa. 17003

Dealers-Foreign

City Gavacenter
  Frederiksberggade 2
  Copenhagen 1459
  Denmark

Das Kleine Hummel Haus
  Post fach 78
  6587 Baumhilder
  W. Germany

Willi Geck
  Silber - und Porzellanhaus
  6200 Wiesbaden
  Bahnhofstrasse 67
  W. Germany

Harry's Gift Shop
  675 Kaiserlautern
  9-11 Mannheimer Strasse
  Postfach 368
  W. Germany

Aa Hyldgaard Jensen
  159 NDR Dragorvey - DK - 2791 Dragor
  Copenhagen, Denmark

McIntosh and Watts, Ltd.
  193 Sparks Street
  Ottawa, Ontario KIP 5B9
  Canada

Scanmark
  3 Krystalgade
  1172 Copenhagen
  Denmark. Tourists only.

R. F. Sowinski
  Export-Import
  3500 Kassel
  Postfach 31 03 21
  W. Germany

Display-Suppliers

Atkins and Merrill, Inc.
Electro Products Division
1 Etna Road
Lebanon, N.H.
603-448-3444
For display lighting.

C-E Morgan Building Products, Division
601 Oregon Street
Oshkosh, Wis.
For display cabinets and materials. Write for information.

Century Display Manufacturing Corp.
11602 West King Street
Franklin Park, Ill. 60131
312-625-1300, call collect.
Display cabinets.

Conco, Industries, Inc.
32 Water Street
West Haven, Conn.
203-934-5271
For display cabinets.

Decoral Division
14660 Arminte Street
Van Nuys, Calif.
For picture frames for plates and shadow boxes. Write for information.

Fetzer's
P.O. Drawer 486
Salt Lake City, Utah
For large display cases.

Hamlin-Overton Frame Company, Inc.
125 Elkenburg Street
South Haven, Mich. 49090
616-637-5266
Frames that hold plates safely.

Howard Displays, Inc.
500 10th Avenue
New York, N.Y.
For display cabinets.

Kotler Picture Frame and Moulding
300 North Oakeley Blvd.
Chicago, Ill.
Write for information concerning shadow boxes and frames for plates.

M and R Specialties
Dept. C, Box 34
Bensenville, Ill. 60106
Shadow boxes, shelves, bases, plate frames; 50¢ for 36-page, illustrated catalog.

Reflector Hardware Corporation
1450 North 25th Avenue
Melrose Park, Ill. 60160
312-345-2500, ext. 700
For special display lighting.

Reliance Picture Frame Company
250 Fifth Avenue
New York, N.Y.
Write for information about picture frames for plates.

Syroco Division
Syracuse, N.Y. 13201
315-635-9911
For display cabinets.

Tall Emporium Products, Inc.
Keystone Park
Emporium, Pa.
814-483-3356
For display lighting.

Dolls

Doll Collectors' Club of America
  1 Chapel Street
  Newburyport, Mass. 01950
  Dorothy P. Burton, President
Margaret Woodbury Strong Museum
  700 Allen Creek Rd.
  Rochester, N.Y. 14618
  Containing the largest collection of dolls in the world - opening
  date to be announced.
Serendipity Shop
  1203 Old Town in the Village
  5500 Grenville Ave.
  Dallas, Tex. 75206
  Have new Hummel dolls.

Insuring & Protecting

Alarm Device Manufacturing Company, Inc.
  Division Pittway Corp.
  165-T Eileen Way
  Syosset, N.Y.
  516-921-6700
Appraisers Association of America
  541 Lexington Avenue
  New York, N.Y.
  Plaza 3-5039
  Write for names in your area.
Brookstone Company
  125 Vose Farm Road
  Peterborough, N.H. 03458
  Marking and other special purpose tools.
Dreml Manufacturing Company
  Department 350
  Racine, Wis. 53406
  414-637-8831
  Engraving tools.
Electronics Corporation of America
  Photoswitch Division
  3 Memorial Drive
  Cambridge, Mass.
  617-864-8000
  For electronic security systems.
F.M. Davy
  39-T Third Street
  Frenchtown, N.J. 08825
  201-996-6496
  Alarms.

Flather and Company, Inc.
888 17th Street, N.W.
Washington, D.C. 20006
202-466-8888
Insuror of fine arts, including porcelain. Write for information.

GBC Closed Circuit TV Corp.
74 Fifth Avenue
New York, New York 10011
212-989-4433 or toll-free 800-221-2240
Magnavox wireless burglar alarms and other alarm systems. Write for information.

Insurance Information Institute
110 William Street
New York, N.Y. 10038
212-233-7650

Mosler Safe Company
1561 Grand Blvd.
Hamilton, Ohio 45012
513-867-4000
Safes for storing valuables.

Napko Security Systems, Inc.
6 Di Tomas Court
Copiaque, N.Y. 11726
516-842-9400

Nu Tone Division
Madison and Red Bank Road
Cincinnati, Ohio 45227
513-527-5100
Write for security systems information.

Potter Electric Signal Company
2083 Craig Road
St. Louis, Mo. 63141
314-878-4321
For security and alarm systems.

Qualified Security Specialists, Inc.
Distributors of Qunaar Security Systems
1559 Monroe Avenue
Rochester, N.Y. 14618
716-442-3630

Simms and Associates
Art and Museum Consultants
18311 S.W. 95th Court
Miami, Fla. 33157
Ultra-violet lamps (black lights) for reading "invisible" identification marks. Also used for checking authenticity of objects.

3-M Company
Security Systems
3-M Center
St. Paul, Minn. 55101
Write for information about their special Intruder Alarm.

Ultra-Violet Products, Inc.
  Walnut Grove Avenue at Grand
  San Gabriel, Calif.
  213-285-3123
  Write for information. Black lights for decoding and defects.
United Security Products, Inc.
  P.O. Drawer 2428
  Dublin, Calif.
  Security systems for protecting your Hummels.
Westminster Collectibles
  6186 Skyline Drive
  East Lansing, Michigan 48823
  517-332-8888
  Sell an "Invisible Marking Pen Kit" $2.50 pp. Read under black light.

Miniatures

Chestnut Hill Studio
  Box 907
  Taylors, S.C. 29867
  1″ to 1′ scale. All furnishings.
L. Kummbrow
  16460 Wagonwheel Dr.
  Riverside, Calif. 92506
  ½″ to 1″ scale. Toys, Tiffany windows, glass, furniture, houses.
Masterpiece Miniatures
  Box 9
  Belle Haven, Va. 23306
  1″ to 1′ scale. Period furniture, drapes, carpets.
The Miniature Mart
  1807 Octavia St.
  San Francisco, Calif. 94109
  1″ to 1′. Furniture, accessories, etc.
Miniature Silver
  317 South Prospect
  Park Ridge, Ill. 60068

  1/12″ scale.

Prints and Postcards

Europe Import Company
    13525 Gratiot
    Detroit, Mich. 48205

Emil Fink Verlag
    15 Heidehofstrafse
    7 Stuttgart
    W. Germany
    Write for catalog. Prints are also available.

Liberty Gifts
    2324 Liberty Street
    Trenton, N.J. 08629
    609-586-6266
    Write for catalog of postcards, prints.

The Lion's Den
    P.O. Box 341774
    Miami, Fla. 33134
    Hummel postcards, prints.

Verlag Ars Sacra, Joseph Müller
    Postfach 360
    8000 Munchen 43
    W. Germany
    Write for catalogs of postcards and prints.

Repairs

Anything Antiques and Art Restoration
770 Harrison Street
San Francisco, Calif. 94107

Rose Behar
2404 University Street
Houston, Tex.

Butterfly Shoppe Studio
637 Livernois
Ferndale, Mich.

Cordier's Fine Arts
1619 South La Cienega Blvd.
Los Angeles, Calif.
Restorers of ceramics and other fine decorative arts.

Craftsmen's Guild
1938 Portland Blvd.
Portland, Ore. 97217

Harry A. Eberhardt and Son, since 1888
2010 Walnut Street
Philadelphia, Pa. 19103
L08-4144
Will repair porcelain figures. Gives estimates on repairs of items sent by mail.

Hess Repairs
200 Park Avenue South
New York, N.Y. 10003
212-260-2255
Repairs porcelain, china, etc.

My Grandfather's Shop
940 Sligo Avenue
Silver Spring, Md. 20910
301-585-4600

Restorations Unlimited
2800 Route 205c, Quadrangle
Dallas, Tex. 75201

Sierra Studios
P.O. 1005
Oak Park, Ill. 60304
312-848-2020
Porcelain, china repair. Specialize in mail order repair work.

Simms and Associates
Art and Museum Consultants
18311 S.W. 95th Court
Miami, Fla. 33157

Vipro Ltd.
10220 Royal Drive
St. Louis, Mo.

Daniel Zalles
580 Sutter Street
San Francisco, Calif.
Restorer of ceramics and other fine and decorative arts.

Repairs, Books on

Cross, Rena. *China Repair and Restoration.* Drake Publishing Company, New York City, 1973.

Encyclopedia of Antique Restoration and Maintenance. Clarkson N. Potter, New York City, 1974.

Grotz, George. *The Antique Restorer's Handbook.* Doubleday, New York.

Porter, Arthur, ed. *Directory of Art and Antique Restoration.*
465 California Street
San Francisco, California 94104

Yates, Raymond. *How to Restore Bric-a-Brac and Small Antiques.* Harper and Row, New York. 1953.

Showrooms — Wholesale and Retail

Chaikalena
1206 West 38th Street
at "26 Doors"
Austin, Tex. 78705
512-459-3187
Large retail display.

Dorothy Dous
1261 University Drive
or P.O. Box 257
Yardley, Pa. 19067
Large retail display. Mail order of rare/old.

Hummel Showrooms
225 5th Avenue
New York, New York
Wholesale only.

W. Goebel Company
Rodental, W. Germany
Factory showroom for visitors

Leo's Jewelry and Gifts
34900 Michigan Avenue
Wayne Mich. 48184
Large retail display of old/rare figurines.

Liberty Gifts
2324 Liberty Street
Trenton, N.J. 08629
Large retail display.

Misty's Gift Gallery
209-217 Fry Blvd., N.W.
Sierra Vista, Arizona 85635
Large display - New, old and rare. Mail orders.

Serendipity Shop
1203 Old Town in the Village
Dallas, Tex. 75206
Old/rare. Large retail display.

Acknowledgments

More than one hundred individuals and organizations have been involved to various degrees and in numerous areas of interest in the creation of this book. Some supplied generous amounts of time. Others contributed samples, pictures, unpublished information, counsel, and even leads to other sources.

The author's right (write) and left hands were many. The "write" hands were Louise Young, Kathy Palokoff, and Marilyn Mallory. Christine Cassidy, editorial assistant, assembled and organized facts, figures, and pictures. Jane Del Cour put unintelligible scribbling into legible form. Another hand, the "Guidance Council," comprised of Robert Miller, Rue Dee Marker, Patrick T. Arbenz, and Dorothy Dous, was instrumental in reviewing ideas and tables and providing an enormous amount of material in a way that only top echelon collectors and experts can do. Examples from the Gerald Busharts' comprehensive collection in Rochester, New York appear in over half the illustrations, with Dorothy Dous and Hummelwerk supplying other important additions. Mary McCarthy's photography is responsible for the translation into color slides.

In addition to the many other hands listed , there were also several others who preferred anonymity.

Helen Adametz, Little Rock, Arkansas

Pauline Alves, Shelton, Connecticut

Patrick T. Arbenz, Sierra Vista, Arizona

David W. Armstrong, Pomona, California

Army Headquarters Air Force Exchange Service, Europe

Arnart Imports, New York, New York

Christine E. Cassidy, Rochester, New York

Donna R. Chaikalene, Austin, Texas

Collectors Showcase, Akron, Ohio

Joseph E. Cramer, Albany, New York

Mary Esther Croker, Grundy Center, Iowa

Das Kleine Hummel Haus, 6587 Baumholder, Germany

Jane DelCour, Rochester, New York

Debbie Dickinson, Rochester, New York

Dorothy Dous, Yardley, Pennsylvania

Robert Dous, Yardley, Pennsylvania

Ross J. Ernst, Omaha, Nebraska

Europe Import Company, Detroit Michigan

Jean Evans, Lewistown, New York

Gunther Flegenheimer, Brecksville, Ohio

Emil Fink, Verlag, F. Stuttgart, W. Germany

Tina Frandson, Denmark

Richard G. Fuller, Jr., New York, New York

Willi Geck, West Germany

The Goebel Collectors' Club, Tarrytown, New York

William Goebel, Rodental, West Germany

Major & Mrs. Charles J. Gray, APO New York

Girards' Antiques, Hot Springs, Arkansas

Jean Grady, Hot Springs, Arkansas

Sally Jean Grady, Hot Springs, Arkansas

Shirley Gremminger, Dallas, Texas

Katherine Gullo, Temple, Texas

Hamlin-Overton Frame Co., Inc., South Haven, Michigan

Harry's Gift Shop, West Germany

Dr. Herbert Herrmann, Boston, Massachusetts

Mrs. Leone Horan, Dallas, Texas

Ann Hotchkiss, Detroit, Michigan

Sam F. Jackson, Tuscaloosa, Alabama

Aa Hyldgaard Jensen, Copenhagen, Denmark

Ju Dee Kay's, Bremen, Indiana

James P. Kelly, Elmsford, New York

Elaine H. Kirkland, Dallas, Texas

Morris Kule, Elmsford, New York

H. M. Lasday, Pittsburgh, Pennsylvania

Faith B. Lasher, Gaithersburg, Maryland

Ruth Laudien, Gary, Indiana

Ann Loyman, Memphis, Tennessee

Leo's Gift Center, Wayne, Michigan

Liberty Gifts, Trenton, New Jersey

Library of Congress, Washington, D. C.

Ben Livingston, Columbus, Ohio

Margaret Woodburg Strong Museum, Rochester, New York

Marilyn Mallery, Rochester, New York

Rue Dee Marker, Bremen, Indiana

Mary McCarthy, Rochester, New York

Jack McDermoth, New York, New York

McIntosh and Watts Ltd., Ottawa, Ontario

Robert L. Miller, Eaton, Ohio

Ruth Miller, Eaton, Ohio

Ruth A. Motsen, Philadelphia, Pennsylvania

Mrs. Louise T. Mroczek, Dallas, Texas

National Potteries, Cleveland, Ohio

Niki's, Marietta, Georgia

Shirley Niz, Hinsdale, Ilinois

The Old World, Dallas, Texas

Olde Towne Colonial Corner, Parma Heights, Ohio

Kathy Palokoff, Rochester, New York

Lars Peterson, Belchertown, Maryland

The Plate Collector, Kermit, Texas

Dr. Gotz M. Pollizien, Munich, Germany

Lillian G. Potter, Portland, Maine

Mr. & Mrs. Paul Preo, Rochester, New York

Chief Myron Raff, New York, New York

Wayne Ranke, Mapleton, Missouri

Rankins, Green Bay, Wisconsin

Mrs. W. Robinson, Poway, California

Rochester Public Library, Rochester, New York

Rue Dee Marker, Bremen, Indiana

Joel Sater, Marietta, Pennsylvania

Schmid Bros., Randolph Massachusetts

Paul A. Schmid, Randolph, Massachusetts

M. Schwartz, Lake Hiawatha, New Jersey

Scottsdale East, Scottsdale, Arizona

Charles Shepherd, Rochester, New York.

Shirley Ann-Tiques, Independence, Missouri

Pauline Sloes, Shelton, Connecticut

L. Sones, Upper Newton Falls, Maryland

R. F. Sowinski, West Germany

Angelo Spadaro, Devon, Pennsylvania

Regina Steele, Wilmington, Delaware

Vera Stoof, Williamsburg, Maryland

Madeline Taylor, Providence, Rhode Island

Tiffany's Treasures Ltd., Poway, California

Tri-State Trader, Knightstown, Indiana

U. S. Bureau of Census, Washington, D. C.

U. S. Dept. of Commerce, Washington, D. C.

University of Rochester Library, Rochester, New York

Pat Upton, Syosset, New York

Mrs. John Wallner, Manchester, Vermont

Joan Welch, Rochester, New York

Patricia Wellenkamp, Rochester, New York

Margaret Whitton, Rochester, New York

Louise Young, Rochester, New York

Vince Zubras, Dallas, Texas

David Zuckerman, Detroit, Michigan

Dorothy Zuckerman, Detroit, Michigan

Bibliography

Books

Anderton, Johanna. *More Twentieth Century Dolls.* North Kansas City, Mo.: Athena Publishing Co., 1974.

Anderton, Johana. *Twentieth Century Dolls.* North Kansas City, Mo.: Athena Publishing Co., 1971.

Angione, Genevieve. *All Bisque and Half Bisque Dolls.* New York: Thomas Nelson, Inc., 1969.

The *Antique Trader Weekly*, editors. "Hummel Update: More Details Presented on These Popular Collectibles," by Claudia Frech. "Hummels, Facts and Fiction," by Allen J.F. Von Geisler. *Annual of Articles on Antiques for 1974.* Dubuque, Ia.: Babka Publishing Co., 1974.

The *Antique Trader Weekly*, editors. "Research Done on Hummels" and "The Goebel Company and Its Other Products," by Claudia Frech. "More Info on Hummels," by Claudia Frech. *Annual of Articles on Antiques for 1973.* Dubuque, Ia.: Babka Publishing Co., 1973.

The *Antique Trader Weekly*, editors. "Trash or Treasure - Hummels," by Philip DeVilbiss. "Hummel Collector Shares Knowledge," by Claudia Frech. *Annual of Articles on Antiques for 1972.* Dubuque, Ia.: Babka Publishing Co., 1972.

Bartels, Nadja, and McKinven, John G., editors. *The Bradford Book of Collector's Plates 1976.* New York: McGraw Hill Book Co., 1977.

Coleman, Dorothy. *Collectors Encyclopedia of Dolls.* New York: Crown Publishers.

Ehrmann, Eric. *Hummel, the Complete Collector's Guide and Illustrated Reference.* Huntington, N. Y.: Portfolio Press Corp., 1976.

Grotz, George. *The Antique Restorer's Handbook.* Garden City, N. Y.: Doubleday and Co., 1976.

Hummel, Berta. *The Hummel Book.* 17th ed. Translated by Lola Ch. Eytel. Stuttgart, Germany: Emil Fink, Verlag, 1973.

Johl, Janet Pagter. *Your Dolls and Mine.* New York: Linquist Publishers, 1952.

Larney, Judith. *Restoring Ceramics.* Cincinnati, Ohio: Watson/ Guptill, 1975.

Marion, Frieda. *China Half-Figures Called Pincushion Dolls.* Newburyport, Mass.: J. Palmer Publishers, 1974.

McGrath, Lee Pariz. *Housekeeping with Antiques.* New York: Dodd, Mead & Co., pp. 137-156.

The Hummel, Drawings by Berta Hummel with Light Verse. Munich, West Germany: Verlag Ars Sacra, Josef Müller, 1972.

Yates, Raymond F. *How to Restore China, Bric-A-Brac and Small Antiques.* New York: Oramercy Publishing Co., 1953.

Periodicals

Allison, Grace. "W. Goebel Porzellanfabrik Commemorates Our 200th Birthday." *National Antiques Review.* August 1976, pp. 20-21.

Arbenz, Pat. "Hummel Facts by Arbenz." *Plate Collector*, July 1976 to present.

Eschenbach, Virginia. "The Merry Wanderer." The *Antique Trader Weekly*, September 15, 1976, pp. 78-79.

"Hummel Collecting, Part 1, Berta's Early Life." *Acquire*, July 1975. pp. 43-44.

"Hummel Dolls." *Tri-State Trader*, September 13, 1975.

Lasher, Faith B. "Hummels or Goebels?" *Joel Saters Antique News*, January 7, 1977, p. 20.

Miller, Robert L. "Recent Rare 'Finds' Enhance Hummel Collecting." The *Antique Trader*, March 2, 1977, pp. 24-25.

Miller, Robert L. "Millers Uncover Extraordinary Hungarian Figurines." *Acquire*, March 1977, pp. 42-43.

"The Miller's Hummel Collection." *Acquire*, May 1976, p. 9.

Monaghan, Nancy. "They Aren't Antiques But Cherubic Hummels Are Prized By Collectors." *Times Union* (Rochester, New York), February 28, 1977, 3rd section, p. 2.

Pfuhl, Nalten "Hummel Wealth Awarded to German Convent." Translated by John Woesner. *Tri-State Trader*, May 18, 1974.

Roye, Josephine S. "Berta Hummel's Figurines." *Sater's Antique News*, May 4, 1973, pp. 8-9

"Trouble at Hummel." *Newsweek.* July 17, 1972, p. 65.

Witt, Louise Schaub. "Along the Collector's Line." *Collector's News.* September 1973, p. 32.

Public Documents

Germany, German Supreme Court. February 22, 1974, as published in *Neue Juristische Wochenschrift* (NJW) 1974, pp. 904-907.

Germany, Lower court decision. 1952 decision published in *Neue Juristische Wochenschrift (NJW), 1952, pp. 784-785. In German.*

State of New York, Department of State, Division of Corporations and State Records, Certificate of Incorporation of Herbert Dubler, Inc., pursuant to Article 2 of the Stock Corporation Law.

United States, Department of Commerce, Bureau of the Census, Foreign Trade Division. Extracts from FT 246, *U.S. Imports for Consumption.* Calendar Years 1971-1975. Presenting date on U.S. Imports of Ceramic Figures.

United States Department of Commerce, Bureau of the Census, Foreign Trade Division. Extracts from IM 146, U.S. Imports for Consumption. Cumulative, January - September 1976. Presenting data on U.S. Imports of ceramic figures.

United States Library of Congress, Copyright Office. Catalog of Copyright Entries: *Third Series.* Volume 29, Parts 7-11A, Number 1. ISSN 0041-7882.

United States, Department of Labor, Bureau of Labor Statistics. *Employment and Earnings.* October 1976.

United States, Department of Labor, Bureau of Labor Statistics. *Estimated Retail Food Prices by City.* 1975 Average Annual and July 1976.

United States, Tariff Commission, *Tariff Schedules of the United States Annotated* (1975). T.C. Publication 706: 1975.

Other Sources

Dous, Dorothy. *Hummel Collectors' Club Newsletter.* Yardley, Pa.: November 1976.

Dous, Dorothy. *International Goebel Collectors' Club Newsletter.* Yardley, Pa.: Dous. April 1975 - July 1976.

Doll Collectors of America. *Doll Collectors Manual.* Newburyport, Massachusetts: Doll Collectors of America, Inc., 1964, pp. 116-119.

R. F. Sowinski to John F. Hotchkiss. February 9, 1976 and July 1, 1976. Personal files of John F. Hotchkiss, Rochester, New York.

Index

Key to Symbols
AT—Ashtray; B—Bell; BE—Bookend; CAN—Candleholder;
CBX—Candy Box; F—Figurine; HWF—Font; LMP—Lamp;
MAD—Madonna; MBX—Music Box; PLQ—Plaque; PLT—Plate.

A

B

C

D

G

H

M

Q

Quartet, PLQ, 66, 75, 92, 124

R

Repairs, 220-221; Black light test, 196

Reproductions, 163-176; Arnart, 166, 175; Dubler, 164, 168-172; Korean, 165, 174; Napco, 169, 175; Picci La Ca, 166-167; unidentified, 171

Retreat to Safety: F, 51, 72, 92, 128; PLQ, 66, 75, 92, 124

Ride into Christmas: F, 51, 72, 92, 135; PLT, 66, 73, 131

Ring Around the Rosie, F, 51, 72, 92, 133

Ring, Ba-Bee, PLQ, 65, 75, 83, 120

Runaway, The, F, 51, 72, 93, 133

S

St. George, F, 52, 72, 92, 121

St. Joseph, F, 52, 72, 92, 129

Schmid Bros. Co., Joseph: and Berta Hummel, 184; annual plate, 140, 157; calendar towel, 145; exclusive rights, 155; 1972 M.D. plate, 158; 1977 catalog, 157; secondary market, 161; types of Hummel products, 30

School Boy, F, 52, 72, 92, 111, 122

School Boys, F, 52, 72, 91, 111, 122

School Girl, F, 52, 72, 92, 111, 122

School Girls, F, 52, 72, 92, 111, 122

Seeman, Margarete, 13, 138, 140

Sensitive Hunter, F, 52, 72, 92, 118

Serenade, F, 52, 72, 92, 123

She Loves Me, She Loves Me Not: F, 53, 72, 92, 104, 127; LMP, 31, 74, 92, 129

Shepherd's Boy, F, 52, 72, 92, 122; old/new, 102

Shining Light, F, 53, 72, 93, 134

Showrooms, wholesale/retail, 221

Signs of Spring, F, 53, 72, 93, 111, 128

Silent Night, CAN, 60, 73, 102, 112, 121

Singing Lesson: CBX, 61, 73, 93, 122; F, 53, 57, 72, 93, 121

Sister, F, 53, 72, 93, 123

Sketch Me, 13, 30, 138

Skier, F, 53, 72, 93, 102, 112, 121

Smart Little Sister, F, 53, 72, 93, 133

Soldier Boy, F, 53, 72, 93, 133

W

X

Y

Z